Australian Scientific Societies and Professional Associations

Edited by
Ian A. Crump

Second Edition

Information Service, CILES
Commonwealth Scientific and Industrial Research Organization
314 Albert Street, East Melbourne, Victoria, Australia 3002
1978

Exclusive Distributor
ISBS, Inc.
P.O. Box 555
Forest Grove, OR   97116

National Library of Australia Cataloguing-in-Publication Entry

Australian scientific societies and professional associations.

Index.
ISBN 0 643 00282 0.

1. Scientific societies - Australia - Directories.
2. Technology - Australia - Societies, etc. - Directories. I. Crump, Ian Alan, 1947-, ed.
II. Commonwealth Scientific and Industrial Research Organization.

506'.94

First published 1971
A previous list was published in 1951 as *CSIRO Documentation Section Pamphlet No. 1*.

Computer typesetting with COMp80 and the COMTEXT software system by CSIRO, Melbourne

Printed by CSIRO, Melbourne

78.179-1000

CONTENTS

FOREWORD

This edition of *Australian Scientific Societies and Professional Associations* is more comprehensive in coverage and content than previous editions. Many more organizations (both established and new) were approached and have provided information for publication.

A directory of bodies as elusive, transitory and changeable as scientific societies and associations inevitably will be incomplete and become outdated. The data for this edition was collected during 1977. All concerned - users, contributors and other interested bodies - are invited to draw our attention to omissions and errors so that these may be rectified.

The co-operation of all who provided information is greatly appreciated.

C. Garrow
Manager
CSIRO Information Service

INTRODUCTION

As has been the practice for many other information files maintained by the CSIRO Information Service, this file has also been converted to and maintained in machine-readable form. This edition of the directory has been produced directly from that file by computer photocomposition. In addition to reference to the directory, subject retrieval is now available using computer programs developed for the CSIRO Selective Dissemination of Information (SDI) System.

Where possible, an entry has been made for the federal body only, with state bodies or subject groups listed as sub-divisions within the entry. The societies and associations are arranged in alphabetical order (conjunctions, prepositions and articles are disregarded). Indexes to subjects, names of societies, publications, and named awards are included. An alphabetic list of initials of society names and their corresponding societies is provided.

The subject index refers to the broad subject fields of societies and is arranged in alphabetic order. The names of societies index refers to both society names and affiliated Australian societies (entries for affiliated societies are shown in italics). The indexes to names of societies, publications and awards are arranged in the same order as the main entries. Initials and acronyms are regarded as words (i.e., CSIRO is regarded as Csiro and comes after the word Council).

Information was obtained from the responses to questionnaires addressed to Society Secretaries. Individual entries may contain information in the following categories:

(i)   *Name of Society*

(ii)   *Address*
                (a) Address of headquarters (including postal address)
                (b) Telephone number

(iii)   *Information*
                (a) Name of Secretary (or equivalent)
                (b) Sub-divisions
                (c) Affiliated societies
                (d) History
                (e) Purpose
                (f) Fields of interest
                (g) Activities (meetings, conferences, seminars, etc.)
                (h) Publications (name of publication and frequency of production)
                (i) Library facilities maintained by society
                (j) Awards (prizes, research grants, medals, lectures, orations and other honours awarded at branch or national level)
                (k) Membership (number of members and types of membership available)

The computer file also contains information which can be used to generate self-adhesive address labels for all or selected entries.

Ian A. Crump
Editor

1 Academy of the Social Sciences in Australia
Second floor, National Library Building, Parkes, A.C.T. 2600.
Telephone: (062) 73 1869

SECRETARY: Dr. C. D. Rowley (Secretary and Director)

HISTORY: The Academy came into existence as a result of decisions of the Social Science Research Council of Australia at its Annual General Meeting on 11th Nov, 1970. The proposal that the Council change its name to Academy of the Social Sciences in Australia and that its members take the title of Fellows was approved by the Registrar of Companies and Incorporated Associations in the A.C.T. on 7th July 1971. Like the Council the Academy is a non-profit organisation, and its functions remain unchanged.

PURPOSE: To encourage the advancement of the social sciences in Australia; to sponsor and organize research; and to assist the publication of studies in the social sciences

INTERESTS: Include anthropology, economics, economic history and business administration, education, geography, history, law, social philosophy, linguistics, political science (including international relations), psychology and sociology (including demography).

ACTIVITIES: Annual General Meeting; quarterly Executive Committee Meetings; Meetings of Research Panels; Meetings of Membership, Research Grants, Finance Committees; meetings of working parties and ad hoc meetings as required.

PUBLICATIONS
Bibliography of Research in the Social Sciences
Annual Report
Annual Lecture
Books and articles resulting from the Academy's major research projects

AWARDS
The Academy obtains funds from government departments, foundations and business for major research projects. Grants are made for research in South East Asia and the South Pacific.

MEMBERSHIP: 150 (fellows, overseas fellows, honorary fellows)

2 Agricultural Engineering Society [Australia]
National Science Centre, 191 Royal Parade, Parkville, Vic. 3052
Telephone: (03) 615 2606

SECRETARY: K.R. Thom

SUBDIVISIONS
Victoria, South Australia, Queensland.

AFFILIATIONS
Australian Institute of Agricultural Science

HISTORY: Founded on 4th May, 1950. Registered as a non-profit society under the Companies Act of Victoria in 1953. In 1969 new Articles of Association were adopted allowing formalization of branches.

PURPOSE: To provide exchange of views and gathering and dissemination of the latest information relating to farm mechanization and agricultural engineering; to promote encourage and co-ordinate the study, development and profession of agricultural engineering and farm mechanization in all its branches; to encourage, promote and undertake investigations and research in agricultural engineering or allied fields of activity; to hold conferences; lectures, field days to discuss subjects affecting agricultural engineering generally, and to publish proceedings of the Society or any other publications which may seem to further the objects of the Society.

ACTIVITIES: Workshops, symposia and field days. Branches meet monthly.

PUBLICATIONS
Agricultural Engineering Australia

AWARDS
Hugh Victor McKay Award (for an outstanding Australian contribution to Agricultural Engineering)
Annual students prize to Longerenong Agricultural College

MEMBERSHIP: 270 (member, honorary member, corporate member)

3   Agricultural Technologists of Australasia
31 Seymour Street, Bathurst, N.S.W.
(P.O. Box 307, Bathurst 2795.)
Telephone: (063) 31 2113, 31 2088

SECRETARY: P.G. Flude

SUBDIVISIONS
New South Wales, Victoria, South Australia,Queensland, Western Australia, Papua New Guinea,
Tasmania and A.C.T.
Sub-branches -
N.S.W - Central Western, Northern Tablelands, Riverina
Vic. - North Eastern, Northern, Western Districts, Wimmera.

HISTORY: Founded in 1969

PURPOSE: To promote advancement of agriculture, of agricultural college graduates, and agricultural
technology.

INTERESTS: Agricultural education; technical advice to farmers and graziers; employment services to
members; employment agency for members; provision of technical information to professional officers.

ACTIVITIES: National symposia, field days, general and Branch meetings

PUBLICATIONS
Agricultural Technologists (quarterly)
Newsletter (quarterly)

MEMBERSHIP: 2100 (members, students)

4   Anthropological Society of New South Wales
The Australian Museum, 6-8 College Street, Sydney, N.S.W.
(Box A285, P.O., Sydney South 2000.)
Telephone: (02) 339 8337

SECRETARY: Dr. J. R. Specht

AFFILIATIONS
Australian Anthropological Association
Canberra Archeological Society

HISTORY: Founded in 1928

PURPOSE: To promote the study of anthropology, particularly to educate the public as well as
professional anthropologists on the conservation of aboriginal heritage.

ACTIVITIES: Monthly meetings.

PUBLICATIONS
Mankind

AWARDS
Frank Bell Memorial Prize (annual)

MEMBERSHIP: 135 (ordinary, student, pensioner, life, corresponding)

5   Anthropological Society of Queensland
Geology Department, University of Queensland, St Lucia, Qld. 4067.

SECRETARY: D. N. Home

HISTORY: Founded in 1948

PURPOSE: To promote the study of anthropology in all its branches especially for the furtherence of knowledge concerning the aborigines of Australia and Tasmania and the indigenous peoples of the Pacific; to create opportunities for friendly intercourse, discussion and co-operation amongst all persons interested in the study and advancement of the science of anthropology; to support any practical policy for the well being of the endigenous peoples of Australia and the Pacific areas, and for the preservation of their culture.

ACTIVITIES: Meetings held monthly.

PUBLICATIONS
Newsletter (monthly)

MEMBERSHIP: 65 (full, ordinary)

6   Anthropological Society of South Australia Incorporated
South Australian Museum, North Terrace, Adelaide, S.A. 5000.
Telephone: (08) 223 8911

SECRETARY: V. Tolcher

AFFILIATIONS
Australian Anthropological Association

HISTORY: Founded in 1926

PURPOSE: To provide the science of anthropology and to take public and official action in the interests of anthropology as may be deemed necessary.

ACTIVITIES: Meetings held monthly from March to November.

PUBLICATIONS
Journal of the Anthropolical Society of South Australia

LIBRARY: Library maintained

MEMBERSHIP: 130 (life, associate, ordinary)

7   Anthropological Society of Victoria
11 Kensington Road, South Yarra, Vic. 3141
Telephone: (03) 24 2242

SECRETARY: Miss V.A. Leeper

AFFILIATIONS
Australian Anthropological Association
Conservation Council of Victoria

HISTORY: Founded in 1934 by Proffessor Wood-James (first President).

PURPOSE: To promote the study of anthropology in all its branches; to take such action in the interests of anthropology as may be deemed desirable and for that purpose to co-operate with other organizations having similar objectives.

ACTIVITIES: Six meetings per annum.

PUBLICATIONS
Four Newsletters per annum. Share in Mankind.

LIBRARY: Books, periodicals, articles, available for loan to members.

MEMBERSHIP: 40 (life, metropolitan, country, family)

8   Anthropological Society of Western Australia
Department of Anthropology, University of W.A., Nedlands, W.A. 6009
Telephone: (092) 80 2853

SECRETARY: J.E. Stanton

HISTORY: Founded in 1958

PURPOSE: To promote the subject of general anthropology, eith emphasis on Australian Aborigines, and in the fields of social and cultural anthropology, physical anthropology, ethnology, archaeology, genetics, linguistics and semantics.

ACTIVITIES: Monthly meetings

PUBLICATIONS
Newsletter

MEMBERSHIP: 100 (general, student)

9   Appita
Clunies Ross House, 191 Royal Parade, Parkville, Vic. 3052
Telephone: (03) 347 2377

SECRETARY: D. F. Lampard

SUBDIVISIONS
Local sections in Burnie (Tas.), Boyer (Tas.), Sydney, Brisbane, Maryvale (Vic.), Auckland (N.Z.)
Appita Forestry Group (Chairman - Mr. J.R. Pollock)
Engineering Group (Chairman - Mr. A. E. Miller)
Wood Products Group (Chairman - Dr. W. P. Macmillan)
Converting Group (Chairman - Mr. G.W. Balstrup)
Appita Printing Group (Chairman - Mr. P. Garnham)

HISTORY: Founded in 1946

PURPOSE: To further the application of science to the pulp and paper industry, promote scientific research, and provide means for the dissemination of scientific and technical knowledge appertaining to the industry.

ACTIVITIES: Annual General Conferences,monthly local section meetings.

PUBLICATIONS
Appita
Standard Methods established by Testing Committee and endorsed by SAA and SANZ.

AWARDS
Appita L. R. Benjamin Award (annual)

MEMBERSHIP: 1025

10   Association of Australasian Palaeontologists
Geological Society of Australia Office, Perpetual Trusts Building, 39
Hunter Street, Sydney, 2000.
Telephone: (02) 231 4696

SECRETARY: Dr. M.R. Walter (Bureau of Mineral Resources, Geology and Geophysics, P.O. Box 378, Canberra, A.C.T. 2601)

AFFILIATIONS
Geological Society of Australia Inc. (A.A.P. is a specialist group with G.S.A.)

HISTORY: Founded on 5th Feb., 1974.

PURPOSE: To promote the interests of palaeontology in the widest sense, arrange conferences and symposia, disseminate information concerning palaeontology and stratigraphy through the publication of a journal, to provide news about the activities of the membership.

PUBLICATIONS
Alcheringa (annual)

MEMBERSHIP: 104 (ordinary, life members)

11   Association for Computer Aided Design Limited
576 St. Kilda Road, Melbourne, 3004
Telephone: (03) 51 9153

SECRETARY: M.V. Jones (National Executive Engineer)

SUBDIVISIONS
N.S.W. Office - Mr. T. Webber (N.S.W. Executive Engineer), Box M270, Sydney Mail Exchange, N.S.W. 2012 (Telephone: (02) 212 2600)
W.A. Office - Mr. K. Kavanagh (Perth Representative), care of- Civil Engineering, University of W.A., Nedlands, W.A. 6009 (Telephone: (092) 80 3071, 80 3074)

HISTORY: Founded in 1970 as the Association of Computer Aided Design of Structures. In 1973 the word Structures was deleted from the title to broaden the interests of the Association.

PURPOSE: To intensify interest and to increase professional competence in the use of computers for the planning, design, construction, maintenance and control of the built environment and to extend knowledge of the techniques available and benefits possible from such use; to initiate, or participate in activities for enhancing the possibility, capability and capacity of members to use computers in their professional work; to provide the means of rationalizing computer programs and systems and of initiating the specification and development of new programs; to provide means for checking and testing programs and systems; to encourage the acceptance of programs checked by the Association and of standards and policy documents published by the Association; to foster discussion and the exchange of experience in computing systems and associated aids.

PUBLICATIONS
Software Index
Standards for Documentation and Checking Computations
Newsletters
Comparative Reports on Software
Comparative Reports on Hardware
Technical Notes
Technical Reports

LIBRARY: Library of programs contributed by members is established on the major bureaux networks

MEMBERSHIP: (individuals, organizations)

12   Association of Medical Directors to the Australian Pharmaceutical Industry
Searle Laboratories, 8 West Street, North Sydney, N.S.W.
(P.O. Box 473, North Sydney 2060)
Telephone: (02) 929 8622

SECRETARY: Dr. A.J. Emmett (Honorary Secretary)

HISTORY: Founded in 1961.

PURPOSE: To promote and encourage the study of those branches or aspects of the medical pharmaceutical and allied sciences with which medical practitioners employed as medical directors or as hereinafter qualified in the Australian Pharmaceutical Industry are particularly concerned in their employment or professional duties; to provide a means and source of advice to the members of the Association on all matters concerning them in their status and liabilities as medical directors employed or engaged as aforesaid; to hold, promote, conduct or arrange for the holding of lectures, conferences, meetings, courses of study and discussions on or concerning matters of interest to members of the Association in their profession or occupation with a view to assisting them in connection with their professional duties; generally to promote, maintain, protect and advance the honour and general and social interest of medical practitioners employed by or engaged in the Australian Pharmaceutical Industry as medical directors.

ACTIVITIES: Annual Meeting, General Meetings (quarterly), Extraordinary Meetings, lectures, conferences, meetings, courses of study.

MEMBERSHIP: 42

13 Association of Officers of the Commonwealth Scientific and Industrial Research Organization
see CSIRO Officers' Association

14 Association of Professional Engineers, Australia
39 a'Beckett Street, Melbourne, Vic.
(P.O.Box 1272L, Melbourne 3001.)
Telephone: (03) 347 5544

SECRETARY: R.A. Corin (Hon. General Secretary)

SUBDIVISIONS
Branches in all States, A.C.T. and N.T.

HISTORY: Founded in 1946

PURPOSE: To represent employee professional engineers in all matters relating to their employment on the basis of their community of interest as members of a seperate professional group; to be concerned not only with the salaries and working conditions of professional engineers but also with the proper organization and administration of their services as professional men and women.

ACTIVITIES: Annual meeting of Federal Executive, bimonthly meetings of the Committee of Management. General meetings of members held annually in each branch.

PUBLICATIONS
PE News (9 editions per year)

MEMBERSHIP: 16,000 professionally qualified engineers plus 2118 affiliates.

15 Association of Professional Scientists of Australia
41 a'Beckett Street, Melbourne, Vic. 3000.
Telephone: (03) 347 4988

SECRETARY: Mr. R.H. Barron (General Secretary)

HISTORY: Founded on 20th November 1962. Recognized by the Commonwealth Conciliation and Arbitration Commission.

PURPOSE: To advance and protect the social and economic interests of its members and employee professional scientists generally.

INTERESTS: Trade unions; employers; government.

PUBLICATIONS
Newsletter (bimonthly) informing members of current industrial relation problems and claims.

MEMBERSHIP: 1500

16   Asthma Foundation of South Australia Inc.
Paringa Buildings, 13 Hindley Street, Adelaide, S.A. 7000
Telephone: (08) 51 4272

SECRETARY: Mrs. L.K. Peel

AFFILIATIONS
Asthma and Allergy Club of S.A.
Asthma and Allergy Club of Ingle Farm
Asthma and Allergy Club of St. Agnes

HISTORY: Founded in 1963.

PURPOSE: To help educate the public on the subject of asthma; to provide funds for grants for research and to help provide units for hospitals.

ACTIVITIES: Monthly Executive Meeting; Annual General Meeting.

PUBLICATIONS
Newsletter (quarterly)

AWARDS
Grants to doctors travelling abroad for research

MEMBERSHIP: 560 (single, family, life)

17   Astronautical Society of Western Australia Inc.
96 Glenelg Avenue, Wembly Downs, W.A.
(Box E 254, G.P.O., Perth, W.A. 6001)
Telephone: (092) 341 1449

SECRETARY: G.D. Davies

SUBDIVISIONS
Geraldton Branch - P.O. Box 941, Geraldton, W.A. 6530
Radio Astronomy Division, operating Mount Gungin Radio Observatory

AFFILIATIONS
International Astronautical Federation

HISTORY: Founded in 1975.

PURPOSE: To encourage an interest in astronautics and the space sciences in W.A.; to assist in the development of astronautics and the space sciences for peaceful purposes in Australia; to cooperate with similar societies and organizations within Australia and overseas.

ACTIVITIES: Monthly meetings, Australian Astronautics Convention (next planned for 1979).

PUBLICATIONS
Astronautical Society of Western Australia News Bulletin
Proceedings of the 1975 Australian Astronautics Convention
European Space Activities
Eclipse '74

LIBRARY: Reference books, films, videotapes.

MEMBERSHIP: 90 (honorary, senior, associate, student members)

18 Astronomers Association of Queensland
Brisbane Planetarium, New Botanic Gardens, Mt. Coot-tha, Brisbane (43
Goldieslie Road, Indooroopilly, Brisbane 4068)
Telephone: (07) 378 1586

SECRETARY: A.J. Russell (General Secretary)

HISTORY: Founded in 1967.

PURPOSE: To foster the advancement of astronomy and observation techniques, to give advice on the construction of instruments, to carry out research and to obtain and disseminate information.

ACTIVITIES: 12 meetings per year.

PUBLICATIONS
Newsletter (monthly)
Annual Proceedings
Astronomy (a technical supplement, 4 issues per year)
Yearbook (published by the Computer Section)

AWARDS
Annual prize for outstanding associate member

MEMBERSHIP: 120 (full membership, associate membership, associate group)

19 Astronomical Society of Albury-Wodonga
379 Wantigong Street, Albury, N.S.W.
(Box 198, G.P.O., Albury 2640)

SECRETARY: J.C. Dick

HISTORY: Founded in 1974.

PURPOSE: To further the interests of the general public in astronomy, space programs and all associated subjects.

INTERESTS: General astronomy, the space programme, astro photography, telescopes.

ACTIVITIES: Monthly meetings, field nights, public viewing nights.

PUBLICATIONS
Geodyssy

LIBRARY: Library maintained.

MEMBERSHIP: 31 (senior, junior, pensioner, country)

20 Astronomical Society of Australia
The Chatterton Astronomy Department, School of Physics, University of
Sydney, Sydney, N.S.W. 2006
Telephone: (02) 692 1122

CSIRO Division of Radiophysics, P.O.Box 76, Epping, N.S.W. 2121
Telephone: (02) 869 1111

SECRETARY: Dr. L.R. Allen (Univ.of Sydney) and Dr. J.B. Whiteoak (CSIRO) (Secretaries)

HISTORY: Founded in 1966

PURPOSE: To promote the advancement of astronomy and closely related sciences, particularly by holding meetings in this country.

ACTIVITIES: Annual General Scientific Meeting and special meetings on specific themes in astronomy.

PUBLICATIONS
Proceedings of the Astronomical Society of Australia

AWARDS
Bernice Page Medal

MEMBERSHIP: 250 (member, student member, corporate member)

21 Astronomical Society of Frankston
1 Brooklyn Avenue, Frankston, Vic. 3199
Telephone: (03) 783 5276, 782 1312

AFFILIATIONS
Astronomical Society of Victoria

HISTORY: Founded in 1968.

PURPOSE: To promote the study of astronomical sciences by amateurs by conducting meetings for the delivery of lectures, by arranging exhibitions and maintaining a library of astronomical materials.

INTERESTS: Observations of variable stars, aurora and meteors; radioastronomy; astrophotography.

ACTIVITIES: Meeting held monthly (except December)

PUBLICATIONS
Journal of the Astronomical Society of Frankston (monthly)

LIBRARY: Mainly magazine subscriptions plus approx. 100 books.

MEMBERSHIP: 30 (honorary members, family members, members, student members)

22 Astronomical Society of Geelong
Breakwater Road, Belmont, Vic.
(P.O. Box 209, Geelong 3220)
Telephone: (052) 9 7667, 9 5508

AFFILIATIONS
Astronomical Society of Victoria

HISTORY: Founded on 30 Sept. 1960.

PURPOSE: To promote astronomical research by amateurs and to generally encourage the study of and practice of astronomy and to disseminate knowledge of the science.

INTERESTS: Variable stars, lunar occultations, astrophotography, telescope mirror making, general amateur astronomy.

PUBLICATIONS
Quasar (quarterly)
Astronomy Notes in Thursday's Geelong Advertiser

LIBRARY: Library maintained.

MEMBERSHIP: 36 (senior, student)

23 Astronomical Society of the Hunter
Newcastle Technical College, Tighes Hill, N.S.W. 2297
Telephone: (049) 61 5448

SECRETARY: J. Tattersall

HISTORY: Founded in 1973.

PURPOSE: To further public interest in the science of astronomy.

ACTIVITIES: Ordinary General Meeting once per month; Committee Meetings once per month.

PUBLICATIONS
Observations of the Astronomical Society of the Hunter (quarterly)

LIBRARY: Library of books and science magazines kept at the Newcastle Technical College.

MEMBERSHIP: 25 (adult, family, junior, student)

24   Astronomical Society of New South Wales
P.O. Box 208, Eastwood, N.S.W. 2122.

SECRETARY: Miss S. Rae

HISTORY: Founded in 1956. Formerly the Sydney Amateur Astronomers (S.A.A.)

PURPOSE: To associate together persons interested in astronomy and allied sciences; to construct and use telescopes and other astronomical or scientific instruments; to assist members in the construction and use of telescopes and other astronomical or scientific instruments and in the study or practice of astronomy and allied sciences; to provide a clubhouse, observatory, workshop and other amenities and things for the use of members; to undertake or participate in, or otherwise assist, any work or project connected with the study or practice of astronomy or allied sciences; to promote and encourage an active interest in amateur astronomy among the general public.

ACTIVITIES: General meetings and discussion meetings on 3rd and 1st Fridays of each month respectively.

PUBLICATIONS
Universe (monthly)
Ephemeris (annual)

LIBRARY: Library maintained.

AWARDS
Yates Award (Junior)
Mc Niven Medal (Senior)
Crago Encouragement Prize

MEMBERSHIP: 120 (full, associate members)

25   Astronomical Society of Queensland
14 Suelin Street, Boondall, Qld. 4034

SECRETARY: A. B. Doran

HISTORY: Founded in 1927

PURPOSE: To promote a popular interest in astronomy and assist in the asvancement of science.

INTERESTS: Astronomical observations and discussions; telescope making; adult education.

ACTIVITIES: Monthly meetings and lectures. Observing nights.

PUBLICATIONS
Astroquest (bimonthly)

AWARDS
Prizes to juniors for lecture and essay competitions

MEMBERSHIP: 150 (city, country, junior, family)

26   Astronomical Society of South Australia Inc.

G.P.O. Box 199, Adelaide, S.A. 5001
Telephone: (08) 79 2936

SECRETARY: U. Rudevics (Hon. Secretary)

HISTORY: Founded in 1892.

PURPOSE: To promote and engage in the study of astronomy, build instruments and encourage public interest in astronomy.

INTERESTS: Telescope making, astronomical education, amateur observation.

ACTIVITIES: General meetings every month.

PUBLICATIONS
Bulletin (monthly)

AWARDS
Sir Kerr Grant Prize (annual)

MEMBERSHIP: 200 approx. (full, concessional)

27   Astronomical Society of Victoria

Box 1059J, G.P.O., Melbourne, Vic. 3001
Telephone: (03) 58 1425

SECRETARY: N.J. Plever

AFFILIATIONS
Astronomical Society of Albury-Wodonga(Mrs J. Dick, 379 Wantigong Street, Albury, N.S.W. 2640.)
Astronomical Society of Geelong (P. F. Cullen, Box 209, P.O., Geelong, Vic 3220.)
Astronomical Society of the Hunter (J. Tatersall, Newcastle Technical College Union, Maitland Road, Tighes Hill, N.S.W. 2297.)
Frankston Astronomical Society (T. B. Tregaskis,21 McGowen Road, Mount Eliza, Vic. 3930.)
Latrobe Valley Astronomical Society (K. Bryant, 20 Hillside, Yallourn, Vic. 3838.)

HISTORY: Founded in 1922

PURPOSE: To promote astronomical research by amateurs; to bring them into closer co-operation; to encourage the study of astronomy; and to disseminate knowledge of this science

INTERESTS: Conduct public demonstrations using trained demonstrators in co-operation with the Science Museum of Victoria. Interested in the study of aurorae, variable stars, novae, astrophotography, instrument making, lunar, solar and planetary research, and computing.

ACTIVITIES: General meetings held monthly, bi annual conventions organized in co-operation with other astronomical societies.

PUBLICATIONS
Journal of the Astronomical Society of Victoria (bi monthly)
Astronomical Yearbook

LIBRARY: Over 1000 titles (continually updated).

MEMBERSHIP: 550 (senior metropolitan, junior metropolitan, student metropolitan, country, institutional)

28   Astronomical Society of Western Australia, Inc.

A.S.W.A. Observatory, Elizabeth Street, Kalamunda, W.A.
(Box S1460, G.P.O., Perth 6001)
Telephone: (092) 67 2942

SECRETARY: A.M. Murray (Telephone: (095) 27 3268)

AFFILIATIONS
British Astronomical Association

HISTORY: Founded in 1950.

PURPOSE: To stimulate popular interest in astronomy and to act as an association of observers, for mutual help and organisation in the work of astronomical observation.

INTERESTS: Amateur astronomical observation; telescope making; discussion of astronomical topics and events.

ACTIVITIES: General Monthly Meeting, monthly Observing Meeting.

PUBLICATIONS
Journal of the Astronomical Society of W.A. (monthly)

AWARDS
Scientific Research Fund
Perpetual Trophy (annual)

MEMBERSHIP: 100 (ordinary, associate, country, junior, honorary life members)

29 Australasian Association for the History and Philosophy of Science

Basser Library, Australian Acadamy of Science, P.O. Box 216, Civic Square, A.C.T. 2608.
Telephone: (062) 48 6011

Royal Society of New Zealand, P.O.Box 12-249, Wellington 4, New Zealand

SECRETARY: Dr. M. E. Hoare

SUBDIVISIONS
Melbourne (Uinversity of Melbourne) and Sydney (University of N.S.W.)

HISTORY: Founded in 1967

PURPOSE: To further the study of the history of the sciences, technology and medicine, of the philosophy of the sciences and related subjects.

ACTIVITIES: Annual conference, Branch meetings.

PUBLICATIONS
Newsletter (annual)

MEMBERSHIP: 100 (ordinary, student)

30 Australasian Association of Philosophy

Philosophy Department, Research School of Social Sciences, A.N.U., Canberra, A.C.T. 2600.
Telephone: (062) 49 3266

SECRETARY: Dr. S.H. Voss

SUBDIVISIONS
Brisbane, Canberra, Melbourne, Newcastle, Perth, Sydney, Auckland and Dunedin.

HISTORY: Founded in 1922

PURPOSE: To promote philosophy

INTERESTS: Philosophy, e.g. philosophy of science, epistemology, logic, ethics, metaphysics, history.

ACTIVITIES: Annually in August, venue variable.

PUBLICATIONS
Australasian Journal of Philosophy

LIBRARY: Small collection maintained.

MEMBERSHIP: 300 (individual, institutional)

31 Australasian College of Dermatologists
271 Bridge Road, Glebe, N.S.W. 2037
Telephone: (02) 660 5392

SECRETARY: R.P. Armati

SUBDIVISIONS
Branches in Queensland, New South Wales, Victoria, South Australia, West Australia and New Zealand.

HISTORY: Founded in 1966. Fostered by the Dermatological Association of Australia, which was dissolved prior to inauguration in May 1967.

PURPOSE: To establish and maintain high standards of learning skill and conduct in the practice of dermatology; and encourage interest and scientific research in dermatological and related fields

INTERESTS: Dermatology, both clinical and practice and scientific research, training of undergraduates and post-graduate students. These fields extend into radiotherapy, clinical medicine, industrial medicine and even into the veterinary sciences.

PUBLICATIONS
Australasian Journal of Dermatology

LIBRARY: Dermatological texts and journals.

MEMBERSHIP: 222 (fellows, associate, honorary and corresponding members)

32 Australasian Corrosion Association
Clunies Ross House, 191 Royal Parade, Parkville, Vic.
(P.O. Box 117, Glen Waverley, 3150)
Telephone: (03) 62 0171

SECRETARY: P.H. Thorpe

SUBDIVISIONS
N.S.W. Branch - Mr. P. Ford (Secretary), School of Metallurgy, University of N.S.W., P.O. Box 1, Kensington, N.S.W.
New Zealand Branch - Mr. L. Boulton (Secretary), P.O. Box 5961, Wellesley Street, Auckland, New Zealand
Newcastle Branch - Mr. M. Thurgood (Secretary), P.O. Box 50, Charlestown, N.S.W.
Qld. Branch - Mr. J.L. Bristow (Secretary), P.O. Box 191, Indooroopilly, Qld.
S.A. Branch - Mr. R.H. Casling (Secretary), 12 Keys Road, Lower Mitcham, S.A.
Tas. Branch - Mr. D.G. Thomas (Secretary), care of- Electrolytic Zinc Co., G.P.O. Box 377D, Hobart, Tas.
Vic. Branch - Mr. J. Tanti (Secretary), Aust. Corrosion Assn, 191 Royal Parade, Parkville, Vic.
W.A. Branch - Dr. N.A. North (Secretary), Conservation Laboratory, W.A. Museum, Finnerty Street, Fremantle, W.A.

HISTORY: Founded as Australian Association for Corrosion Prevention; Melbourne Branch founded in 1955, Sydney Branch in 1956, Queensland Branch in 1958. The New Zealand Corrosion Prevention Association joined as a branch in 1960; name changed to present title in 1960.

PURPOSE: To promote co-operation of industrial, government organizations and interested individuals leading to a more complete awareness of the problems of corrosion and to its understanding and mitigation and to enable all interested individuals, companies and government bodies to study and solve those problems.

ACTIVITIES: Annual Australasian Conference; monthly branch meetings; symposia held regularly by all branches. International Congress on Metallic Corrosion held in 1975.

PUBLICATIONS
Corrosion Australasia
Australasian Corrosion Directory

AWARDS
Australasian Corrosion Medal
P.F. Thompson Memorial Lecture (annual)
Annual best paper awards

MEMBERSHIP: 804 (ordinary, student, company members)

33   Australasian Institute of Metal Finishing
Clunies Ross House, 191 Royal Parade, Parkville, Vic. 3052
Telephone: (03) 347 2526

SECRETARY: C.M. Whittington

SUBDIVISIONS
Branches in Adelaide, Brisbane, Melbourne, Sydney.

AFFILIATIONS
Electroplaters and Metal Polishers Group, New Zealand (Auckland Manufacturers Association, P.O. Box 28-090, Auckland)

HISTORY: Founded in 1969

PURPOSE: Advancement and dissemination of knowledge in the field of electroplating and other fields related to the finishing of metals.

INTERESTS: Electrodeposition and other industrial applications of electrochemistry; the pretreatment and organic coating of metals; plant, equipment and processes related to metal finishing.

ACTIVITIES: Monthly branch meetings; annual national conferences.

PUBLICATIONS
Metals Australia (11 times per year)
Electroplating and Metal Finishing (monthly)
Branch newsletters (10 times per year)

LIBRARY: Library maintained at Head Office.

AWARDS
Lawrence Smith Award (best two student papers, annually)
Electrofin Award (Apprentice award, Collingwood Technical School, Vic.)
Westinghouse Prize (best paper in 'Metals Australia' annually)

MEMBERSHIP: 600 (ordinary, student, corporate members)

34   Australasian Institute of Metals
191 Royal Parade, Parkville, Vic. 3052
Telephone: (03) 347 2526

SUBDIVISIONS
Branches in Adelaide, Brisbane, Melbourne, Newcastle, Perth, Port Kembla, Sydney and New Zealand.
Divisions in Central Victoria, Rockhampton and Townsville.

HISTORY: Incorporated in 1936, previously Metals Treatment Society

PURPOSE: To encourage the study of metals at all levels; to assist the metallurgical industry and profession; to strengthen the relationship between metallurgy and other scientific and technological interests.

ACTIVITIES: Monthly meetings all branches, annual conferences, special conferences.

PUBLICATIONS
Journal of the Australasian Institute of Metals
Metals Australia
Institute of Metals Handbook
Data Sheets

LIBRARY: Library maintained.

AWARDS
Metallographic exhibition, student subsidies, branch and federal awards.

MEMBERSHIP: 2000 (company, ordinary, student members)

35   Australasian Institute of Mining and Metallurgy
Clunies Ross House, 191 Royal Parade, Parkville, Vic.
(P.O. Box 310, Carlton South, 3053)
Telephone: (03) 347 3166

SECRETARY: W.E. Vance (Chief Executive Officer)

SUBDIVISIONS
34 branches throughout Australia, New Zealand, Papua New Guinea, Fiji.

AFFILIATIONS
Australian Geomechanics Society (joint technical unit with the Institution of Engineers, Australia)

HISTORY: Founded in 1893.

PURPOSE: To promote engineering with special reference to mining and metallurgy.

INTERESTS: Geology, exploration, mining, mineral beneficiation, extractive metallurgy, physical metallurgy, educational research, metals, non-metallic bodies, coal, petroleum.

ACTIVITIES: Annual conference, annual meeting, monthly meetings of branches, periodical symposia, seminars.

PUBLICATIONS
Bulletin of Australasian Institute of Mining and Metallurgy (monthly)
Proceedings of Australasian Institute of Mining and Metallurgy (quarterly)
Monographs of Australasian Institute of Mining and Metallurgy (periodically)
Annual conference and symposia series.

LIBRARY: Reference library maintained

AWARDS
Australasian Institute of Mining and Metallurgy Medal (annually)
President's Award (annually)
Students' Essay prizes (annually)

MEMBERSHIP: 6,281 (members, associate members, juniors, affiliates, students, company members)

36   Australasian Institute of Radiography
Suite No. 1, 228 Clarendon Street, East Melbourne, Vic.
(P.O. Box 278, East Melbourne 3002)
Telephone: (03) 419 3336

SECRETARY: W. Gilbert-Purssey (General Secretary)

SUBDIVISIONS
N.S.W., Qld, S.A., Tas., Vic., W.A.

AFFILIATIONS
New Zealand Society of Radiographers
Society of Radiographers (U.K.)
American Registry of Radiologic Technologists
Canadian Society of Radiological Technicians
Nederlandse Vereniging van Radiologisch Laboranten (Holland)
International Secretariat of Radiographers and Radiological Technicians

HISTORY: Incorporated under the Companies Act, 1936 (N.S.W.) on 20th Feb., 1950

PURPOSE: To promote, encourage and provide for advancement and regulation of the practice of medical radiography (and radiotherapy) and allied sciences; to cultivate and maintain the highest principles of practice and ethics.

ACTIVITIES: Annual National Technical Conference; monthly state branch meetings; regional sub-branch meetings, occasional joint 'mini-conferences.'

PUBLICATIONS
Radiographer (quarterly)
AIR-ab Monthly (monthly appointments bulletin)

LIBRARY: Federal archives and branch libraries in Vic, Tas and S.A.

AWARDS
Wat-Vic Award of Merit (for outstanding service to Radiography)
Cecil E. Eddy Memorial Oration (annually, during Annual National Technical Conference)
Edgar J. Rouse Post-graduate Lectureships
Education Fund to provide for travelling scholarships etc. - usually associated with overseas travel. The same fund finances continuing education schemes (eg. Fellowship examinations etc.)

MEMBERSHIP: 1980 (fellow, ordinary, student, associate, honorary members)

37   Australasian Society of Clinical and Experimental Pharmacologists
Department of Medicine, University of Melbourne, Parkville, Vic. 3052
Telephone: (03) 342 7702

SECRETARY: Dr. J. Shaw

SUBDIVISIONS
New Zealand membership administered by Subcommittee of Council. Dr. W.M. Smeeton (Secretary), P.O. Box 23-244, Papatoetoe, Auckland, New Zealand.

AFFILIATIONS
International Union of Pharmacology
National Committee for Pharmacology

HISTORY: Founded in 1967.

PURPOSE: To promote and advance the study and application of pharmacology in all its aspects

INTERESTS: Medicine, pharmacology, clinical pharmacology, pharmaceutical science, veterinary science, biological science.

ACTIVITIES: Scientific meetings in Australia and New Zealand; annual general meeting; council meetings

PUBLICATIONS
Publications in clinical and experimental pharmacology and physiology.

MEMBERSHIP: 395 (ordinary, honorary members)

38 Australasian Society of Engineers

Federal Office, 2nd floor, 422-424 Kent Street, Sydney, N.S.W.
(Box 2195, P.O., Queen Victoria Buildings, Sydney 2000)
Telephone: (02) 29 4147

SECRETARY: T.L. Addison (Federal Secretary)

SUBDIVISIONS
N.S.W. - A.R. Honeyman (State Secretary), 422-424 Kent Street, Sydney, N.S.W. 2000 (Telephone: (02) 29 8288)
Vic. - F. Boswell (State Secretary), 15 Drummond Street, South Carlton, Vic. 3053 (Telephone: (03) 347 4188)
S.A. - A.R. Griffiths (State Secretary), 38-40 Sturt Street, Adelaide, S.A. 5000 (Telephone: (08) 51 5484)
W.A. - N. Xavier (Acting State Secretary), 318 Lord Street, Perth, W.A. 6000 (Telephone: (092) 28 4799)
Tas. - J.E. Foster (State Secretary), 265 Macquarie Street, Hobart, Tas. 7000 (Telephone: (002) 23 6173)

HISTORY: Founded on Feb. 4, 1890.

PURPOSE: To service the members for the good of those workers working within Australia.

ACTIVITIES: Federal Council, Federal Conference.

PUBLICATIONS
Australasian Society of Engineers Federal Journal

MEMBERSHIP: 38 000 financial members

39 Australian Academy of Science

P.O.Box 783, Canberra City, A.C.T. 2601
Telephone: (062) 48 6011

SECRETARY: H.A.W. Southon (Executive Secretary)

AFFILIATIONS
The Academy represents Australia in a number of international non-government scientific organizations.
International Council of Scientific Unions

HISTORY: Established by Royal Charter in 1954.

PURPOSE: Similar to national academies of science in many countries. Its purpose is to review scientific matters of national importance, act as a consultant by the Australian government on scientific matters, disseminate scientific knowledge, establish and maintain contacts between Australian Scientists and international bodies and help administer funds for purposes of scientific research.

INTERESTS: The natural sciences in Australia.

ACTIVITIES: Annual General Meeting; international and national scientific conferences (3 or 4 per year); Science and Industry Forum (twice yearly); many committees.

PUBLICATIONS
Records of the Australian Academy of Science (annual)
Reports of the Australian Academy of Science (occasional)
Calendar of Scientific Meetings in Australia (twice yearly)
Science and Industry Forum Reports (occasional)
Biological Science. The Web of Life (school text)
Year book
Reports to international bodies
Proceedings of scientific conferences (occasional)

LIBRARY: Adolph Basser Library specialising in the history of Australian Science.

AWARDS
Matthew Flinders Lecture
Burnet Lecture
Thomas Ranken Lyle Medal
Pawsey Medal
Selby Fellowship
Geoffrey Frew Fellowship
Gottschalk Medal
Rudi Lemberg Travelling Fellowship

MEMBERSHIP: 167 fellows; 4 corresponding members (overseas)

40   Australian Academy of Technological Sciences
191 Royal Parade, Parkville, Vic. 3052
Telephone: (03) 347 3166

SECRETARY: Miss B.E. Jacka (Administrative Officer), Dr. H.K. Worner (Secretary)

HISTORY: Founded in 1976

PURPOSE: To promote in Australia the application of scientific knowledge to practical purposes and to provide in Australia a forum for discussion and advice to government and the community in relation to the application of scientific knowledge; to initiate and sponsor multi-disciplinary studies related to and necessary for the better understanding of the social and economic implications of technological sciences; to encourage research and education in technological sciences and the education and training of appropriate professional and technological staff for such research and for the practice of technological sciences; to provide an incentive for the pursuit in Australia of technological sciences by the election to Fellowship of the Academy of persons of proven ability and achievement in technological sciences; to develop an effective liaison with other Australian Academies concerned with the natural sciences, social sciences, humanities, and the arts; to collaborate with professional institutes and other learned societies and educational institutions in matters of mutual interest; to establish and maintain relations between the Academy and overseas bodies having essentially the same objectives in technological sciences as the Academy.

INTERESTS: Technology, natural resources, environment, national security, natural disasters.

ACTIVITIES: Annual Conference and Symposium; Annual Meeting; Council Meetings (6 times per year)

PUBLICATIONS
Presidential Address of the Australian Academy of Technological Sciences (annual)
Annual Report
Newsletter (quarterly)

MEMBERSHIP: 111 (Royal fellow, honorary fellow, fellows)

41   Australian Acoustical Society
Science Centre, 35 Clarence Street, Sydney, N.S.W. 2000
Telephone: (02) 29 7747

SECRETARY: W.A. Davern, Division of Building Research, CSIRO Graham Road, Highett, Vic. 3190

SUBDIVISIONS
N.S.W. - Science Centre, 35 Clarence Street, Sydney, N.S.W. 2000
Vic. - National Science Centre, 191 Royal Parade, Parkville, Vic. 3052
W.A. - G. Yates, Physiology Department, University of W.A., Nedlands, W.A. 6009
S.A. - D.H. Woolford, Engineering, Australian Broadcasting Commission, 85 North East Road, Collinswood, S.A. 5081

HISTORY: Founded in 1964 as a federal society with divisions in New South Wales and Victoria. Membership in states has continued to increase and divisions were formed in Western Australia in May, 1972 and in South Australia in March 1976

PURPOSE: To promote and advance the science and practice of acoustics in all its branches and to facilitate the exchange of information and ideas in this field.

INTERESTS: Sound, noise, vibration, architectural acoustics, hearing, underwater sound, ultrasonics, bi-acoustics, music.

ACTIVITIES: One major conference or symposium each year; divisional technical meetings.

PUBLICATIONS
Quarterly bulletin

MEMBERSHIP: Approximately 300 (honorary, fellows, members, affiliates, subscribers, students)

42   Australian Agricultural Economics Society
Suite 302, Clunies Ross House, 191 Royal Parade, Parkville, Vic. 3052
Telephone: (03) 347 1277

SECRETARY: H.J. Plunkett

SUBDIVISIONS
Branches in New South Wales, Victoria, Australian Capital Territory, Queensland, Western Australia and New Zealand.

HISTORY: Founded in 1957

PURPOSE: To encourage the pursuit of study, research, and extension work in the discipline of agricultural economics.

ACTIVITIES: Annual conference in 2nd week in February; Branches hold regular and special meetings and symposia

PUBLICATIONS
Australian Journal of Agricultural Economics
Branch newsletters and monographs

AWARDS
Journal article prize (one per year)
Masters thesis award (one per year)
Papua New Guinea studentship (one per year)

MEMBERSHIP: 1300 (students, library, ordinary, corporate members).

43   Australian Animal Technicians' Association
P.O. Box 4, P.H.H. Little Bay, N.S.W. 2036
Telephone: (02) 661 0111 ext 326

SECRETARY: T. Smith (National Secretary)

SUBDIVISIONS
Branches in Australian Capital Territory, Victoria, Queensland, South Australia, Tasmania.

HISTORY: Founded by a few dedicated technicians who envisaged that a training programme was needed for employees working with animals used for research purposes. Founded in 1963 in South Australia, Queensland in 1963, A.C.T. and N.S.W. in 1964, W.A. in 1965, Victoria in 1971.

PURPOSE: To promote and further the interest of its members and raise the standards of scientific animal care and investigation; to arrange tuition in animal care - to this and courses in animal care have been arranged at technical colleges in each Australian state.

ACTIVITIES: Conferences (held bi-annually in different states in turn); monthly branch meetings.

PUBLICATIONS
Whyalla (quarterly)

AWARDS
Jack Loftus Memorial Award (for best student completing animal care course)
Prizes, certificates and diplomas issued to students who have successfully completed stages of the animal care course, together with set periods of employment in an approved animal establishment.

MEMBERSHIP: Approximately 500 (affiliates, ordinary members, associates, students, qualified personnel, fellows)

44 Australian Association of Clinical Biochemists
Biochemistry Department, Royal Prince Alfred Hospital, Camperdown, N.S.W. 2050
Telephone: (02) 51 0444

SECRETARY: Dr. J.B. Whitfield

SUBDIVISIONS
Branches in New South Wales, Victoria, South Australia, Queensland, Western Australia, Tasmania.

AFFILIATIONS
International Federation of Clinical Chemistry

HISTORY: Founded in 1961

PURPOSE: To advance the study and practice of clinical biochemistry; to disseminate knowledge of the principles and practice of clinical biochemistry; to protect and promote the interests of clinical biochemistry.

ACTIVITIES: Annual general and scientific meeting; branch meetings.

AWARDS
Roman Memorial Lectureship (annual)

MEMBERSHIP: 500 (honorary fellows, fellows, members, associates, sustaining members)

45 Australian Association of Dieticians
Box 331, Civic Square, Canberra, A.C.T. 2608

SECRETARY: Mrs. E. Richardson

AFFILIATIONS
Dietetic Association of New South Wales
Dietetic Association of Victoria
Dietetic Association of Western Australia
Dietetic Association, South Australia
Dietetic Association, Australian Capital Territory
Dietetic Association of Queensland

HISTORY: Founded in 1976 (Replaced the Australian Dietetic Council which was founded in 1949)

PURPOSE: To foster and develop dietetic work in Australia; to unify the profession of dietetics; to improve standards of training; to improve efficiency in the profession; to communicate with similar bodies overseas.

ACTIVITIES: Annual meeting; 7th International Congress of Dietetics (to be held in Sydney, May 1977).

AWARDS
Margaret Shoobridge Memorial Lecture (triennial)

MEMBERSHIP: Full, provisional, student membership in 6 affiliate associations.

46 Australian Association of Gerontology
Science Centre, 35-43 Clarence Street, Sydney, N.S.W. 2000
Telephone: (02) 29 7747

SECRETARY: Mrs. R.J. Inall

SUBDIVISIONS
Branches in all states.

HISTORY: Founded in 1964

PURPOSE: To promote gerontological research; to promote co-operation between organizations and individuals interested in gerontology; to promote the training of persons in the fields of gerontology.

ACTIVITIES: Annual conference, meetings held by individual societies in each state.

PUBLICATIONS
Proceedings of the Australian Association of Gerontology

LIBRARY: Library at Lidcombe State Hospital

MEMBERSHIP: 750 (individual, corporate members)

47   Australian Association of Mathematics Teachers
Education Department, Construction House, 37 Havelock Street, West Perth, W.A. 6005
Telephone: (092) 22 6722

SECRETARY: R. McCreddin

AFFILIATIONS
Mathematical Association of South Australia
New England Mathematical Association
Queensland Association of Mathematics Teachers
Canberra Mathematical Association
Mathematical Association of Tasmania
Newcastle Mathematical Association
Mathematical Association of Victoria
Mathematical Association of Western Australia
Mathematical Association of New South Wales
Northern Rivers Mathematical Association

HISTORY: Founded in 1966

PURPOSE: To promote interest in mathematical education at all levels; to promote research in the teaching of mathematics; to publish and distribute a journal; to hold conferences; to speak and act on national matters related to mathematical education.

ACTIVITIES: Biennial conferences in even numbered years.

PUBLICATIONS
Australian Mathematics Teacher

AWARDS
Australian Association of Mathematics Teachers Prize (for research and practice in mathematics)

MEMBERSHIP: 2,500 (branch, honorary, individual, institutional members)

48   Australian Association of Neurologists
Suite 5, 5th Floor, North Shore Medical Centre, 66-80 Pacific Highway, St. Leonards, N.S.W. 2065
Telephone: (02) 43 5533

SECRETARY: Dr. P.M. Williamson

SUBDIVISIONS
State committees in New South Wales, Victoria, Queensland, South Australia, Western Australia.

HISTORY: Founded in 1950

PURPOSE: To bring together physician neurologists and scientific workers in the field of the nervous system and its diseases, for their mutual benefit, and better understanding of the nervous system and its diseases.

ACTIVITIES: Conferences and meetings; annual scientific and annual ordinary business meetings.

PUBLICATIONS
Proceedings of the Australian Association of Neurologists (annually)

MEMBERSHIP: 133 (provisional, ordinary, associate, honorary members)

49   Australian Association of Occupational Therapists Inc.
18 Mahara Street, Bardon, Qld, 4065
Telephone: (072) 36 1223

SECRETARY: Miss E.L. Watson (Honorary Secretary)

SUBDIVISIONS
Member Associations - New South Wales Association of Occupational Therapists

AFFILIATIONS
Victorian Association of Occupational Therapists
South Australian Association of Occupational Therapists
Western Australian Association of Occupational Therapists
Queensland Association of Occupational Therapists
Tasmanian Association of Occupational Therapists
World Federation of Occupational Therapists

HISTORY: Founded in New South Wales in 1956, incorporated in Western Australia.

PURPOSE: To promote the science and art of occupational therapy and the development, use, practice and ethics of the same in Australia. To educate and inform public and governmental opinion as to the practice of occupational therapy.

INTERESTS: Education of occupational therapists; research into techniques of occupational therapy; reciprocity with W.F.O.T. member countries in work and educational standards.

ACTIVITIES: Annual council meeting; biennial conference.

PUBLICATIONS
Australian Occupational Therapy Journal
National Occupational Therapy News (newsletter)
State newsletter printed in New South Wales, Victoria and Western Australia.

LIBRARY: State Occupational Therapy Association libraries.

AWARDS
Sylvia Docker Lecture

MEMBERSHIP: Approximately 700 (full members, associate or country members, honorary members, students)

50   Australian Association of Social Workers
11 Ferguson Street, Abbotsford, Vic.
(P.O. Box 1059, North Richmond, 3121)
Telephone: (03) 41 6960 and 41 4797

SECRETARY: A. Sutherland (P.O. Box 366, Woden, A.C.T. 2606)

SUBDIVISIONS
Victoria - Miss B. Brown (Hon. Secretary), care of - Mrs. G. Hawkins, P.O. Box 1059, Richmond North 3121.
Tasmania - Mr. W. Inglis (Hon. Secretary), care of - Miss M. Darmody, G.P.O. Box 356D., Hobart 7000.
South Australia - Hon. Secretary, AASW S.A. Branch, G.P.O. Box 278D., Adelaide 5000.
Australian Capital Territory - Mr. A. Sutherland, Social Work Department, Woden Valley Hospital, Woden 2606.
Queensland - Ms. J. Zubevitch, care of - Mrs. N. Ives, 302 Bennetts Road, Norman Park 4170.
Western Australia - Rev. Fr. B. Hickey, 25 Victoria Square, Perth 6000.
New South Wales - Ms. V. Chivell, care of - Mrs. M. Fennell, P.O. Box N10, Grosvenor Street, Sydney 2000.
Northern Territory - Miss D. McLean, P.O. Box 1640, Darwin 5794.

AFFILIATIONS
Australian Council of Social Service
International Federation of Social Workers

HISTORY: Founded in 1946

PURPOSE: To foster the values, knowledge and skills of the social work profession in Australia; to promote and develop professional social work practice which is primarily concerned with the optimum welfare of the individual and the community.

INTERESTS: Social policy, social planning and administration; social work and social welfare education; community development, rights and needs of minorities and disadvantaged peoples.

ACTIVITIES: A.A.S.W. national conference (biennial); branch general meetings, conferences and many informal group meetings to develop particular fields of professional interest.

PUBLICATIONS
Australian Social Work (quarterly journal)
Monthly branch newsletters in South Australia, Victoria and New South Wales; quarterly branch newsletters in Western Australia and Queensland

LIBRARY: Library at Federal Office, mainly international social work journals and reference material on social work education throughout the world.

AWARDS
Norma Parker Award (annual, for best assignment by a social work student)
Wilga Fleming Prize (annual, for best professional entry published in 'Australian Social Work')
Isobel Straughan Prize (annual, final year field work prize, Melbourne University)

MEMBERSHIP: 1,600 (members, associates, student affiliates)

51 Australian Association of Speech and Hearing
253 Hampton Street, Hampton, Vic. 3188
Telephone: (03) 598 0097

SECRETARY: Mrs. A. Manolitsas (General Secretary), A.I. Brown (Honorary Secretary)

SUBDIVISIONS
A.C.T. Branch - Hon. Secretary, 169 Millers Street, O'Connor, A.C.T. 2601
N.S.W. Branch - Hon. Secretary, P.O. Box 105, Roseville, N.S.W. 2069
Qld. Branch - Hon. Secretary, P.O. Box 235, North Brisbane, Qld. 4000
S.A. Branch - Hon. Secretary, P.O. Box 35, North Adelaide, S.A. 5006
Tas. Branch - Hon. Secretary, P.O. Box 117, South Launceston, Tas. 7250
Vic. Branch - Hon. Secretary, care of- School of Human Communication Disorders, Lincoln Institute, 625 Swanston Street, Carlton, Vic. 3053
W.A. Branch - Hon. Secretary, P.O. Box 224, Subiaco, W.A. 6008

HISTORY: Founded in 1953 as Australian College of Speech Therapists. Name changed in 1975.

PURPOSE: To promote the profession of speech pathology and its inter-relation with any allied science in particular medical, surgical, psychological, physical and educational.

INTERESTS: Human communication and related disorders.

ACTIVITIES: Annual study conference in alternate states; branch meetings, seminars and workshops.

PUBLICATIONS
Australian Journal of Human Communication Disorders (twice per year)
Speech Pathology in Australia

LIBRARY: Library facilities in each state.

AWARDS
Journal prize for article submitted to Australian Journal of Human Communications Disorders by a member

MEMBERSHIP: 600 (practising, subscriber, non-practising, fellow)

52   Australian Association of Surgeons
Great Pacific House, 55 Lavender Street, Milson's Point, N.S.W.
(P.O. Box 821, North Sydney 2060)
Telephone: (02) 922 3022

SECRETARY: G. Arthur (Executive Director)

SUBDIVISIONS
Victoria - Mr K.G. Grenfell-Hoyle (Executive Secretary), 19 Landsdowne Street, East Melbourne, Vic. 3002 (Telephone: (03) 662 2277)
State Committee is elected annually in each State

HISTORY: Founded in 1972.

PURPOSE: To promote and safeguard the professional interests of surgeons and to this end to maintain and improve the conditions of service of surgeons in carrying out their duties to the community.

ACTIVITIES: Annual meeting.

PUBLICATIONS
Principles of Surgical Care (quarterly)
Newsletters to members

AWARDS
Justin Fleming Memorial Medal

MEMBERSHIP: 1450 (ordinary, honorary)

53   Australian Biochemical Society
Division of Human Nutrition, CSIRO, Kintore Avenue, Adelaide, S.A. 5000
Telephone: (08) 223 5511

SECRETARY: Dr. F.J. Ballard

AFFILIATIONS
Federation of Asian and Oceanian Biochemists
International Union of Biochemists

HISTORY: Founded in 1955

PURPOSE: The advancement of the science of biochemistry.

ACTIVITIES: Annual conference; specialist workshops

PUBLICATIONS
Proceedings of the Australian Biochemical Society

AWARDS
R.K. Morton Scholarships

MEMBERSHIP: 1,300 (ordinary, honorary, student, sustaining members)

54   Australian Cancer Society
Suites 311-312, 155 King Street, Sydney, N.S.W.
(G.P.O. Box 4708, Sydney 2001)

SECRETARY: Mr. G. Pickford (Executive Director)

AFFILIATIONS
Clinical Oncological Society of Australia

HISTORY: Founded in 1961 as a federation of the State Cancer Councils.

INTERESTS: Cancer research; professional and public education in cancer; service to cancer patients.

ACTIVITIES: Bi-annual meeting of Australian Cancer Society's council and committees; annual meeting of the Clinical Oncological Society of Australia.

PUBLICATIONS
Cancer Forum (4 monthly journal)
Annual Report
Tar and Nicotine Contents of Cigarettes (pamphlet, annually)
Sunscreen Lotions in Order of Effectiveness (pamphlet, annually)

AWARDS
Postdoctoral research fellowship awarded annually.

MEMBERSHIP: Australian Cancer Society - 7 State Cancer Councils; Clinical Oncological Society of Australia - 600 members.

55   Australian Capital Territory Association of Occupational Therapists
Occupational Therapy Department, Woden Valley Hospital, P.O.Box 11, Woden, A.C.T. 2606
Telephone: (062) 81 0433

SECRETARY: Mrs. J. Gretton

HISTORY: Founded in 1973

PURPOSE: To promote the profession of occupational therapy and the development, use, practice and ethics of same.

INTERESTS: Professional communication, education and development, and the community and health care.

MEMBERSHIP: 27 (full, associate members)

56   Australian Ceramic Society
Department of Ceramic Engineering, University of New South Wales, P.O. Box 1, Kensington, N.S.W. 2033
Telephone: (02) 531 3457

SECRETARY: K.D. Reeve (Federal Secretary)

SUBDIVISIONS
Victorian Branch - Brick Development Research Institute, School of Architecture and Building, University of Melbourne, Parkville, 3052
New South Wales Branch - same address as headquarters

HISTORY: Founded in 1970 by amalgamation of Australian Ceramic Societies in New South Wales and Victoria.

PURPOSE: Promotion of research and technology of ceramics.

ACTIVITIES: Monthly meetings conducted by each branch; biennial technical conference.

PUBLICATIONS
Journal of the Australian Ceramic Society

LIBRARY: Library at headquarters

AWARDS
Scholarship in Ceramic Engineering (University of New South Wales)

MEMBERSHIP: Approximately 300 (ordinary, company, student members, subscribers)

57   Australian Chiropody Association (Vic.)
245 Punt Road, Richmond, Vic. 3121
Telephone: (03) 42 5027

HISTORY: Chiropodists Association of Victoria founded in 1929 and the Australian Institute of Chiropodists founded in 1932; merged in 1962. In 1968, they merged with the National Society of Chiropodists, which had been founded in 1947.

PURPOSE: To advance and encourage the profession of chiropody in Victoria, in co-operation with other chiropody associations in Australia.

ACTIVITIES: Monthly membership lectures; seminars; conventions.

PUBLICATIONS
Australian Podiatrist

LIBRARY: Library maintained

MEMBERSHIP: 446 (full, retired, honorary members)

58   Australian Chiropractors Association, A.C.T. Council
13 Theodore Street, A.C.T.
(Box 124, Curtin, A.C.T. 2605.)
Telephone: (062) 81 4740 (A.H. - 54 7266)

SECRETARY: F. Wyss, 54 Longeronong Street, Farrer, A.C.T.

SUBDIVISIONS
Branches in each state which are affiliated with a federal body

HISTORY: Founded in the A.C.T. in 1973

PURPOSE: To further the chiropractic profession, obtain registration and to protect members by setting minimum standards

INTERESTS: Chiropractic health care, particularly of handicapped children, maintaining a high professional standard of practice.

ACTIVITIES: Annual and bi-annual meetings and seminars

PUBLICATIONS
Federal and state journals

MEMBERSHIP: (Practising, non-practising and honorary members)

59   Australian Clay Minerals Society
C.S.R. Research Pty. Ltd., 28 Barcoo Street, Roseville, N.S.W.
(P.O. Box 39, Roseville, 2069)
Telephone: (02) 407 0271

SECRETARY: Dr. J.H. Patterson

HISTORY: Founded in 1962

PURPOSE: To further the study of clay minerals and allied substances, stimulating interest in clay mineralogy and encouraging the practical applications of clay minerals research.

ACTIVITIES: Biennial conference

PUBLICATIONS
Conference abstracts, conference proceedings.

MEMBERSHIP: Approximately 80 (ordinary, student, visiting, honorary, company members)

60   Australian College of Allergists
98 Kermode Street, North Adelaide, S.A. 5006

SECRETARY: Dr. S. Birdseye

SUBDIVISIONS
Branches in each state of Australia.

AFFILIATIONS
Australian Medical Association

HISTORY: Founded in 1953

PURPOSE: To advance and maintain the highest possible standards amongst those engaged in the practice of allergy; to set and maintain standards for qualification of practitioners engaging in the practice of allergy and applied immunology as a speciality

ACTIVITIES: Annual general meeting and conference.

AWARDS
Proceedings, papers, letters

MEMBERSHIP: 97 (fellows, honorary fellows, members, associate members)

61   Australian College of Medical Administrators
293 Royal Parade, Parkville, Vic. 3052
Telephone: (03) 347 6127

SECRETARY: Mrs. E. Hunter

SUBDIVISIONS
State Committees in all States and Territories

HISTORY: Founded in 1967.

PURPOSE: To advance the standard of medical administration by post graduate and continuing education.

ACTIVITIES: Annual national conference, numerous scientific meetings conducted in each capital city.

AWARDS
Bernard Nicholson Prize (to outstanding examinee)

MEMBERSHIP: 322 fellows

62 Australian College of Veterinary Scientists
A.V.A. House, 70 Station Road, Indooroopilly, Qld. 4068
Telephone: (07) 378 5720

SECRETARY: Dr. G.I. Alexander

HISTORY: Founded in 1971

PURPOSE: To advance the study of veterinary science and to bring together members of the veterinary profession for their common benefit; to hold conduct or arrange examinations of professional proficiency.

ACTIVITIES: Monthly executive meeting; bi-annual council meeting; annual general meeting.

PUBLICATIONS
College brochure; college newsletter

AWARDS
Australian College of Veterinary Science Prize (for outstanding contributions of veterinary science in any field)

MEMBERSHIP: Approximately 500 (ordinary, life members, honorary fellows)

63 Australian Computer Society Incorporated
C.S.A. Centre, 460 Pacific Highway, St.Leonards, N.S.W.
(P.O. Box 640, Crows Nest, 2065)
Telephone: (02) 439 2434

SECRETARY: K. Arter

SUBDIVISIONS
Branches in New South Wales, Australian Capital Territory, Victoria, Queensland, South Australia, Western Australia, Tasmania.

HISTORY: Founded in 1966 by amalgamation of five previously existing local computer societies. Western Australian branch admitted later.

PURPOSE: To extend the knowledge and appreciation of digital and analogue computers, automatic data processing systems and computer based automatic control systems, and related theory; to further the study and application of computer science and technology, information processing and related subjects; to maintain a code of ethics and to define standards of knowledge in the computer field; to promote the integrity and develop the competence of persons engaged in the science, technology and practice of computing and information processing.

ACTIVITIES: Australian Computer Conferences; monthly branch meetings; Professional Development Seminars.

PUBLICATIONS
Australian Computer Journal (3 issues per year)
Australian Computer Bulletin (10 issues per year)

LIBRARY: Small libraries maintained by Council and some branches.

AWARDS
Australian Computer Society Lecture of the Year
Australian National Committee on Computation and Automatic Control Prize
Australian Computer Society Case Study Prize

MEMBERSHIP: 6669 personal members, 150 institutional members

64   Australian Conservation Foundation Incorporated
364 Albert Street, East Melbourne, Vic. 3002
Telephone: (03) 419 3366

SECRETARY: Dr. J.G. Mosley (Director)

SUBDIVISIONS
Western Chapter - Perth based
North east Chapter - Brisbane based
N.S.W. Office - Laureton

HISTORY: Founded in 1965; Secretariat established in 1966

PURPOSE: To promote the understanding and practice of conservation throughout Australia and its territories.

INTERESTS: The total environment, including the urban environment.

ACTIVITIES: Council meetings; seminars and symposia; membership functions; annual general meeting.

PUBLICATIONS
Habitat (bimonthly)
Viewpoint Publications
Conservation Directory
ACF Newsletter (monthly)
Special publications; other ACF publications; annual report

LIBRARY: Library open to public

AWARDS
Grants given for the purpose of carrying out the objects of the foundation.

MEMBERSHIP: 8400 (ordinary, life members, member bodies, national sponsors, benefactors)

65   Australian Consumers' Association
28 Queen Street, Chippendale, N.S.W. 2008
Telephone: (02) 698 9200

SECRETARY: Ms. G. Ettinger (Executive Officer)

AFFILIATIONS
Australian Federation of Consumer Organizations
International Organization of Consumer Unions

HISTORY: Founded in 1959

PURPOSE: To promote consumer education and protection; to conduct comparative tests of goods and services available and to publish results. To prepare and make submissions to government enquiries; to promote consumer education.

ACTIVITIES: Periodic meetings of local consumer groups and IOCU biennial world meetings.

PUBLICATIONS
Choice
Choice with car supplement, a quarterly reprint from the journal of A.C.A.'s British counterparts.

LIBRARY: Periodicals library for members' use

MEMBERSHIP: 150,000 (ordinary, associate members)

66   Australian Council for Educational Research
9 Frederick Street, Hawthorn, Vic.
(P.O. Box 210, Hawthorn, 3122)
Telephone: (03) 81 1271

SUBDIVISIONS
Each state has an autonomous State Institute for Educational Research, which nominates one member
to the Council, which is the governing body of A.C.E.R. The state institute members are not members
of A.C.E.R.

PURPOSE: To promote and undertake research into education; to further the results of research and to
assist educational experiments.

ACTIVITIES: Annual council meeting.

PUBLICATIONS
Australian Journal of Education
Australian Education Review
A.C.E.R. Research Series
Occasional papers.

LIBRARY: Library for staff and inter-library loans

MEMBERSHIP: 13 members

67 Australian Council for Health, Physical Education and Recreation
P.O.Box 1, Kingswood, S.A. 5062
Telephone: (08) 272 1700

SECRETARY: G. Dodd (National Secretary)

SUBDIVISIONS
W.A. Branch - Mr. L. Pavey (President), care of- Physical Education Branch, Education Department,
W.A.
Vic. Branch - Mr. P. Fryar (President), care of- Ballarat College of Advanced Education, Ballarat,
Vic.
Tas. Branch - Mr. B. Stewart (President), care of- Physical Education Branch, Education Department,
Tas.
S.A. Branch - Mr. B.J. Stanton (President), care of- Physical Education Branch, 101 Crenmore Street,
Unley, S.A.
Qld. Branch - Miss P. Dickson (President), Kelvin Grove College of Advanced Education, Kelvin
Grove, Qld.
N.S.W. Branch - Dr. A. Colvin (President), care of- Curriculum Research and Development Branch,
N.S.W. Education Department, Sydney

HISTORY: Founded in 1954 as the Australian Physical Education Association

PURPOSE: To study and advance physical education, health education and recreation as disciplines of
educational, biological and sociological worth.

ACTIVITIES: Biennial national conference; regular state branch meetings of a professional nature.

PUBLICATIONS
Australian Journal of Physical Education (4 per year)
Bimonthly Bulletins in each State.

MEMBERSHIP: 1800 (full, associate, student, honorary, life members)

68 Australian Council on Hospital Standards
P.O. Box 144, St. Leonards, N.S.W. 2065
Telephone: (02) 439 5099

SECRETARY: E. Pickering

HISTORY: Founded in 1973.

PURPOSE: To act in a consultative role to hospitals.

INTERESTS: Hospital standards.

ACTIVITIES: Council meets quarterly; workshops conducted regularly.

PUBLICATIONS
Accreditation Guide for Australian Hospitals

LIBRARY: Limited to area of hospital standards and quality assurance.

MEMBERSHIP: 8 member organizations

69   Australian Dental Association
116 Pacific Highway, North Sydney, N.S.W. 2060
Telephone: (02) 92 0682, 92 0683

SECRETARY: Dr. C.H. Wall (Federal Secretary)

SUBDIVISIONS
Branches in New South Wales (R.B. Newland - Secretary), Queensland (A.H. Jackson - Secretary), South Australia (B. Blunt - Secretary), Tasmania (T.D. Crisp - Secretary), Victoria (A.H. Proud - Secretary) and Western Australia (R.C. Ward - Secretary).

AFFILIATIONS
Australian Society of Implant Dentistry
Australian and New Zealand Society of Oral Surgeons
Australian Society of Orthodontists
Australian Society of Periodontology
Australian Society of Prosthodontists
Australian Society of Endontology
Federation Dentaire Internationale

HISTORY: Australian Dental Association founded in 1909 as a federation of dental societies. Name changed to National Dental Association in 1910 and reverted to original title in 1927.

PURPOSE: To encourage the improvement of the health of the public and to promote the art and science of dentistry.

ACTIVITIES: Dental congress held every 3 years.

PUBLICATIONS
Australian Dental Journal
Australian Dental Association Dental Directory
Facts and Figures
Federal News Bulletin

LIBRARY: Libraries housed in New South Wales and Victorian branches

MEMBERSHIP: 4,492 (active, student, restricted, honorary members)

70   Australian Dried Fruits Association
24 Jeffcott Street, West Melbourne, Vic.
(Box No. 4524, Melbourne 3001)
Telephone: (03) 328 3019

SECRETARY: L.P. Burgess (General Secretary-Manager)

SUBDIVISIONS
Branches are established in the dried fruits producing areas of N.S.W., Vic., S.A. and W.A. In the larger areas of production, such as Sunraysia, Branches meet together as District Councils. Delegates from all Branches meet annually at Federal Council to receive the report of the Board of Management for the previous year.

HISTORY: In 1895 the Mildura and Renmark Dried Fruits Trusts met to establish minimum prices for their products. The two Trusts amalgamated in 1907 to form the Australian Dried Fruits Association.

PURPOSE: To preserve the dried fruits industry, the welfare of growers and the uniform marketing of dried fruits products.

INTERESTS: Marketing, processing, viticultural practices and research.

ACTIVITIES: Board of Management meets 8 times each year.

PUBLICATIONS
Australian Dried Fruits News (5 times per year)

AWARDS
Access to the Dried Fruits Research Fund which is financed by a levy on production and subsidized on a $-for-$ basis by the Commonwealth Government. The Association has a majority of members on the controlling Committee.

MEMBERSHIP: 4600 (grower, packer, agent)

71 Australian Electrical Vehicle Association
National Secretariat, 95 Collins Street, Melbourne, Vic. 3000
Telephone: (03) 63 0491

SECRETARY: C.J. Bain (National Secretary)

SUBDIVISIONS
Branches in Adelaide, Brisbane, Melbourne, Perth, Sydney, Townsville

HISTORY: Founded in Sept. 1973.

PURPOSE: To provide a forum for technical and social communications between persons and organisations interested in electric vehicles; to encourage electric vehicle research, development and use and to establish standards and quality of performance; to become the authoritative source of information on electric vehicles in Australia.

ACTIVITIES: Branch meetings bi-monthly; National Council meetings quarterly; Annual conferences held concurrently with Annual general meeting.

PUBLICATIONS
Electric Vehicle News (quarterly)

LIBRARY: Extensive library on electric vehicles, lead batteries and related fields at National Secretariat, 95 Collins Street, Melbourne.

MEMBERSHIP: 85 (corporate, ordinary, corporate overseas, ordinary overseas, student)

72 Australian Entomological Society
Plant Research Institute, Swan Street, Burnley, Vic. 3121
Telephone: (03) 81 1487

SECRETARY: Dr. T.G. Amos

AFFILIATIONS
Entomological Society of Queensland
Royal Zoological Society of New South Wales
Entomological Society of Victoria
Entomological Society of Australia (N.S.W.)

HISTORY: Founded in 1965

PURPOSE: The advancement and dissemination of entomological knowledge in all its aspects, particularly but not exclusively in relation to the Australian fauna.

ACTIVITIES: General and scientific meetings held usually in association with successive congress of A.N.Z.A.A.S.

PUBLICATIONS
Journal of the Australian Entomological Society
Australian Entomological Society News Bulletin
Miscellaneous publications

AWARDS
Annual awards to students in entomology

MEMBERSHIP: 551 (ordinary, honorary, sustaining, affiliate members)

73 Australian Farm Management Society
13th Floor, O'Connell House, 15 Bent Street, Sydney, N.S.W. 2000

SECRETARY: J. Chudleigh

SUBDIVISIONS
Branches in Perth, Merredin, Esperance, Albany, W.A.; Ballarat, Vic.; Albury-Wodonga, N.S.W.-Vic.; Adelaide, S.A.; Orange, Sydney, Armidale, N.S.W.; Brisbane, Qld.

HISTORY: Founded in 1971

PURPOSE: To establish an effective liaison between primary producers and those who service primary production.

ACTIVITIES: Branch meetings and a national annual conference.

PUBLICATIONS
Australian Farm Management Society Newsletter (10 per year)

AWARDS
Prizes for students at agricultural colleges.

MEMBERSHIP: 844 full members

74 Australian Federation of Construction Contractors
110 Alfred Street, Milsons Point, N.S.W.
(Box 427, P.O. Milsons Point, 2061.)
Telephone: (02) 92 5466, 92 4777

SECRETARY: G.G. Mathews (Executive Director); A.E. Holmes (Assistant Director)

SUBDIVISIONS
Branches in Queensland, New South Wales, Victoria, Tasmania, South Australia, Western Australia.

HISTORY: Founded 1959 by amalgamation of Associations of Civil Engineering Contractors in Victoria and New South Wales. In 1968 the Civil Engineering Contractors Association, Queensland merged with the Federation and now forms the Queensland Branch. In 1971 Australian Federation of Civil Engineering Contractors became by resolution of the general membership the Australian Federation of Construction Contractors operating under new rules. AFCC became an industrially registered organization under the Conciliation and Arbitration Act.

PURPOSE: To raise the status and advance the interests of civil engineering and heavy construction contractors and to provide an authorised voice on matters of common interest; to establish a code of ethics for construction contractors, and to make membership of the Federation a reasonable assurance to the public of the skill, integrity and responsibility of its members. Exchange of technical information amongst members; establishment of good industrial relations between members and their employees; encouragement of economics of construction through cooperative action and promotion and support of laws and regulations affecting construction contracts, and the interests of the community. Training courses are also conducted on subjects of interest to the industry at large.

ACTIVITIES: Regular meetings of the Council of the Federation and branches and committees thereof. Annual meetings; special general meetings; field days. Biennial convention held by Federation.

PUBLICATIONS
Manual of Dayworks Incidental to Contracts
Bonding of Construction Contractors
Case Against Day Labour Construction (booklet and summary)
Annual Report

LIBRARY: Library maintained.

AWARDS
Construction Achievement Award (annual)

MEMBERSHIP: 168 (full, associate members)

75 Australian Federation for Medical and Biological Engineering
Department of Electrical Engineering, University of Melbourne, Parkville, Vic. 3052
Telephone: (03) 341 6686

SECRETARY: Dr. D.J. Dewhurst

SUBDIVISIONS
Society for Medical and Biological Engineering (Victoria); L.J. Dally (Secretary), Department of Physiology, University of Melbourne, Parkville, 3052
New South Wales Society for Medical and Biological Engineering; K.L. Dingeldei (Secretary), 67 Stacey Street, Bankstown, 2200
South Australian Society for Medical and Biological Engineering; N.W. Martin (Secretary), 14a Hanson Avenue, Heathpool, 5068
Society for Medical and Biological Engineering (Tasmania); R.D. Sutherland (Secretary), Electronic Engineering Department, Cardiac Investigation Centre, Argyle Street, Hobart, 7000
Society for Medical and Biological Engineering (Queensland); Dr. A. Morton (Secretary), Repatriation Department, Repatriation General Hospital, Newdegate Street, Greenslopes, 4120

AFFILIATIONS
International Federation of Medical and Biological Engineering

HISTORY: Society for Medical and Biological Engineering (Victoria) founded in 1959; South Australian and New South Wales Societies founded in 1966; Australian Federation for Medical and Biological Engineering founded in 1966; Society in Tasmania in 1969; Society in Queensland in 1972.

PURPOSE: To promote progress of medical and biological engineering, to improve its status and to encourage research in it.

ACTIVITIES: Meetings of Australian Federation as required.

MEMBERSHIP: 350 (ordinary, honorary members)

76 Australian Federation of Medical Women
12 Brae Street, Coorparoo, Qld, 4151

SECRETARY: Dr. G. Lennon

SUBDIVISIONS
State branches in New South Wales, Queensland, Victoria, Tasmania, South Australia, Western Australia

AFFILIATIONS
Australian Medical Association
Mecical Women's International Association

HISTORY: Founded in 1929

PURPOSE: To promote the interests of medical women throughout Australia and to affiliate with the Medical Women's International Association

ACTIVITIES: State societies meet four or more times per year. The Federation holds triennial general meetings of Council and members. The Executive Council headquarters pass from state to state in rotation. Executive Council meets annually. The Federation is represented at Congress of Medical Women's International Association held in different countries throughout the world every two years.

MEMBERSHIP: Approximately 600 (full, associate members)

77 Australian Fire Protection Association
40 Chetwynd Street, West Melbourne, Vic. 3003
Telephone: (03) 329 5577

SECRETARY: D.A. Sandy (Executive Director)

SUBDIVISIONS
Interstate Representative Committees in all States, A.C.T. and N.T.

HISTORY: Founded in 1960 as a non-profit technical and educational organisation.

PURPOSE: To safeguard life and property against fire.

ACTIVITIES: Day seminars, National Conferences.

PUBLICATIONS
Fire Journal
Fire News
AFPA Monthly Bulletin
Technical Papers

LIBRARY: Technical reference library maintained.

MEMBERSHIP: 1200 (sponsors, associate members, full members, honorary life members)

78 Australian Foundry Institute (New South Wales Division)
8 Crofts Avenue, Hurstville, N.S.W. 2220
Telephone: (02) 570 1580

SUBDIVISIONS
Newcastle branch.

HISTORY: Founded in 1943

PURPOSE: To provide means of advancing foundry knowledge.

ACTIVITIES: Monthly meetings

PUBLICATIONS
Casting: a Journal for Foundrymen

MEMBERSHIP: Approximately 300 (members, company, associate, student members)

79 Australian French Association of Professional and Technical Specialists
383 George Street, Sydney, N.S.W.
(G.P.O. Box 512, Sydney 2001)
Telephone: (02) 29 4230

SECRETARY: D. Maurel-Roussel

AFFILIATIONS
Agence pour la Co-operation Technique Industrielle et Economique (A.C.T.I.M.)

HISTORY: Founded in 1963.

PURPOSE: To continue the benefits obtained through contact with French colleagues as a consequence of an A.C.T.I.M. fellowship granted by the French Government, and vice-versa with those French engineers and undergraduates who have been granted a fellowship in Australia; to promote scientific, educational and social activities between previous fellowship holders and other technical or professional people who have had an interest in these aspects of the French way of life; to create opportunities where previous and future scholars can meet and exchange ideas and experience, and scientific information relating to the two countries.

ACTIVITIES: Monthly guest evenings; lectures, seminars, film sessions.

MEMBERSHIP: (full member, associate member (individual), associate member (principal: firms, associations), student member, sponsor)

80   Australian Gas Association

Administrative Offices, Civic Permanent Centre, 32 Allara Street,
Canberra City, A.C.T.
(P.O. Box 155, Civic Square 2608) (Telex: AA62137)
Telephone: (062) 47 3955

SECRETARY: C. Dorning (General Manager)

SUBDIVISIONS
Technical Department - H. Hartmann (Chief Technical Officer), 320 St. Kilda Road, Melbourne, Vic. 3004 (Telephone: (03) 699 4344; Telex: AA34092)

HISTORY: Founded as the National Gas Association of Australia in 1935; name changed to present name in 1962.

PURPOSE: To promote and develop the gas industry in all its branches; to protect the interests of the industry and the public by setting standards.

ACTIVITIES: Annual Convention; Marketing and Industrial Seminars; Operating Seminars; Gas Workshops.

PUBLICATIONS
Australian Gas Journal (quarterly)
Directory of the Australian Gas Industry (annual)
Project material - Gas in Australia
Papers presented at Annual Conventions and other conferences

MEMBERSHIP: 654 (utility, manufacturer, associate, individual)

81   Australian Geography Teachers' Association

Adelaide College of Advanced Education, Kintore Avenue, Adelaide,
S.A. 5000
Telephone: (08) 223 8011

SECRETARY: R. Smith

SUBDIVISIONS
Geography Teachers Association of South Australia, care of- 163A Greenhill Road, Parkside, S.A.
Geography Teachers Association of New South Wales, care of- Science House, Glouscester Street, Sydney, N.S.W. 2000
Geography Teachers Association of Victoria, care of- P.O.Box 346, Carlton South, Vic. 3053
Geography Teachers Association of Queensland, care of- P.O.Box 84, North Brisbane, Qld. 4000
Tasmanian Geography Teachers Association, care of- Launceston Matriculation College, Paterson Street, Launceston, Tas. 7250
Geography Teachers Association of Western Australia, care of- P.O.Box 152, Nedlands, W.A. 6009
A.C.T.Geography Secretariat, care of- P.O.Box 20, Civic Square, A.C.T. 2608

HISTORY: Founded in 1967

PURPOSE: To promote the teaching and study of geography in Australian schools; to provide an organization through which teachers of geography may express opinions on educational matters and to promote research into geographical education.

ACTIVITIES: Council meetings held twice yearly. National conference held biennially.

PUBLICATIONS
Geographical Education
Geography Education Monograph Series
Readings in Geographical Education Vols. I&II
Geography in Education
Taminga (G.T.A.S.A.)
Geography Bulletin (G.T.A.N.S.W.)
Geography Teacher (G.T.A.V.)
G.T.A.Q.Journal
Geography Courier (T.G.T.A.)
Bulletin, G.T.A.W.A.

AWARDS
Australian Geography Teachers' Association Award (issued for outstanding books and materials
produced in Australia contributing to geography teaching)

MEMBERSHIP: Approximately 3000 members

82   Australian Geomechanics Society
Institution of Engineers, Australia, 11 National Circuit, Barton, A.C.T.
2600
Telephone: (062) 73 3633

SECRETARY: E.D. Storr

SUBDIVISIONS
Branches in each state capital and Newcastle.

AFFILIATIONS
International Association of Engineering Geology
International Society for Rock Mechanics
International Society of Rock Mechanics and Foundation Engineering

HISTORY: Founded in 1970

PURPOSE: To promote and advance the science and practice of geomechanics.

ACTIVITIES: National conferences held yearly; local meetings arranged by local groups and branches.

PUBLICATIONS
Australian Geomechanics Journal

MEMBERSHIP: Approximately 400 (corporate members, graduates, associates, affiliates)

83   Australian Geosciences Information Association
Australian Mineral Foundation, Conyngham Street, Glenside, S.A.
(P.O. Box 97, Glenside 5065)
Telephone: (08) 79 7821

SECRETARY: Mrs. J. Jones (Consolidated Goldfields Aust. Ltd., Goldfields House, Sydney Cove, N.S.W.
2000. Telephone: (02) 2 0512

SUBDIVISIONS
Melbourne - Miss H. Cameron, Australian Anglo American Ltd., 500 Collins Street, Melbourne, Vic.
Adelaide - Mr. J. Keeling, Department of Mines, P.O. Box 151, Eastwood, S.A.
Brisbane - Mrs. M. Emery, Utah Development Corporation, G.P.O. Box 1389, Brisbane, Qld.
A.C.T. - Mrs. H. Hughes, Department of National Resources, Tasman House, Hobart Place, Canberra
City, A.C.T.

HISTORY: Inaugural meeting in August 1976.

PURPOSE: To initiate, and improve the exchange of information in the earth sciences and related areas
through mutual co-operation among users and processors of earth sciences and resource information
both in Australia and internationally.

ACTIVITIES: Branch meetings in Sydney, Adelaide, Melbourne every two months, National meetings - at least one per year.

PUBLICATIONS
A.G.I.A. Newsletter (quarterly)

MEMBERSHIP: 50 (individual, organization)

84   Australian Institute of Agricultural Science
Suite 302, Clunies Ross House, 191 Royal Parade, Parkville, Vic. 3052
Telephone: (03)347 1277, 347 1154, 347 1424

SECRETARY: Mrs. H. Carrol (Office Manageress)

SUBDIVISIONS
Branches in New South Wales, Australian Capital Territory, Victoria, Queensland, South Australia, Northern Territory, Western Australia, Tasmania.

AFFILIATIONS
Agricultural Engineering Society [Australia]
Australian Agricultural Economics Society
Australian Association of Agricultural Faculties
Australian Farm Management Society
Australian Society of Animal Production
Australian Society of Dairy Technology
Grasslands Society of Victoria
Tropical Grassland Society of Australia
Weed Science Society of South Australia
Weed Science Society of New South Wales
Weed Science Society of Victoria

HISTORY: Founded in 1935

PURPOSE: To promote agricultural science; to encourage interchange of ideas; to promote progress in agriculture.

ACTIVITIES: Average of 10 meetings per year in each of the branches

PUBLICATIONS
Journal of the Australian Institute of Agricultural Science
Australian Journal of Experimental Agriculture and Animal Husbandry
Manual of Australian Agriculture

AWARDS
Australian Medal of Agricultural Science
Branch student prizes.

MEMBERSHIP: 2,994 (fellow, corporate, student, emeritus members, company associates)

85   Australian Institute of Building
217 Northbourne Avenue, Turner, A.C.T.
(P.O. Box 1467, Canberra City 2601)
Telephone: (062) 47 7433

SECRETARY: A.H. Gordon (Executive Director)

SUBDIVISIONS
N.S.W. Chapter - Master Builders Association Building, 1 King Street, Newtown, N.S.W. 2042
New Zealand Chapter - P.O. Box 1796, Wellington, New Zealand
Qld. Chapter - G.P.O. Box 646, Brisbane, Qld. 4001
S.A. Chapter - P.O. Box 33, Eastwood, S.A. 5063
Tas. Chapter - G.P.O. Box 992K, Hobart, Tas. 7001
Vic. Chapter - 332 Albert Street, East Melbourne, Vic. 3002
W.A. Chapter - 44 Outram Street, West Perth, W.A. 6005

HISTORY: Founded in 1951. Incorporated in 1955 and incorporated by Royal Charter in 1969.

PURPOSE: To promote the study and advance the science and practice of building and of all kindred matters, arts and sciences and to facilitate the exchange of information and ideas in relation thereto.

INTERESTS: Education in building, research, dissemination of knowledge in building.

ACTIVITIES: Biennial Conference and Seminar. Seminars, Chapter Meetings, Technical Discussion groups at Chapter level.

PUBLICATIONS
Chartered Builder (quarterly)
Chapter Newsheets
Practice Notes

AWARDS
Australian Institute of Building Medal
Chapter Honour Award
Chapter Award
Florence M. Taylor Medal
Sir Manuel Hornibrook Travel Grant
Fred Wilson Memorial Prize
Australian Institute of Building Research and Education Foundation and individual chapter awards.

MEMBERSHIP: 2224 (honorary member, honorary life fellow, fellow, associate, licentiate, student, affiliate, retired member)

86   Australian Institute of Building Surveyors
12 Leindan Court, Mount Eliza, Vic. 3930
Telephone: (03) 787 3702

SECRETARY: D.J. Moore

SUBDIVISIONS
South Australia (Interim Committee); B.A. Nelson (Secretary), 12 Branson Avenue, Clearview, 5085

HISTORY: Founded in 1962, taking over the interests of the Institute of Municipal Building Surveyors.

PURPOSE: To improve and elevate the technical and general knowledge of building surveyors, inspectors and persons intending to become building surveyors or inspectors.

INTERESTS: Building surveying and building inspection.

ACTIVITIES: Annual conference

PUBLICATIONS
Publications in building and construction issued periodically

MEMBERSHIP: 208 (fellows, associates, affiliates, students)

87   Australian Institute of Cartographers
P.O. Box 1292, Canberra City, A.C.T. 2601

SECRETARY: R.G. Roberts (Hon. Gen. Secretary), G.P.O. Box 1922, Adelaide, S.A. 5001

SUBDIVISIONS
Sub-divisions in Victoria, New South Wales, South Australia, Australian Capital Territory, Tasmania, Queensland, Western Australia.

AFFILIATIONS
International Cartographic Association

HISTORY: Founded in 1923 in Victoria

PURPOSE: To improve the knowledge and standards of cartography; to set standards for admission of members; to protect and conserve the interests of members, but not as an industrial organization.

INTERESTS: Every action connected with the making of maps from original survey to printing.

ACTIVITIES: Meetings of divisions and Bi-annual Conferences

PUBLICATIONS
Cartography

MEMBERSHIP: 1,113 (honorary fellows, members, associate members, fellows, students, affiliate and company members)

88   Australian Institute of Engineering Associates Limited
P.O. Box 408, North Sydney, N.S.W. 2060
Telephone: (02) 84 2856

SECRETARY: J.A. Nash

SUBDIVISIONS
Divisions:-
Sydney, P.O.Box 857, Parramatta, N.S.W. 2150
Newcastle, P.O.Box 59, Waratah, N.S.W. 2298
Queensland, P.O.Box 590, South Brisbane, Qld. 4101
Western Australia, Box T1751, G.P.O., Perth, W.A. 6001
Tasmania, P.O.Box 228, Sandy Bay, Tas. 7005
Victoria, P.O.Box 183, Eltham, Vic. 3095
South Australia, P.O.Box 110, St.Peters, S.A. 5069
Branches:-
Orange, Broken Hill - N.S.W.
Brisbane, Rockhampton, Townsville - Queensland
Launceston - Tasmania
Canberra - A.C.T.

HISTORY: Founded in 1963 as the Association of Certificate Engineers, Australia and in 1964 amalgamated with the Association of Diploma Engineers (W.A.)

PURPOSE: To further the aims of engineering associates, to enable them to gain their status in the community.

INTERESTS: All engineering disciplines.

ACTIVITIES: Regular meetings.

PUBLICATIONS
Engineering Associate

MEMBERSHIP: (fellow, member, graduate, student)

89   Australian Institute of Food Science and Technology
Clunies Ross House, 191 Royal Parade, Parkville, Vic. 3052

SECRETARY: Dr. J.G. Fairbrother (P.O. Box 1384, North Sydney, N.S.W. 2060 (business telephone: (02) 92 4885)

SUBDIVISIONS
New South Wales Branch; Southern Branch; Queensland Branch; South Australian Branch.

HISTORY: In 1949, formed Australian Southern Section and Australian Northern Section of Institute of Food Technologists of U.S.A. Formed independent Australian Institute of Food Science and Technology in April, 1967.

PURPOSE: To promote the standing, usefulness and welfare of the profession of food science and technology; to encourage education, investigation and research in food science and technology; to protect the interests of members and provide facilities for lectures, reading of papers and dissemination of knowledge to the public.

ACTIVITIES: Annual convention; combined convention with New Zealand body every four years; regular monthly branch or group meetings or seminars

PUBLICATIONS
Food Technology in Australia (monthly)

AWARDS
AIFST Young Members Award
AIFST Award of Merit (annual)
Food Industry Innovation Award (irregular)
Donations or prizes to educational bodies and careers organizations.

MEMBERSHIP: 1350 (fellows, associates, honorary fellows, life members, graduate members, licentiate members, affiliates, student members)

90   Australian Institute of Health Surveyors
69 Australia Street, Camperdown, N.S.W.
(P.O. Box 97, Camperdown 2050)
Telephone: (02) 516 2419, 516 2559

SECRETARY: P.S. Taylor

SUBDIVISIONS
Divisions in N.S.W., Qld., Tas., S.A., Vic. and W.A.

HISTORY: Founded in 1936.

PURPOSE: To improve and preserve residential and industrial hygienic environments and housing for individuals and communities, and to improve and preserve public health and allied matters by the application of modern preventative science and practice.

ACTIVITIES: National Conference each year and Annual Conferences in each Division. Quarterly meetings of groups within each Division.

PUBLICATIONS
Australian Health Surveyor
Conference Reports from each Annual Conference

AWARDS
Prizes are awarded by Divisions annually through the various Colleges

MEMBERSHIP: 2300 (fellow, associate fellow, member, associate, student member)

91   Australian Institute of Horticulture Incorporated
National Council, 26 Lindley Avenue, Narrabeen, N.S.W. 2101
Telephone: (02) 982 2615

SUBDIVISIONS
A.C.T. Branch - Mrs. A. Rudd (Secretary), P.O. Box 75, Lyneham, A.C.T. 2602 (Telephone: (062) 41 3547)
N.S.W. Branch - Mrs. J. Hynes (Secretary), 24 Lindley Avenue, Narrabeen, N.S.W. 2101 (Telephone: (02) 982 2615)
S.A. Branch - Mr. M. Campbell (Secretary), 48 Millswood Crescent, Millswood, S.A. 5034 (Telephone: (08) 272 3517)
Vic. Branch - Mr. N. Rivett (Secretary), 371 Wattletree Road, Malvern, Vic. 3144 (Telephone: (03) 509 5557)
W.A. Branch - Mr. L. Murnane (Secretary), 77 Second Road, Armadale, W.A. 6112 (Telephone: (092) 72 2183)

HISTORY: Founded in August 1959.

PURPOSE: To provide horticulturists with a central professional body; to encourage the advancement of the profession and to assist and promote education in this field.

INTERESTS: All matters pertaining to horticulture, including nursery, landscape, parks.

ACTIVITIES: Annual meetings of national body; committee meetings monthly in all states; general meetings in all states every two months.

PUBLICATIONS
Journal of Australian Institute of Horticulture (quarterly)

LIBRARY: New South Wales state council operate a small library.

AWARDS
Prizes awarded to students at horticultural colleges in all states each year.

MEMBERSHIP: 450 (fellows, full members, associates, students)

92   Australian Institute of Hospital Administrators
Federal Registrar, Ryde Hospital, Denistone Road, Eastwood, N.S.W. 2122
Telephone: (02) 85 1211

SUBDIVISIONS
Branches in New South Wales, Victoria, Tasmania, South Australia, Western Australia, Queensland and A.C.T.

HISTORY: Founded in 1945. Previously separate organizations existed in Victoria and New South Wales.

PURPOSE: To promote the interests of hospital administrative officers and to uphold the status of the profession of members; to teach subjects pertaining to administration and management of hospitals; to grant certificates and diplomas; to conduct examinations

ACTIVITIES: Annual general meeting; branch meetings; seminars; conferences; national congress.

PUBLICATIONS
Hospital and Health Administration

AWARDS
Annual prizes awarded by School of Health Administration, University of New South Wales.

MEMBERSHIP: 700 (life members, honorary fellows, fellows, associates, provisional associates, licentiates, students)

93   Australian Institute of Industrial Psychology
Suite 1002, 10th Floor, Kindersley House, 33-35 Bligh Street, Sydney, N.S.W. 2000
Telephone: (02) 232 5063

SECRETARY: Miss R. Weir

HISTORY: Founded in 1928 by Department of Psychology, University of Sydney.

PURPOSE: Distribution and collection of knowledge of psychology as it is applied to commerce, education and clinical - medical areas.

INTERESTS: Commerce and industry; vocational guidance for employment at any level.

ACTIVITIES: Quarterly meetings; annual conference

PUBLICATIONS
Test News Bulletin

LIBRARY: Small library in operation

AWARDS
H.F. Benning Prize (bi-annual for best company careers brochure)

MEMBERSHIP: 572 (commercial, educational members)

94   Australian Institute of Landscape Architects
P.O. Box 677, Canberra City, A.C.T. 2601

SUBDIVISIONS
Groups in all states and Australian Capital Territory.

HISTORY: Founded in 1966

PURPOSE: To advance the study of landscape architecture and the related arts and sciences; to promote
the development of urban and rural areas on sound principles of landscape design

ACTIVITIES: Biennial conference.

PUBLICATIONS
Landscape Australia (quarterly)

MEMBERSHIP: 198 (honorary fellows, associates, fellows, students, affiliates, retired members)

95   Australian Institute of Management
Suite 2, 65 Queens Road, Melbourne, Vic. 3004
Telephone: (03) 267 3450

SECRETARY: A.L. Warrick (Executive Officer)

SUBDIVISIONS
Queensland Division - R. Sadler, General Manager (Telephone: (07) 29 2866), Management House,
Cnr Boundary and Rosa Streets, Spring Hill, Qld. 4000, has branches in Toowoomba, Rockhampton,
Mackay, Townsville and Darwin
Victorian Division - R. Gilchrist, Director (Telephone: (03) 94 8181), Management House, 10 St.
Leonards Avenue, St. Kilda, Vic. 3182, has branches in Ballarat, Bendigo, Latrobe Valley.
Tasmanian Division - K. Ulmer, Director (Telephone: (002) 23 7715), 2nd Floor, 52 Macquarie Street,
Hobart, Tas. 7001, has branches in Northern Region, North-West Region.
N.S.W. Division - P. Peterson, Chief Executive (Telephone: (02) 92 0791) has branches in Wollongong
and Newcastle.
South Australian Division - R. Denniston, General Manager (Telephone: (08) 272 1877), Management
House, 136 Greenhill Road, North Unley, S.A. 5001, has a branch in Mt Gambier and Whyalla.
W.A. Division - G. Lapsley, Manager (Telephone: (092) 86 7077), 20-22 Stirling Highway, Nedlands,
W.A. 6009 with branch at Kalgoorlie.
Canberra Division - P.O. Box 928, Canberra City, A.C.T. 2601.

HISTORY: Founded in 1941 as the Institute of Industrial Management. Name changed to present title
in 1950

PURPOSE: To promote the art and science of management, through establishing and maintaining the
highest standards of management in the country.

ACTIVITIES: General Management Conference, National marketing Conference, Annual Report Award
held annually. States hold their own conferences and other activities.

PUBLICATIONS
Management Education in Australia
Executive Salary Survey
Each division publishes its own management news

LIBRARY: Each division has its own management library.

AWARDS
John Storey Medal
William Gueale Lecture
Some divisions present prizes for students involved in areas of management education.

MEMBERSHIP: 17000 (individual, company members)

96   Australian Institute of Marine and Power Engineers
14 Quay Street, Sydney, N.S.W. 2001
Telephone: (02) 212 1666

SECRETARY: J.R. Cleworth (Federal Secretary)

SUBDIVISIONS
Branches in Sydney, Newcastle, Brisbane, Melbourne, Adelaide and Fremantle.

AFFILIATIONS
Australian Council of Trade Unions
Australian Council of Salaried and Professional Associations
Officers (Merchant Navy) Federation, London

HISTORY: Founded in 1881

PURPOSE: To promote the interests of marine engineering in all areas; improving conditions of employment and education of members

ACTIVITIES: Monthly meetings

PUBLICATIONS
On watch

MEMBERSHIP: 4,000 (seagoing, ashore, cadets, honorary)

97   Australian Institute of Medical Technologists
2 Ferndale Street, Floreat Park, W.A. 6014
Telephone: (092) 87 1457

SECRETARY: B. Chandler

SUBDIVISIONS
N.S.W. - Miss C. Van Zijl, Secretary, Box 2657, G.P.O., Sydney, N.S.W. 2001.
Vic. - Miss J. Mathiesen, Secretary, Bacteriology, Mercy Maternity Hospital, East Melbourne, Vic. 3002.
Qld. - Mr. L. Freney, Secretary, 52 Cassandra Street, Chapel Hill, Qld. 4069.
S.A. - Mr. B. Gormley, Histopathology, Diagnostic Laboratory Services, Flinders Medical Centre, Bedford Park, S.A. 5042.
W.A. - Mr. J. Cale, Secretary, Haematology, Sir Charles Gairdner Hospital, Shenton Park, W.A. 6008.
Tas. - Mr. B. Angle, Secretary, Pathology, Launceston General Hospital, Launceston, Tas. 7250.

HISTORY: Founded in 1914

PURPOSE: To promote, support, further and advance the character, status and the common interests of medical technologists throughout Australia.

INTERESTS: Pathology, medical technology

ACTIVITIES: National Annual Scientific Meeting, monthly branch meetings.

PUBLICATIONS
Australian Journal of Medical Technology (4 per annum)
AIMT Newsletter (4 per annum)
Branch Newsletters (monthly)

LIBRARY: Maintained in each state branch

AWARDS
Wellcome Prize ($500 annual award for Institute Fellowship examination)
Sundry scientific awards in branches to successful students in courses of training at Colleges of Advanced Education.

MEMBERSHIP: 1670 (fellow, associate, graduate, student, affiliate)

98 Australian Institute of Navigation
Box 2250, G.P.O., Sydney, N.S.W. 2001
Telephone: (02) 94 4399

SECRETARY: A. P. Davey

HISTORY: Founded in 1949

PURPOSE: To advance the science and practice of navigation and to unite into one society those so interested.

INTERESTS: All forms of navigation in the space, aviation and marine fields.

ACTIVITIES: Monthly meetings held in Sydney

PUBLICATIONS
Navigation (annual)
Newsletter (monthly)

MEMBERSHIP: 450 (ordinary, student, corporate)

99 Australian Institute of Non-Destructive Testing
NATA, 191 Royal Parade, Parkville, Vic. 3052
Telephone: (03) 317 222, 92 2384 (A.H.)

SECRETARY: J.H. Cole

SUBDIVISIONS
N.S.W. Branch, Science Centre, 35-43 Clarence Street, Sydney, N.S.W. 2000
Qld. Branch, P.O. Box 202, Rocklea, Qld. 4106
S.A. Branch, Clunies Ross Memorial Foundation, Australian Minerals Foundation Building, Conyngham Street, Glenside, S.A. 5065
Vic. Branch, NATA, 191 Royal Parade, Parkville, Vic. 3052
W.A. Branch, 259 Star Street, Welshpool, W.A. 6106

AFFILIATIONS
International Committee for Non-destructive Testing.
Pan Pacific Committee for Non-Destructive Testing

HISTORY: Founded in N.S.W. in 1963, federal constitution adopted in 1967

PURPOSE: To promote the science and practice of non-destructive testing by dissemination of knowledge and inculcation of sound practice, by the holding of meetings and publication of literature; to promote education in non-destructive testing and related subjects and conduct examinations.

ACTIVITIES: Annual 3-5 day conference. Branches hold regular meetings, plant visits and symposia.

PUBLICATIONS
Non-Destructive Testing - Australia (monthly)

LIBRARY: N.S.W., S.A. and Vic. branches each have a library.

AWARDS
Philips Award (annual)

MEMBERSHIP: 450 (corporate, ordinary, student members)

100 **Australian Institute of Nuclear Science and Engineering**
Lucas Heights, N.S.W.
(Private Mail Bag, P.O., Sutherland, N.S.W. 2232)
Telephone: (02) 531 0111

SECRETARY: E.A. Palmer (Executive Officer)

HISTORY: Founded in 1958

PURPOSE: To assist research and training in nuclear science and engineering and to make available the facilities (reactors, accelaerators, etc.) at Lucas Heights for use by the Universities and other organizations

INTERESTS: Radiation biology, radiation chemistry, plasma physics, nuclear physics, neutron diffraction, nuclear materials, aspects of economics relevant to the nuclear field, applications of nuclear technology.

AWARDS
AINSE Grants (annual grants for the support of research and training in the nuclear field)
AINSE Research Fellowships (post-doctoral awards tenable in Australian universities and Lucas Heights)
AINSE Research Studentships (post graduate awards for higher degree studies)

MEMBERSHIP: 18 organizations

101 **Australian Institute of Packaging**
P.O. Box 20, Chatswood, N.S.W. 2067

SECRETARY: D. Moriarty (National Secretary)

SUBDIVISIONS
Divisions in N.S.W., Vic. and Qld.

HISTORY: Founded in 1962.

PURPOSE: To serve as a professional institute; to advance the science and technology of packaging; to establish the confidence of the community in the profession; to encourage the study of packaging technology; to watch over and promote the interests of the profession; to establish divisions of the institute for the purpose of conducting the affairs of the institute.

ACTIVITIES: Monthly technical meetings at each Division, seminars, workshops, plant visits.

PUBLICATIONS
Divisional newsletters each month
New items and technical papers published in 'Australian Packaging', 'Packaging News' and 'Australian Lithographer and Packager'

LIBRARY: At the Packaging Centre, National Materials Handling Bureau, Department of Productivity, 105-115 Delhi Road, North Ryde, N.S.W.

AWARDS
Australian Packaging (prize for technical papers)
Australian Institute of Packaging Award (for technical excellence in a package)

MEMBERSHIP: 250 (fellow, member, associate, affiliate, student)

102 **Australian Institute of Parks and Recreation**
302A St Georges Road, Thornbury, Vic.
(P.O. Box 18, Northcote, 3070.)
Telephone: (03) 874 1893

SECRETARY: U.F. Davies (Executive Director)

SUBDIVISIONS
Divisions in W.A., S.A., Tas., Vic., Hume (Northern and Southern N.S.W.), A.C.T. region, N.S.W. and Qld.

AFFILIATIONS
International Federation of Parks and Recreation Associations

HISTORY: Founded in 1926 as the Victorian-Tree Planters Association. 1956 to 1962 Institute of Park Administration of Victoria. 1963 to 1966 Australian Institute of Park Administration. Present title adopted in 1967.

PURPOSE: To provide a central organization of persons and organizations associated with public parks, recreation centres, botanic gardens, national parks and open spaces, and to promote co-operation between them; to promote the study of matters associated with the management of public parks, recreation centres and botanic gardens; to raise the standard and status of their work, to safeguard and advance the interests of parks and recreation management.

ACTIVITIES: Annual conference, monthly; bimonthly or quarterly meetings of Divsions.

PUBLICATIONS
Australian Parks and Recreation (quarterly)
Newsletter published in months when Australian Parks is not published.

MEMBERSHIP: 613 (corporate, sustaining, trade, student, retired members)

103   Australian Institute of Petroleum Ltd.
227 Collins Street, Melbourne, Vic. 3000
Telephone: (03) 63 2756

SECRETARY: J.M. Flower

SUBDIVISIONS
N.S.W. Branch - P.O. Box W1, Hayes Street, Neutral Bay, N.S.W. 2089
Vic. Branch - 227 Collins Street, Melbourne, Vic. 3000
Qld. Branch - Box 1180, G.P.O., Brisbane, Qld. 4001
S.A. Branch - P.O. Box 139, Eastwood, S.A. 5063
Petroleum Institute Environmental Conservation Executive (PIECE)
Petroleum Marketing Engineers' Advisory Committee (PMEAC)
Various other committees concerned with standards, health, safety and other petroleum industry affairs

AFFILIATIONS
World Petroleum Congress
Institute of Petroleum (U.K.)

HISTORY: Founded in 1976. Incorporated in Vic. and registered in all other States and Territories. Absorbed the former Petroleum Information Bureau (Aust.).

PURPOSE: To promote, encourage and co-ordinate study in relation to petroleum, its products and their uses, and matters of public interest concerned therewith; to represent and advance the interests of the petroleum industry generally; and to serve the interests of individual members.

INTERESTS: Petroleum science, technology and economics. Other energy-supply industries and energy resources in general. Related industries such as transport, chemicals. Public relations.

ACTIVITIES: Subdivisions hold conferences, seminars, etc. on an ad hoc basis. State Branches have regular meetings, usually monthly.

PUBLICATIONS
Petroleum Gazette (three times yearly)
Oil and Australia - the Figures Behind the Facts (annual)
Petroleum Search in Australia (every 2 years)
Codes of practice, health and safety bulletins, other technical publications and a range of educational booklets for teachers and students

LIBRARY: Comprises 1800 volumes, copies of 250 periodicals and extensive reference files. Loans restricted to AIP members and accredited libraries.

MEMBERSHIP: 684 (corporate, individual, institutional)

104 Australian Institute of Physics
Science Centre, 35-43 Clarence Street, Sydney, N.S.W. 2000
Telephone: (02) 29 7747

SECRETARY: Dr. J.R. Bird

SUBDIVISIONS
Branches in A.C.T., N.S.W., Qld., S.A., Tas., Vic. and W.A.
Biophysics Group, Nuclear and Particle Physics Group, Vacuum Physics Group

HISTORY: Founded in 1962, incorporated in 1963, taking over the responsibilities and activities of the former Australian Branch of the Institute of the Physical Sciences (London)

PURPOSE: To promote the development of pure and applied physics; to facilitate the exchange, dissemination, and discussion of information and ideas relating to physics and its applications; and to express the views of physicists in Australia on matters relating to the science and the profession of physics.

ACTIVITIES: Meetings arranged by all branches and groups.

PUBLICATIONS
Australian Physicist (monthly)

MEMBERSHIP: 1800 (fellow, member, graduate, associate, student, subscriber, group affiliate, company subscriber)

105 Australian Institute of Quantity Surveyors
37-43 Alexander Street, Crows Nest, N.S.W.
(P.O. Box 534, Crows Nest 2065.)
Telephone: (02) 43 1277

SECRETARY: J. Silversmith

SUBDIVISIONS
Sydney, Canberra, Brisbane, Melbourne, Adelaide and Perth.

AFFILIATIONS
Royal Institution of Chartered Surveyors
Institute of Rhodesian Quantity Surveyors
Jamaican Society of Quantity Surveyors
Association of South African Quantity Surveyors
Quantity Surveyors Institute of New Zealand

HISTORY: Founded by amalgamation of the Australian Institute of Quantity Surveyors and the Institute of Quantity Surveyors of Australia, in January 1971.

PURPOSE: The advancement of quantity surveying; the unity of quantity surveyors on an Australia-wide basis; the improvement and elevation of the technical knowledge of persons engaged in or about to engage in the profession of quantity surveying and to secure uniformity in methods throughout Australia.

ACTIVITIES: Annual Session of Federal Council, monthly Chapter Council meetings, seminars.

PUBLICATIONS
Building Economist

AWARDS
Australian Institute of Quantity Surveyors Medal

MEMBERSHIP: 940 (fellow, associate, probationer, student, retired)

106 Australian Institute of Refrigeration, Air Conditioning and Heating (Inc.)

191 Royal Parade, Parkville, Vic.
(P.O. Box 52, Parkville 3052.)
Telephone: (03) 347 4941

SECRETARY: Mrs. M.A. Hessey

SUBDIVISIONS
Queensland Division - S. Collinson (Secretary)
New South Wales Division - L.G. Farrar (Secretary)
Victorian Division - Mrs. M.A. Hessey (Secretary)
South Australian Division - C.W. Gensch (Secretary)
Western Australian Division - N.A. Steketee (Secretary)
Tasmanian Division - P.A. Wallbank (Secretary)

AFFILIATIONS
American Society of Heating, Refrigeration and Air Conditioning Engineers, Inc.
Institute of Refrigeration, London
New Zealand Institute of Refrigerating Engineers
International Institute of Refrigeration

HISTORY: Founded in 1920 as the Victorian Institute of Refrigeration. Name changed in 1935 to the Australian Institute of Refrigeration. In 1940 it amalgamated with the N.S.W. Institute of Refrigerating Engineers and the N.S.W. Society of Refrigerating Engineers under the name of the Australian Institute of Refrigeration. Name changed to present title in 1959.

PURPOSE: To promote the science and practice of refrigeration, air conditioning and heating in all their branches and usefulness and efficiency of persons engaged therein.

ACTIVITIES: Annual conference, monthly technical and general meetings in each state division.

PUBLICATIONS
Australian Refrigeration Air Conditioning and Heating

LIBRARY: Library at present incorporated into the Library of the School of Mechanical Engineering, University of N.S.W.

AWARDS
James Harrison Award

MEMBERSHIP: 2050 (full, associate, affiliate, junior, student)

107 Australian Institute of Science Technology Inc.

University of Adelaide, North Terrace, Adelaide, S.A. 5000
Telephone: (08) 223 4333

SECRETARY: A.G. Ewart (Federal Secretary)

SUBDIVISIONS
Adelaide - Mr. R.J. Dunsford (Secretary), 7 Catherine Drive, Redwood Park, S.A. 5097.
Melbourne - Mr. A.J. Douglas (Secretary), Mechanical Engineering Department, University of Melbourne, Vic. 3052.
Sydney - Mr. J. Dixon (Secretary), Architectural Science, University of Sydney, Sydney, N.S.W. 2006.
Canberra - Mr. R.A. Goodman (Secretary), Physical Biochemistry Department, J.C.S.M.R., A.N.U., P.O. Box 334, Canberra City, A.C.T. 2601.
Armidale - Mr. R. Plant (Secretary), P I *Chemistry Department, University of New England, Armidale, N.S.W. 2350.*

HISTORY: Founded in 1957 as the Australian Science Technicians Association. Reconstituted under present title in 1966

PURPOSE: To encourage technical education in all fields of science technology; to develop the knowledge and expertise of its members; to provide advice and assistance to members in professional and technical matters and to promote the general, professional and technical causes of science technology.

ACTIVITIES: Regular lectures, seminars, exhibitions of scientific apparatus and equipment, tours of scientific and industrial laboratories. The Australian Conference on Science Technology.

PUBLICATIONS
Science and Australian Technology
Branch Newsletters and Bulletins.

MEMBERSHIP: 500 (fellows, associates, members and non-corporate members)

108 Australian Institute of Steel Construction
118 Alfred Street, Milsons Point, N.S.W.
(P.O. Box 434, Milsons Point 2061)
Telephone: (02) 929 6666

SECRETARY: G.A. Day (Director)

SUBDIVISIONS
Victorian office - 10th floor, 140 William Street, Melbourne, Vic. 3000.
Membership branches in Brisbane, Adelaide, Perth, Melbourne and Sydney.

HISTORY: Founded in 1962, incorporated in 1972.

PURPOSE: To foster the use of fabricated steelwork.

INTERESTS: Engineering design, steel fabrication and erection, student education, codes and standards.

ACTIVITIES: Regular branch meetings in all states. Occasional conferences, seminars, tutorial classes, and overseas lectures.

PUBLICATIONS
Steel Construction (quarterly)
Steel Fabrication Journal (quarterly)
Numerous text books, manuals etc.

LIBRARY: 3000 books and pamphlets, 50 serials.

AWARDS
Fund established to provide one year's membership to interested students who graduate in civil engineering.

MEMBERSHIP: 1000 (fabricator, individual, associate members and student register)

109 Australian Institute of Systems Analysts
Box 1308, G.P.O., Sydney, N.S.W. 2001

Box 1773Q, G.P.O., Melbourne, Vic. 3001

SUBDIVISIONS
Branches in Sydney and Melbourne; currently being formed in Brisbane; others to follow

HISTORY: Founded in Sept. 1968.

PURPOSE: To promote a broader understanding and acceptance of the systems function as a component of effective management. (The systems function embraces any organised approach, technique or device which can be shown to improve managerial and organisational performance); to support and advance the character, status and interests of the members collectively and to provide for the personal development of individual members.

ACTIVITIES: Monthly meetings

PUBLICATIONS
Catalyst

LIBRARY: Library maintained.

MEMBERSHIP: 340 approx. (general or ordinary, student)

110   Australian Institute of Urban Studies
A.N.U. Buildings, Childers Street, Turner, A.C.T.
(P.O. Box 809, Canberra City 2601.)
Telephone: (062) 47 6155

SECRETARY: D.P. Cartwright (Director)

SUBDIVISIONS
Division in each State.

HISTORY: The Social Science Research Council of Australia and the Royal Australian Planning Institute formed a Joined Committee for an Australian Institute of Urban Studies which first met in 1965. The Institute was inaugurated in 1967 and a permanent secretariat established in 1970.

PURPOSE: To support, stimulate, sponsor and undertake research into urban affairs in Australia, particularly urban problems, and to disseminate research findings.

INTERESTS: Include urban development, urban settlement and facilities, physical environment, population and social characteristics, economics, transportation movement and communications, government, administration.

ACTIVITIES: Annual conference, meetings of State divisions, seminars, Board meetings.

PUBLICATIONS
AIUS Conference Proceedings
Australian Urban Studies (quarterly)
Urban Issues (quarterly, published by Qld. Division)
More than 60 publications (List available)

MEMBERSHIP: 546 (councillors, members, corporate members)

111   Australian Kidney Foundation
Hutton Street, Canberra, A.C.T.
(P.O. Box 1850, Canberra City 2601)
Telephone: (062) 47 6784

SECRETARY: Dr. R.W. Greville (Medical Director)

SUBDIVISIONS
N.S.W. - 20th Level, 1 York Street, Sydney, N.S.W. 2000
Vic. - care of- Marquand and Co., 51 Queen Street, Melbourne, Vic. 3000
Qld. - 62 Astor Terrace, Brisbane, Qld. 4000
S.A. - care of- Peat, Marwick, Mitchell and Co., 124 Waymouth Street, Adelaide, S.A. 5000
W.A. - 236 St. George's Terrace, Perth, W.A. 6000
Tas. - care of- 130 Collins Street, Hobart, Tas. 7000

HISTORY: Founded in 1968.

PURPOSE: To raise funds to reduce the prevalence of diseases of the kidney, urinary tract and related organs in Australia by means of:- improvement of early diagnosis of these diseases; stimulation and support of research into their causes, prevention detection and treatment; education of the public and provision of information to medical practitioners; support of kidney transplantation and dialysis registries.

ACTIVITIES: Meetings of various general and scientific committees.

PUBLICATIONS
Annual Report, pamphlets on kidney disease and associated subjects

AWARDS
Grant-in-aid research funds, Research Fellowships and Vacation Scholarships

MEMBERSHIP: 100 approx.

112   Australian Lead Development Association

95 Collins Street, Melbourne, Vic. 3000
Telephone: (03) 63 0491

SECRETARY: J.H. McAuliffe

SUBDIVISIONS
Battery Technologists Group
Cable Technologists Group

HISTORY: Founded in 1962.

PURPOSE: To disseminate technical-educational information on the uses and industrial applications of lead and lead products, technical support for industry and encouragement of latest technology.

ACTIVITIES: Technical symposia held regularly in major Australian and New Zealand cities for groups of up to 650 people. In-plant seminars and consultations, and technologists group meetings held regularly in Melbourne and Sydney.

PUBLICATIONS
A wide range of technical manuals, reference works and technical-promotional publications on all major industrial applications for lead. Circulation of bi-monthly Lead Abstracts, a review of current world technical literature on lead. Full text of articles abstracted supplied free on request.

LIBRARY: Extensive lead technical library facilities.

MEMBERSHIP: 6 member companies engaged in mining and smelting of lead.

113   Australian Leather Institute

122 Walker Street, North Sydney, N.S.W.
(P.O. Box 577, North Sydney 2060)
Telephone: (02) 922 1622

AFFILIATIONS
Federated Tanners' Association of Australia (P.O. Box 1525, Canberra City, A.C.T. 2601)

HISTORY: Founded in 1974 by the Federated Tanners' Association of Australia as a non-trading, promotional body.

PURPOSE: To promote leather in all its many applications and to encourage widespread use and recognition of the international leather symbol.

PUBLICATIONS
What is leather (general information booklet)
Various point of sale and promotional leaflets

MEMBERSHIP: 30 member companies (full, associated)

114   Australian Licensed Aircraft Engineers' Association

926A Botany Road, Mascot, N.S.W. 2020
Telephone: (02) 667 0690, 667 0698

SECRETARY: J.C. Hardy (Federal Secretary)

HISTORY: Founded in January 1957.

PURPOSE: To advance aircraft maintenance engineers.

INTERESTS: Practical and technical training and welfare.

ACTIVITIES: Federal Executive - 2 monthly; Conference triennially.

PUBLICATIONS
Aircraft Engineer
Newsletters

AWARDS
Best Apprentice Awards
Funds to technical institutions

MEMBERSHIP: 1720

115 Australian Littoral Society
P.O. Box 82, St. Lucia, Qld. 4067
Telephone: (07) 378 6077

SECRETARY: Ms. D. Tarte.

SUBDIVISIONS
N.S.W. Division, P.O. Box A285, Sydney South 2000.
Townsville Branch, School of Biological Sciences, James Cook University, Townsville, Qld. 4811

HISTORY: Founded in 1965

PURPOSE: To educate the public on the principles and values of effective conservation; to provide scientific advice to the government, private organisations and teaching bodies; to save the Barrier Reef - prevent its destruction and ensure its wisest use; to investigate the extent and effects of water pollution in Australia; to study and protect wetland areas important to recreational and commercial fishing; to encourage and assist artificial reef projects; to discourage and oppose wanton destruction and-or over-exploitation of aquatic resources and protect endangered habitats, animals and unique areas.

INTERESTS: Tidal wetlands research; water pollution research; Great Barrier Reef research, management and conservation.

ACTIVITIES: Bi-monthly general meetings.

PUBLICATIONS
Operculum (quarterly)
Newsletters

LIBRARY: Limited reference library

MEMBERSHIP: 688 (life, individual, student, institutional, library)

116 Australian Mammal Society Incorporated
Arthur Rylah Institute, 123 Brown Street, Heidelberg, Vic. 3084

SECRETARY: R.M. Warneke

AFFILIATIONS
Australian and New Zealand Association for the Advancement of Science Incorporated

HISTORY: Founded in 1958

PURPOSE: To promote scientific study of the mammals of the Australian region.

INTERESTS: The biology and conservation of mammals

ACTIVITIES: Annual General Meeting in May, general meetings in association with ANZAAS

PUBLICATIONS
Australian Mammalogy
Australian Mammal Society Inc. Bulletin

AWARDS
Adolph Bolliger Award

MEMBERSHIP: (ordinary, honorary life, subscription members)

117   Australian Marine Sciences' Association
The Australian Museum, College Street, Sydney, N.S.W.
(P.O. Box A285, Sydney South 2000.)
Telephone: (02) 339 8111

SECRETARY: Dr. R.J. King, School of Botany, University of N.S.W., P.O. Box 1, Kensington, N.S.W.
2033

SUBDIVISIONS
Branches in all states

HISTORY: Founded in 1962

PURPOSE: To promote, develop and assist in the study of all branches of marine science in Australia
and, by means of publications, meetings, symposia and such other methods as may be considered
appropriate, to provide for the exchange of information and ideas between those concerned with
marine sciences.

ACTIVITIES: General Meeting and Conference held once a year. Other meetings from time to time.

PUBLICATIONS
Australian Marine Science Bulletin

AWARDS
Student Prize for best paper presented by a student ($50).
Junior Travel Award for best paper prepared for presentation by a young scientist at an AMSA
Conference.

MEMBERSHIP: 500 (Ordinary, student, associate, corresponding, corporate, sustaining members)

118   Australian Mathematical Society
Melbourne State College, 757 Swanston Street, Carlton, Vic. 3053.
Telephone: (03) 347 5122

HISTORY: Founded in 1956

PURPOSE: To promote and extend mathematical knowledge and its applications.

ACTIVITIES: Annual General Meeting and Conferences; Summer Research Institute.

PUBLICATIONS
Journal of the Australian Mathematical Society
Bulletin of the Australian Mathematical Society
Australian Mathematical Society Gazette

MEMBERSHIP: 600 (ordinary, honorary, institutional, reciprocal members)

119   Australian Medical Association
77-79 Arundel Street, Glebe, N.S.W.
(P.O. Box 20. Glebe 2037.)
Telephone: (02) 660 6466

SECRETARY: Dr. G. D. Repin (Secretary General)

SUBDIVISIONS

New South Wales - Dr. N. Larkins, Medical Secretary, P.O. Box 121, St. Leonards, N.S.W. 2065 (Telephone: (02) 439 8822).

Victoria - Dr. W.M.G. Leembruggen, Medical Secretary, 293 Royal Parade, Parkville, Vic. 3052 (Telephone: (03) 347 8722).

Queensland - Mr. M. Hudson, Secretary, 88 L'Estrange Terrace, Kelvin Grove, Qld. 4059 (Telephone: (07) 356 0628).

South Australia - Mr. I. Dobbie, Secretary, 80 Brougham Place, North Adelaide, S.A. 5006 (Telephone: (08) 267 4355).

Western Australia - Mr. R.G. Hayward, Secretary, 8 Kings Park Road, West Perth, W.A. 6005 (Telephone: (092) 21 7898).

Tasmania - Dr. H.McP. Cartledge, Hon. Medical Secretary, 2 Gore Street, Hobart, Tas. 7000 (Telephone: (002) 23 2047).

AFFILIATIONS

Australian Association of Physical Medicine and Rehabilitation
Australian College of Allergists
Australian College of Ophthalmologists
Australian Society of Anaesthetists
Australian Federation of Medical Women
Australian Postgraduate Federation in Medicine
Australasian College of Dermatologists
Australian and New Zealand College of Psychiatrists
Australian and New Zealand Society of Occupational Medicine
Australian Association of Neurologists
Royal Australasian College of Radiologists
Association of Medical Directors to the Australian Pharmaceutical Industry
Australian Orthopaedic Association
Australian Society of Plastic Surgeons
Australian Assocation of Surgeons
Provincial Surgeons' Association
Australian Rheumatism Association
National Association of Medical Specialists
National Association of General Practitioners of Australia

HISTORY: Founded in 1962. Previously each Branch had been a Branch of the British Medical Association

PURPOSE: To promote medical and allied sciences; to promote, maintain and extend the honour and interests of the medical profession and of the Branches of the Association and of any body affiliated with it.

ACTIVITIES: Annual Assembly Meeting, Annual Meetings, Federal Council Meetings, Executive Committee Meetings, Seminars

PUBLICATIONS
Medical Journal of Australia
A.M.A. Gazette
Monthly Branch Bulletins

AWARDS
John G. Hunter Prize
A.M.A. Press Award

MEMBERSHIP: (ordinary, honorary, overseas, associate, extraordinary)

120   Australian Meteorological Association Inc.
196 Walkerville Terrace, Walkerville, S.A. 5008
Telephone: (08) 44 6521

SECRETARY: Mrs. J. Bannister

AFFILIATIONS
Meteorological Society of N.S.W.
Canberra Meteorological Society

HISTORY: Founded in 1969

PURPOSE: To promote interests in meteorology

ACTIVITIES: Meetings held bi-monthly

PUBLICATIONS
Monana (annual)

MEMBERSHIP: 117 (full, affiliate, student, junior, pensioner members)

121   Australian National Committee on Large Dams

Australian Department of Construction, 17 Yarra Street, Hawthorn, Vic.
(G.P.O. Box 2807 AA, Melbourne, 3001)
Telephone: (03) 81 0271

SECRETARY: R.B. Johnson

AFFILIATIONS
International Commission on Large Dams

HISTORY: Founded in 1936

PURPOSE: To stimulate interest in and promote knowledge of the design, construction, maintenance
and operation of dams.

ACTIVITIES: Annual General Meeting

PUBLICATIONS
ANCOLD Bulletin
Occassional publications such as Current Technical Practices

MEMBERSHIP: 76 (member organizations, associate members, subscribers)

122   Australian and New Zealand Association for the Advancement of Science Incorporated (ANZAAS)

Science House, 157 Gloucester Street, Sydney, N.S.W. 2000.
Telephone: (02) 27 2620, 27 9193

SECRETARY: A.G. Cairns (Executive Officer)

SUBDIVISIONS
Divisions in all Australian States and Territories, in New Zealand and in Niugini.

AFFILIATIONS
Affiliated through institutional membership with the Universities in Australia and New Zealand and
with Australian and New Zealand learned and specialist Societies and Institutions.

HISTORY: Founded in 1888 as the Australasian Association for the Advancement of Science, name
changed to present title in 1930.

PURPOSE: The advancement of science and scholarship through the communication of knowledge; and
the promotion of a spirit of cooperation among scientific workers, scholars and those in sympathy with
science and scholarship, especially in Australia and its Territories, in New Zealand, and in Niugini.

ACTIVITIES: Federal congresses; regional meetings.

PUBLICATIONS
Search (formerly Australian Journal of Science)

AWARDS
ANZAAS Medal
Mueller Medal

MEMBERSHIP: Over 2,700 (ordinary, student, institutional, retired)

123 Australian and New Zealand College of Psychiatrists

Maudsley House, 107 Rathdowne Street, Carlton, Vic. 3053
Telephone: (03) 347 6466

SECRETARY: Dr. G.L. Lipton (Honorary Federal Secretary)

HISTORY: Founded in 1946 as the Australian Association of Psychiatrists

PURPOSE: To promote the study of psychiatry and ancillary sciences; to conduct courses and technical training; to grant qualifications to medical practitioners

PUBLICATIONS
Australian and New Zealand Journal of Psychiatry (quarterly)

MEMBERSHIP: 926 (fellows, members, corresponding members)

124 Australian and New Zealand Society for Epidemiology and Research in Community Health

Salisbury College of Advanced Education, Smith Road, Salisbury, S.A.
5108
Telephone: (08) 258 3000

SECRETARY: J.R. Whimp

SUBDIVISIONS
Branches in N.S.W., Vic., Qld., W.A., Tas. and N.Z.

PURPOSE: To encourage epidemiological research and research in community health.

INTERESTS: Distribution, determinants and significance of health, sickness and disability. Structure and function of health services and organizations. Politics and economics of health.

ACTIVITIES: Annual Conference in May each year; monthly State Branch meetings.

PUBLICATIONS
Annual Conference Proceedings and other occasional publications

MEMBERSHIP: 420 (full financial, student)

125 Australian and New Zealand Society of Nuclear Medicine

A.A.E.C., Private Mailbag, Sutherland, N.S.W. 2232
Telephone: (02) 531 3511

SECRETARY: R.E. Boyd

SUBDIVISIONS
Qld., N.S.W., Vic., Tas., S.A., W.A. and New Zealand

AFFILIATIONS
Royal Australian College of Physicians

PURPOSE: To promote the advancement of knowledge in the use of radionuclides in medicine and the biological sciences.

ACTIVITIES: Annual Scientific meeting held in May; State branches have meetings from time to time.

MEMBERSHIP: 270 (honorary, associate, sustaining)

126 **Australian and New Zealand Society of Occupational Medicine**
26 Koetong Parade, Mt. Eliza, Vic. 3930

SECRETARY: Dr. D.F. Potter (Federal Secretary)

SUBDIVISIONS
In New Zealand and all States.

AFFILIATIONS
Permanent Commission and International Association of Occupational Health
Asian Association on Occupational Health

HISTORY: Founded in 1969, as a result of a joint meeting in Canberra 1968 of the Sections of Occupational Medicine of the N.S.W. and Vic. Branches of the Australian Medical Association. Both sections were formed in 1952.

PURPOSE: To promote the standing, knowledge and practice of occupational medicine in Australia and New Zealand

ACTIVITIES: Regular Branch Meetings; Annual Branch Meetings; 3-4 Federal Council Meetings per year; Annual Society Scientific Conference in Sept.-Oct. (venue rotates)

PUBLICATIONS
Scientific Proceedings of Annual Meetings

MEMBERSHIP: 289 (members, life members)

127 **Australian and New Zealand Society of Oral Surgeons**
97 Remuera Road, Remuera, Auckland, New Zealand

SECRETARY: Dr. W. Marsden Bell

SUBDIVISIONS
In all states except Tasmania, and in New Zealand.
Australian Secretary - Dr. P. Bowker, 110 Collins Street, Melbourne, Vic. 3000 (Telephone: (03) 63 9453)

HISTORY: In 1958 a N.S.W. Society of Oral Surgeons was formed and with this Society as a nucleus arrangements were made to hold a national meeting in 1959. Australian and New Zealand Society of Oral Surgeons founded in 1961.

PURPOSE: To study and advance oral surgery and to promote its furtherence as a distinct dental speciality, and in particular to establish formal post graduate training programmes in Australia and New Zealand.

PUBLICATIONS
Proceedings of Clinical Meetings.

MEMBERSHIP: (full, associate, honorary, honorary life members)

128 **Australian Nurserymen's Association Limited**
Lot 6, Annangrove Road, Rouse Hill, N.S.W.
(P.O. Box 99, Round Corner 2154)
Telephone: (02) 628 1472

SECRETARY: K.E. Gallard

SUBDIVISIONS
Queensland Nurserymen's Association Ltd.
N.S.W. Association of Nurserymen Ltd.
Tasmanian Association of Nurserymen Ltd.
South Australian Association of Nurserymen Ltd.
Nurserymen's Association of Western Australia Inc.
Nurserymen's and Seedsmen's Association of Victoria

HISTORY: Formed from the Federation of Australian Nurserymen in October 1975.

PURPOSE: To promote and further the interests of nurserymen and allied industries in Australia and to promote the advancement of horticulture.

ACTIVITIES: Annual General Meeting.

PUBLICATIONS
Australian Nurserymen (quarterly)
Horticultural Research in Australia (annual)

LIBRARY: Lot 6, Annangrove Road, Rouse Hill, N.S.W.

MEMBERSHIP: 900 (full, allied trade)

129 Australian Optometrical Association
Suite 1, 611 St. Kilda Road, Melbourne, Vic. 3004
Telephone: (03) 51 2218, 529 1040

SECRETARY: Dr. D.P. Smith (Executive Director)

SUBDIVISIONS
Victoria - Miss L. Noble, 30 Essex Road, Surrey Hills, Vic. 3127.
N.S.W. - Mrs. N. Samin, 26 Nithsdale Street, Sydney, N.S.W. 2000
S.A. - B.C. Marsden, 38 Grenfell Street, Adelaide, S.A. 5000
W.A. - P.E. Middleton, 44 Outram Street, West Perth, W.A. 6005
Qld. - R. Scott, P.O. Box 254, Towong, Qld. 4066.
Tas - N.B. Sims, 18 Elizabeth Street, Hobart, Tas. 7000

HISTORY: Constituted in 1918 by amalgamation of independent state societies and institutes.

PURPOSE: To promote the educational, scientific, technical, political and general advancement of the optometrical profession, to promote research in visual science and its clinical application, and to promote and protect standards of community eye and vision care.

ACTIVITIES: Monthly meetings of State Executive Committees; quarterly meetings of Federal Executive Council: frequent scientific meetings; annual scientific State congresses; triennial, national professional conference; quadrennial international scientific congresses

PUBLICATIONS
Australian Journal of Optometry (Monthly since 1917)
Irregular newsletters

LIBRARY: 'Wright Library' maintained by federal office and smaller ad hoc libraries maintained by individual State branches

AWARDS
Waterworth Memorial Lecture. (Section 7, ANZAAS Congress)
Post-graduate scholarship offered annually
Under-graduate scholarships offered annually in S.A., W.A. and Tas.
Research grants awarded on application and on merit
Study and Travel grants awarded on application and on merit

MEMBERSHIP: 856 (full, honorary life, associate members)

130 Australian Organisation for Quality Control
Industry House, 370 St. Kilda Road, Melbourne, Vic 3004.
Telephone: (03) 698 4268, 698 4111

SECRETARY: T.H.K. Sheahan (Executive Secretary)

SUBDIVISIONS
N.S.W. Division - J. Latham, 60 York Street, Sydney, N.S.W. 2000 (Telephone: (02) 290 0700).
Victorian Division - T.H.K. Sheahan (address as above)
S.A. Division - F. Thomson, Industry House, 12 Pirie Street, Adelaide, S.A. 5000. (Telephone - (08) 212 4691)
Qld. Division - G. Kimball, Manufactures' House, 375 Wickham Terrace, Brisbane, Qld. 4000 (Telephone - 072 21 1699)
Regional Groups in Albury-Wodonga, Ballarat and Geelong.

HISTORY: Victorian and N.S.W. organisations formed in 1967 combined with S.A. into a national body in 1970. Qld. joined in 1973.

PURPOSE: To promote throughout industry and the community the principles and practice of quality control; to improve the fitness for use of products and services at a national level.

INTERESTS: Prevention of defects, through the use of systematic methods of appraisal of raw materials; processes, finished products and services in relation to the needs of consumers, customers and users. Promotion of economic management and improved profitability through the adoption of effective quality control practices. Improvement of product reliability and customer satisfaction.

ACTIVITIES: Monthly meetings of each State Division, seminars, conventions, training courses, workshops and other educational aids.

PUBLICATIONS
Monthly newsletters published by State Divisions.

LIBRARY: Each State Division maintains a collection of text books, journals and technical papers.

MEMBERSHIP: 1500 (individual, company, student, honorary members)

131 Australian Orthopaedic Association
Fifth Floor, 139 Macquarie Street, Sydney, N.S.W. 2000.
Telephone: (02) 27 8154

SECRETARY: F.J. Harvey (Hon. Secretary)

SUBDIVISIONS
Sydney, Melbourne, Brisbane, Adelaide, Perth, Hobart.

AFFILIATIONS
Boards of Studies in Orthopaedics and Trauma in each State.

HISTORY: Founded in 1936.

PURPOSE: To advance orthopaedic surgery; to provide a national and authoritative body of experts to act, advise and cooperate in all matters affecting the welfare of cripples, and the prevention and relief of crippling disabilities arising during peace or as a result of war.

ACTIVITIES: Annual General Meetings at capital cities.

PUBLICATIONS
Guide to Orthopaedic Training in Australia

LIBRARY: Library is maintained

AWARDS
Australian Orthopaedic Association Research Fund
L.O. Betts Memorial Prize

MEMBERSHIP: 373 (active, honorary, associate, affiliate, corresponding, emeritus members)

132   Australian Paediatric Association

Institute of Child Health, Royal Alexandra Hospital for Children,
Camperdown, N.S.W. 2050.
Telephone: (02) 519 4643

SECRETARY: Dr. B. Storey

AFFILIATIONS
Australian Paediatric Research Association

HISTORY: Founded in 1950

PURPOSE: To promote the advancement of paediatrics in Australia.

ACTIVITIES: Annual meeting held in Canberra for 3 days.

PUBLICATIONS
Australian Paediatric Journal

MEMBERSHIP: 400 (ordinary, honorary)

133   Australian Petroleum Exploration Association Ltd.

London Assurance House, 20 Bridge Street, Sydney, N.S.W.
(G.P.O. Box 834, Sydney, 2001.)
Telephone: (02) 27 6718

SUBDIVISIONS
Branches in N.S.W., Vic., Qld., S.A., and W.A.

AFFILIATIONS
Petroleum Exploration Society of Australia

HISTORY: Founded in 1959

PURPOSE: To maintain, develop, preserve, protect and promote the petroleum industry in Australia and
also anywhere else in the World; to protect and promote the interests of persons engaged in
prospecting, drilling, refining, exploring, or developing petroleum or other minerals.

ACTIVITIES: Annual Scientific conference

PUBLICATIONS
APEA Journal

MEMBERSHIP: 121 (full (exploratory), service companies)

134   Australian Pharmaceutical Sciences Association

Pharmacy School, S.A.I.T., North Terrace, Adelaide, S.A. 5000.

SECRETARY: Dr. B.H. Stock

SUBDIVISIONS
Committee members in all States.

HISTORY: Founded in 1962

PURPOSE: To bring together all persons interested in any aspect of pharmaceutical science.

INTERESTS: Advancement of drug science and technology.

ACTIVITIES: Annual meeting.

PUBLICATIONS
Newsletter

MEMBERSHIP: 200 ordinary members

135   Australian Physiological and Pharmacological Society
Division of Animal Production, CSIRO, P.O. Box 239, Blacktown,
N.S.W. 2148.
Telephone: (02) 631 8022

SECRETARY: Dr. J.R.S. Hales

AFFILIATIONS
International Union of Physiological Sciences
International Union of Pharmacology

HISTORY: Founded in 1960

PURPOSE: To advance the sciences of physiology and pharmacology.

ACTIVITIES: Two meetings per year, rotating between Australian Universities.

PUBLICATIONS
Proceedings of the Australian Physiological and Pharmacological Society (one volume per annum)

MEMBERSHIP: 400 (normal, sustaining)

136   Australian Physiotherapy Association
201 Balaclava Road, Caulfield, Vic. 3161
Telephone: (03) 527 5041

SECRETARY: S. Komesarook

SUBDIVISIONS
Branches in N.S.W., Qld., S.A., Tas., Vic., W.A. and A.C.T.

HISTORY: Founded in 1905

PURPOSE: To promote the science and practice of physiotherapy and to maintain the honour and interests of practising physiotherapists.

INTERESTS: Post graduate education, laws relating to the physiotherapy profession, general and social interests of members of the profession, and ethical conduct.

ACTIVITIES: Federal Council meetings; Biennial Congress

PUBLICATIONS
Australian Journal of Physiotherapy

MEMBERSHIP: 3500 individual members

137   Australian Plant Pathology Society
Plant Research Institute, Department of Agriculture, Burnley Gardens,
Burnley, Vic. 3121
Telephone: (03) 81 1487

SECRETARY: Dr. P.R. Merriman

SUBDIVISIONS
N.S.W. Branch - Dr. J.W. Bowyer, University of Sydney, (Telephone: (02) 660 8528)
Qld. Branch - Dr. D.S. Teakle, University of Qld. (Telephone: (07) 370 6627)
Vic. Branch - Dr. R.G. Garrett, Plant Research Institute, Burnley Gardens (Telephone: (03) 81 1487)
S.A. Branch - Dr. B.G. Clare, Waite Agricultural Research Institute (Telephone: (08) 79 7901)
W.A. Branch - Dr. G.D. McLean, Department of Agriculture, S. Perth (Telephone: (092) 67 0111)
Tas. Branch - Mr. P.F. Williams, Department of Agriculture, Devonport (Telephone: (004) 24 1461)
A.C.T. Branch - Dr. K.M. Harrower, Australian National University (Telephone: (062) 49 3525)
N.T. Branch - Mr. R.N. Pitkethley, Animal Industry and Agriculture Branch, Darwin (Telephone: (089) 84 3093)
New Zealand Branch - Prof. F.J. Newhook, University of Auckland (Telephone: 7 4740)
P.N.G. Branch - Dr. T.V. Price, University of P.N.G.

HISTORY: Founded in 1969

PURPOSE: To advance and disseminate plant pathology knowledge and practice, particularly in relation to Australia

INTERESTS: Plant pathology and related fields bearing on the relationships between pathogenic microorganisms and plants

ACTIVITIES: National Plant Pathology Conferences and specialist workshop meetings

PUBLICATIONS
Australian Plant Pathology Society Newsletter (quarterly)

AWARDS
Daniel McAlpine Memorial Lecture

MEMBERSHIP: 360 (ordinary, honorary, sustaining)

138   Australian Pneumatic and Hydraulic Association
32 Buckingham Street, Surry Hills, N.S.W. 2010
Telephone: (02) 69 7955

SECRETARY: M.J. Farley (Executive Officer)

HISTORY: Constituted in October 1971.

PURPOSE: To actively promote the technology of pneumatics and hydraulics; to establish and maintain an active relationship between members.

INTERESTS: Standards and tariff.

ACTIVITIES: Federal Committee Meetings quarterly.

PUBLICATIONS
Occasional newsletter (as necessary)

MEMBERSHIP: 29 companies (full, agency-distributorship)

139   Australian Postgraduate Federation in Medicine
25 Lucas Street, Camperdown, N.S.W. 2050.
Telephone: (02) 519 1522

SECRETARY: G.W. Hunt

AFFILIATIONS
Australian Medical Association
Victorian Medical Postgraduate Foundation
Postgraduate Committee in Medical Education, University of New South Wales
Postgraduate Committee in Medicine, Australian National University
South Australian Postgraduate Medical Education Association Inc.
Postgraduate Committee in Medicine, University of Sydney
Postgraduate Medical Education Committee, University of Queensland
Postgraduate Medical Education Committee, University of Western Australia
Postgraduate Medical Committee of the Northern Territory
Tasmanian Postgraduate Committee in Medicine

HISTORY: Founded in 1946

PURPOSE: To promote in Australia postgraduate education study, work and research in medicine and the advancement of the art and science of medicine.

ACTIVITIES: Annual (ordinary general) meeting; Forum and Victor Coppleson Memorial Lecture.

PUBLICATIONS
Courses of Training and Instruction in Postgraduate Medicine available in Australia and Summary of Postgraduate Degrees and Diplomas
Directory of Australian Resident Medical Officer and Registrar Appointments (1970)
General Information for Medical Graduates Proceeding Abroad to the U.K. and the U.S.A.
Fellowships and Grants for Postgraduate Medical Study (1970)
Newsletter (quarterly)

AWARDS
Mayo Fellowships
Searle Travel Grants

140   Australian Psychological Society
191 Royal Parade, Parkville, Vic. 3052.
Telephone: (03) 347 2720

SECRETARY: Dr. F.D. Naylor (General Secretary), P.G. Power (Executive Officer)

SUBDIVISIONS
Branches in A.C.T., Newcastle, New England (Armidale), Qld., S.A., Sydney, Tas., Vic. and W.A.
Divisions - Counselling Psychologists, Clinical Psychologists, Educational Psychologists, Occupational Psychologists

AFFILIATIONS
Australian Council of Social Service
Australian National Committee on Illumination
International Union of Psychological Science

HISTORY: Founded in 1966, as the successor to the Australian Branch of the British Psychological Society.

PURPOSE: To advance the scientific study and professional practice of psychology ; the promotion of the public welfare by encouraging the development of all branches of psychology; promoting and improving research in psychology; promoting high standards of professional ethics, competence, conduct, education, qualifications and achievement amongst psychologists; promoting the dissemination of psychological knowledge and thought through meetings, lectures, professional contacts, reports, papers, discussions and publications; advancing scientific interest and inquiry in psychology and all related areas of knowledge and practice.

ACTIVITIES: Annual Conference, Branch and Division meetings.

PUBLICATIONS
Australian Journal of Psychology (thrice yearly)
Australian Psychologist (thrice yearly)
Directory of members (available to members)

AWARDS
A.P.S. Prize (awarded to students)
Free Student Subscriber Awards

MEMBERSHIP: 3030 (fellows, honorary fellows, members, associate members, affiliates, student subscribers, foreign affiliateships)

141 Australian Rangeland Society
54 Broome Street, Cottesloe, W.A. 6011
Telephone: (092) 31 1464

SECRETARY: A.L. Payne, Department of Agriculture, Jarrah Road, South Perth, W.A. 6151.

HISTORY: Founded in 1975

PURPOSE: To foster the art and science of the use of Australias rangeland resources commensurate with their continued productivity or stability.

ACTIVITIES: Annual conference

PUBLICATIONS
Range Management Newsletter (quarterly)
Australian Rangeland Journal (biannual)
Quarterly newsletter and Annual journal (planned)

MEMBERSHIP: 200 ordinary members

142 Australian Remedial Education Association
703 Burke Road, Camberwell, Vic.
(G.P.O. Box 334, Camberwell 3124.)
Telephone: (03) 82 1659

SECRETARY: Mrs. B.C. Keir

SUBDIVISIONS
N.S.W. Branch, 15 Bronte Road, Bondi Junction, N.S.W. 2022

HISTORY: Founded in 1966

PURPOSE: To improve the professional status and competance of remedial teachers and to facilitate closer interdisciplinary communications.

INTERESTS: All fields relating to diagnosis, remediation and educational management of children with learning problems, including medical and psychological as well as educational fields.

ACTIVITIES: Meetings for all classes of members. Conference (approx 1 per year) for the public.

PUBLICATIONS
Australian Journal of Remedial Education

LIBRARY: Journals of allied associations (Aust. and overseas)

MEMBERSHIP: 257 (full, associate, student, organisation members)

143 Australian Science Teachers Association
A.C.E.R., 9 Frederick Street, Hawthorn, Vic.
(P.O. Box 210, Hawthorn, Vic 3122.)
Telephone: (03) 81 1271

SECRETARY: M.J. Rosier

AFFILIATIONS
New South Wales Science Teachers Association
Science Teachers Association of Victoria
Science Teachers Association of Queensland
South Australian Science Teachers Association
Science Teachers Association of Western Australia
Science Teachers Association of Tasmania
Science Teachers Association of the A.C.T.
International Council for Associations of Science Education

HISTORY: Founded in 1952 as a federal body

PURPOSE: To foster an interest in Science education

INTERESTS: Teaching of science, curriculum development, research in science education, communication among teachers and others interested in science education

ACTIVITIES: Annual Conference (CONASTA - Annual Conference of ASTA)

PUBLICATIONS
Australian Science Teachers Journal (3 issues per year)

MEMBERSHIP: approx 4000 (members of affiliated societies)

144   Australian Society of Anaesthetists
86 Elizabeth Bay Road, Elizabeth Bay, N.S.W.
(P.O. Box 525, Potts Point, 2011.)
Telephone: (02) 358 2298

SECRETARY: Dr. J. Keneally (Acting Hon. Federal Secretary)

SUBDIVISIONS
Branches in N.S.W., Vic., Qld., S.A., W.A. and Tas.

HISTORY: Founded in 1934

PURPOSE: To advance the science and art of anaesthetics in Australia.

ACTIVITIES: Annual General Meeting; Quarterly meetings of State Branches.

AWARDS
Jackson Rees Research Grant
Gilbert Troups Prize

MEMBERSHIP: 1,150 (ordinary, honorary, associate, life members)

145   Australian Society of Animal Production
191 Royal Parade, Parkville, Vic 3052.
Telephone: (03) 347 1277

SECRETARY: Dr. P.D. Mullaney

SUBDIVISIONS
Branches in N.S.W., Vic., Qld., S.A., N.T., W.A., Naracoorte (S.A.), New England (N.S.W.), Hunter Valley (N.S.W.), Southern Tablelands (N.S.W.) and Riverina (N.S.W.)

AFFILIATIONS
Australian Institute of Agricultural Science
World Association of Animal Production

HISTORY: Founded in 1950

PURPOSE: To promote the advancement and further the interests of animal production in Australia, and to promote and encourage the interchange throughout the Commonwealth and overseas countries.

ACTIVITIES: National Biennial Conference, Branches hold meetings and seminars throughout the year.

PUBLICATIONS
Proceedings of the Australian Society for Animal Production

MEMBERSHIP: 2000 (fellows, honorary, student concession)

146   Australian Society of Cosmetic Chemists
P.O. Box 503, Darlinghurst, N.S.W. 2010.

SECRETARY: B. Browne

SUBDIVISIONS
Victorian Chapter. - R. Feben, 8 Pakenham Street, Blackburn, Vic. 3130

AFFILIATIONS
International Federation of Societies of Cosmetic Chemists

HISTORY: Founded in 1964. Victorian Chapter founded in 1967

PURPOSE: To further the status of those professionally and technically engaged in the chemical division of the cosmetic industry.

ACTIVITIES: Annual General Conference, lectures in Sydney and Melbourne during the year.

MEMBERSHIP: 330 (full, associate members)

147   Australian Society of Dairy Technology (Inc.)
Dairy Industry House, 576 St. Kilda Road, Melbourne, Vic.
(P.O. Box 1657N, Melbourne, 3001)
Telephone: (03) 64 0111

SECRETARY: R.W. Gilbert (Federal Secretary)

SUBDIVISIONS
Divisions in Qld., N.S.W., Vic., Tas., S.A., W.A.
Sections - Northern District, East Gippsland, Western District, Central Gippsland, North Eastern, Darling Downs, Wide Bay, Richmond Tweed, Manning River, Nepean Hawkesbury, Hunter Valley, Bunbury, South Eastern, Mt. Gambier.

HISTORY: Founded in 1945

PURPOSE: To promote the advancement of dairy technology

INTERESTS: Research, technical and commercial

ACTIVITIES: Yearly conferences, Federal Council meetings, Division and Section meetings (monthly).

PUBLICATIONS
Australian Journal of Dairy Technology (quarterly)

LIBRARY: CSIRO Dairy Research Laboratory, Highett, Vic.

AWARDS
Scholarships and awards

MEMBERSHIP: 1500 (corporate, associate, life, honorary)

148   Australian Society of Endontology
Australian Dental Association, 116 Pacific Highway, North Sydney, N.S.W. 2060.

SECRETARY: Dr. I.A. Stewart, 220 Collins Street, Melbourne, Vic. 3000

SUBDIVISIONS
Branches in N.S.W., Qld., S.A., Vic., W.A.

AFFILIATIONS
Australian Dental Association

HISTORY: Founded in 1967.

PURPOSE: To study and advance endontology.

INTERESTS: Diseases of the dental pulp and related structures.

ACTIVITIES: Triennial general meeting, periodic conferences.

AWARDS
Essay prize to final year dental students.

MEMBERSHIP: 250 (full, honorary members)

149   Australian Society of Exploration Geophysicists
Science Centre, 35 Clarence Street, Sydney, N.S.W. 2000
Telephone: (02) 29 7747

SECRETARY: P.M. Cooney

SUBDIVISIONS
Branches in S.A. and W.A.

AFFILIATIONS
Society of Exploration Geophysicists (U.S.A.)

HISTORY: Founded in Sydney in 1970.

PURPOSE: To promote the science of geophysics especially its application to exploration. To promote the standing and professionalism of geophysicists.

INTERESTS: Coal, hydrocarbon and mineral exploration; education and training of geophysicists.

ACTIVITIES: Six ordinary meetings and one annual general meeting each year plus occassional extraordinary meetings.

PUBLICATIONS
Bulletin of the Australian Society of Exploration Geophysicists (quarterly)

AWARDS
ASEG scholarship of $200 is issued annually to an outstanding undergraduate to enable him to continue in his studies of geophysics.

MEMBERSHIP: 356 (active, corporate, student, associate)

150   Australian Society for Fish Biology
Australian Museum, 6-8 College Street, Sydney, N.S.W. 2000
Telephone: (02) 339 8111

SECRETARY: Dr. D.F. Hoese

SUBDIVISIONS
Sydney

HISTORY: Founded in 1971.

PURPOSE: To promote the study of fish and fisheries in Australia, particularly research and educational activities and to provide a medium for the interchange of information between Australians studying fishes.

ACTIVITIES: Annual Conference, with presentation of scientific papers and general business. Sydney Branch - Monthly seminars.

PUBLICATIONS
Newsletter (twice yearly)

LIBRARY: Very small, housed at Australian Museum.

AWARDS
Gilbert P. Whitley Award (an award of $50 for the best student paper delivered at the annual conference)

MEMBERSHIP: 200 (ordinary, student, foreign)

151   Australian Society of Herpetologists
Department of Histology and Embryology, Anderson Stuart Building. F13, University of Sydney, Sydney, N.S.W. 2006.
Telephone: (02) 692 1122 ext. 2491

SECRETARY: Dr. L.A. Moffat

HISTORY: Founded in 1964

PURPOSE: To promote the scientific study of amphibians and reptiles.

ACTIVITIES: Meetings held approx. once a year, often in conjunction with ANZAAS.

PUBLICATIONS
Newsletter (twice yearly).

LIBRARY: Small collection of reprints and journals held by Secretary-Treasurer.

MEMBERSHIP: 106 (ordinary, honorary)

152   Australian Society for Limnology
Zoology Department, University of Adelaide, Adelaide, S.A. 5000
Telephone: (08) 223 4333 ext. 2576

SECRETARY: R.T. Buckney

HISTORY: Founded in 1961

PURPOSE: To establish effective liaison between all persons interested in any aspect of fresh or brackish water in Australia; to promote the study of, and encourage these interests in State and Australian Government Research Institutes and Departments and educational institutions.

ACTIVITIES: Annual Congress, Annual General Meeting.

PUBLICATIONS
Special Publications (irregular)
Newsletter (quarterly)

AWARDS
Hilary Jolly Award (recipient delivers the Hilary Jolly Memorial Lecture at the Annual Congress)

MEMBERSHIP: 320 (ordinary, sustaining, student, affiliated body)

153   Australian Society for Medical Research
145 Macquarie Street, Sydney, N.S.W. 2000

SECRETARY: Dr. G.D. Duggin

SUBDIVISIONS
Branches in N.S.W., Qld., S.A., Vic., W.A.

HISTORY: Founded in 1961

PURPOSE: To foster interests in medical research; to provide an opportunity to meet others in related fields; to provide research workers in medical and allied sciences with a forum; to encourage recent graduates to undertake research.

ACTIVITIES: Annual Conference

PUBLICATIONS
Proceedings of the Australian Society for Medical Research.

MEMBERSHIP: 650 (regular, senior)

154   Australian Society for Microbiology Inc.
CSIRO Division of Food Research, P.O. Box 52, North Ryde, N.S.W. 2113.
Telephone: (02) 888 1333

SECRETARY: Dr. J.A. Howard (National Secretary)

SUBDIVISIONS
Branches in all states except Tasmania and in the A.C.T.

AFFILIATIONS
International Association of Mircobiological Societies

HISTORY: Founded in 1959.

PURPOSE: To advance the science of microbiology.

INTERESTS: Bacteriology, virology, mycology, immunology.

ACTIVITIES: Annual Scientific Meeting held in May; branch meetings on monthly and annual basis.

AWARDS
Sydney Rubbo Memorial Oration (delivered at each Annual Scientific Meeting)
Neil Goldsworthy Memorial Lecture (N.S.W.)
Prizes awarded to students by most Branches

MEMBERSHIP: 1100 (members, associate members, student members, honorary members and sustaining members)

155   Australian Society for Operations Research Incorporated
CSR Limited, G.P.O. Box 483, Sydney, N.S.W. 2001.
Telephone: (02) 2 0515

SECRETARY: Dr. R. Webb

SUBDIVISIONS
New South Wales Chapter - Mr. Les Whale (Secretary), Administrative Building 1, 12th Floor, QANTAS, Mascot, N.S.W. 2020
Victorian Chapter - Dr. J. Adams (Secretary), Clunies Ross House, 191 Royal Parade, Parkville, Vic. 3052
A.C.T. Chapter - Mr. R.B. Mitchell (Secretary), School of Information Sciences, Canberra College of Advanced Education, P.O.Box 1, Belconnen, A.C.T. 2616
South Australian Chapter - Dr. R.G.J. Mills (Secretary), School of Mathematics and Computer Studies, S.A. Institute of Technology, P.O.Box 1, Ingle Farm, S.A. 5095
Western Australian Chapter - Dr. D.G. Stevenson (Secretary), Westrail, Cnr. William and Murray Streets, Perth, W.A. 6000
Queensland Chapter - Dr. R. Lane (Secretary), Department Manager, University of Queensland, St. Lucia, Qld. 4067

HISTORY: Founded in 1971 from the amalgamation of seven separate operations research societies.

PURPOSE: To foster the development of the science of operations research; to foster the application of operations research wherever appropriate; to foster the widest possible exchange of information and ideas on operations research and related subjects; to define standards of knowledge in and to further the study of operations research.

ACTIVITIES: National Conferences, Chapter meetings.

PUBLICATIONS
Proceedings of National Conferences.
Chapter Newsletters

AWARDS
Conference Prize Paper Award.

MEMBERSHIP: approx 700 (fellow, associate, member, student)

156 Australian Society of Orthodontists
179 St. Georges Terrace, Perth, W.A.

SUBDIVISIONS
Branches in all states except Tasmania.

AFFILIATIONS
Australian Dental Association

HISTORY: Founded in 1927. Commenced to refunction on a constitutional basis in 1950.

PURPOSE: To promote the study and advancement of orthodontics, guidance in post graduate training for orthodontists and Denattal Board Specialist Registration.

INTERESTS: In conjunction with the Commonwealth Bureau of Dental Standards, an interest in materials used in orthodontics

ACTIVITIES: State Branch meetings held monthly or bimonthly and regular Federal Council Meetings. Triennial Orthodontic Congress is held in rotation around States.

PUBLICATIONS
Australian Orthodontic Journal (twice yearly)
Newsletter

AWARDS
Australian Society of Orthodontists Foundation for Research and Education sponsers overseas Lectures for Australian tours and gives research grants.

MEMBERSHIP: 204 (honorary life, state honorary, full, provisional, associate, student, corresponding)

157 Australian Society for Parasitology
CSIRO Long Pocket Laboratories, Private Bag No. 3, Indooroopilly, Qld. 4068
Telephone: (07) 371 3322

SECRETARY: Dr. I.G. Wright

AFFILIATIONS
Australian and New Zealand Association for the Advancement of Science Incorporated
World Association for the Advancement of Veterinary Parasitology.
World Federation of Parasitologists

HISTORY: Inaugural meeting Canberra Jan. 1964.

PURPOSE: To foster association of persons interested in parasitology, and by facilitating intercourse and discussion, to promote investigation and advance knowledge of parasitology.

ACTIVITIES: Annual or biannual meetings, Register of Live Parasite Cultures.

PUBLICATIONS
International Journal for Parasitology (Pergamon Press)

MEMBERSHIP: 190 (fellowship, ordinary)

158   Australian Society of Periodontology
145 Collins Street, Melbourne, Vic. 3000
Telephone: (03) 63 3616

SECRETARY: Dr. L.G. O'Brien

SUBDIVISIONS
Qld. Branch - Dr. G.M. Newcomb (Secretary), Dental School, Turbot Street, Brisbane, Qld. 4000 (Telephone: (07) 221 8044)
N.S.W. Branch - Dr. B. Pearlman (Secretary), 148 New South Head road, Edgecliff, N.S.W. 2027 (Telephone: (02) 32 0876)
Vic. Branch - Dr. D. Hurley (Secretary), 36 Garden Street, Geelong, Vic. 3220 (Telephone: (052) 9 5811)
S.A. Branch - Dr. L. Anaf (Secretary), 170 North Terrace, Adelaide, S.A. 5000 (Telephone: (08) 51 3770)
W.A. Branch - Dr. I. Grant (Secretary), 23 Park Street, Como, W.A. 6152 (Telephone: (092) 60 2506)
Tas. Branch - Dr. P. Crowe (Secretary), Dental Clinic, Rosebury, Tas., 7470

AFFILIATIONS
Australian Dental Association

HISTORY: Founded in 1961

PURPOSE: To promote the study and advancement of periodontology

ACTIVITIES: Scientific Meeting and General Meeting held at each Triennial Congress of the Australian Dental Association; State Branches hold bi-monthly meetings.

PUBLICATIONS
Newsletter (quarterly)

AWARDS
R.G. Williams Memorial Prize (triennially)

MEMBERSHIP: 337 (specialists, ordinary, honorary)

159   Australian Society of Plant Physiologists
School of Biological Sciences, (A12), University of Sydney, N.S.W. 2006
Telephone: (02) 692 1122 ext 2275

SECRETARY: Dr. W.J. Cram

SUBDIVISIONS
Active State Chapters in S.A., Vic. and W.A.

HISTORY: Founded in 1958.

PURPOSE: To advance the science of plant physiology.

ACTIVITIES: Annual meetings; occassional local meetings organized by State Chapters.

AWARDS
J.G. Wood Memorial Lecture
P.L. Goldacre Award

MEMBERSHIP: 560

160   Australian Society of Prosthodontists
Department of Restorative Dentistry, Royal Adelaide Hospital, North
Terrace, Adelaide, S.A. 5000.
Telephone: (08) 223 0230 ext. 8005

SECRETARY: Dr. P. Penhall

SUBDIVISIONS
Branches in N.S.W., Qld., W.A., Southern (includes Adelaide and Melbourne).

AFFILIATIONS
Australian Dental Association

HISTORY: Founded in 1961

PURPOSE: To promote the study of prosthodontics.

ACTIVITIES: Regular Branch meetings throughout the year. Triennial Scientific Meetings.

PUBLICATIONS
News Bulletin

MEMBERSHIP: 170 (ordinary, associate, corresponding, honorary members)

161   Australian Society for Reproductive Biology
Animal Research Institute, Department of Agriculture, Werribee, Vic.
3030
Telephone: (03) 741 1300

SECRETARY: Dr. I.A. Cumming

HISTORY: Founded in 1969

PURPOSE: To promote the study of reproductive biology by holding of an Annual Conference and by
publication of the Proceedings thereof.

ACTIVITIES: Annual Conference and Symposia.

PUBLICATIONS
Theriogenology

MEMBERSHIP: 237 (ordinary, honorary, sustaining)

162   Australian Society of Soil Science Incorporated.
N.S.W. Department of Agriculture, Agricultural Research Institute,
Private Bag, Wagga Wagga, N.S.W. 2650
Telephone: (069) 23 0999

SECRETARY: G.D. Batten (Federal Secretary)

SUBDIVISIONS
Branches in Qld., N.S.W., Vic., A.C.T., Riverina, S.A. and W.A.

HISTORY: Founded in 1955 as a federation of 5 branches. Riverina and W.A. joined at a later date.

PURPOSE: To advance soil science; to provide a link between soil scientists and members of kindred
bodies within Australia and in other countries.

PUBLICATIONS
Soils News (as newsletter)
Special publications; special reports; presidential addresses.

AWARDS
Prescott Award (annual)

MEMBERSHIP: 600 (ordinary, honorary members)

163   Australian Speleological Federation
P.O.Box 36, Lindisfarne, Tas. 7015

SECRETARY: A.C. Culberg

AFFILIATIONS
Societies in each state

HISTORY: Founded in 1956

PURPOSE: To further speleology in all its aspects on a national level, to gather together Australian speleologists and formulate national policies in furtherence of these aims.

ACTIVITIES: Biennial Conference and other seminars on a random basis

PUBLICATIONS
ASF Newsletter
Speleo Handbook
Proceedings of Conferences
Occasional papers on specific topics

LIBRARY: Library maintained

AWARDS
Edie Smith Award (biennial)

MEMBERSHIP: (full, associate, fellow)

164   Australian Systematic Botany Society
Herbarium Australiense, CSIRO, P.O. Box 1600, Canberra City, A.C.T. 2601

SUBDIVISIONS
Branches in Adelaide, Brisbane, Canberra, Melbourne, Perth, Sydney

HISTORY: Founded in 1973.

PURPOSE: To promote the study of systematics.

INTERESTS: Taxonomy of Australian plants.

ACTIVITIES: Symposia, contributed papers and General Meeting held at least once every two years.

PUBLICATIONS
Newsletter (four times per year)

MEMBERSHIP: 250 approx.

165   Australian Technical Millers Association
Box 274, Strathfield, N.S.W. 2135
Telephone: (02) 660 1233

SECRETARY: L.M. Youdale. (Henry Simen Aust., 40 Francis Street, Glebe, N.S.W.)

SUBDIVISIONS
Queensland Technical Millers Association - P.O. Box 77, Brisbane Markets, Qld. 4106
Victorian Technical Millers Association - 327 Collins Street, Melbourne, Vic. 3000

HISTORY: Founded in 1960 as Technical Millers Group of N.S.W. Name changed in 1970 to recognise considerable interstate membership. Qld. and Vic. groups formed in 1974.

PURPOSE: To bring together members of the flour milling and allied industries; to encourage technical interest and knowledge to the betterment of the interest.

INTERESTS: Flour and stockfeed milling, rice and oat milling, starch manufacture, cereal processing generally.

ACTIVITIES: Biannual National Technical Seminar. State meetings approx. bimonthly, Committee meetings monthly.

PUBLICATIONS
Information through 'Australian Baker and Millers Journal'

MEMBERSHIP: 97 (full, associate); QTMA and VTMA membership not included

166   Australian Telecommunications Development Association
60 York Street, Sydney, N.S.W.
(G.P.O. Box 3968, Sydney 2001)
Telephone: (03) 290 0700

SECRETARY: J.P. Kevans (Executive Officer)

HISTORY: Founded in 1934 and incorporated as a company limited by guarantee.

PURPOSE: To develop the use, manufacture and improvement of all telecommunications and associated equipments and their components and to promote the science of electronics applicable to this particular sector of industry. To promote the general welfare of the industry; to improve its services to its customers; to co-operate with the Government and its Departments, and to carry out any or all other objectives and or research programmes as may be conducive to the advancement and development of the industrial resources of Australia.

ACTIVITIES: Policy Committee, Council and General meetings held as required.

PUBLICATIONS
Telecommunications 1976 (Annual Report)

AWARDS
Sponsor eight scholarships at North Sydney Technical College covering the Electronics and Communications Certificate course, three scholarships with the Dept. of Further Education in the Radio Trades course and award Annual prizes to state Institutes of Technology in electronics engineering

MEMBERSHIP: 38

167   Australian Tunnelling Association
Institute of Engineers, Australia, 11 National Circuit, Barton, A.C.T.
2600
Telephone: (062) 73 3633

SECRETARY: E.D. Storr

AFFILIATIONS
International Tunnelling Association

HISTORY: Founded in 1972

PURPOSE: To promote and advance the science and practice of tunnelling

ACTIVITIES: National Conference held biennially

PUBLICATIONS
Tunnelling Information (Literature review - monthly)

MEMBERSHIP: Approx.30 members (corporate bodies) and 20 affiliates (individuals)

168 Australian Urban and Regional Information Systems Association
93 Dumaresq Street, Hamilton, Newcastle, N.S.W.
(P.O. Box 337, Hamilton 2303)
Telephone: (049) 69 1851

SECRETARY: Ms W. Jarvie

HISTORY: Founded in 1975 at the 3rd URPIS Conference.

PURPOSE: To promote research into the development and use of information systems as related to all aspects of urban and regional administration and planning; to advance the interests of members by facilitating the acquisition, dissemination and exchange of information relating to developments in their fields or interest; to provide for corporate representation of members on matters involving their common interests; to encourage international exchange of concepts and techniques by establishing liaison with associations in countries having similar objectives.

ACTIVITIES: Council meets as required during the year. Annual conference - URPIS - the Australian Conference on Urban and Regional Planning Information Systems. (URPIS ONE was held in 1973).

PUBLICATIONS
AURISA Newsletter (quarterly)
Proceedings of the Australian Conference on Urban and Regional Planning Information Systems (annual)

MEMBERSHIP: Approx. 200 members (ordinary, corporate, student)

169 Australian Veterinary Association
134-136 Hampton Road, Artarmon, N.S.W. 2064
Telephone: (02) 411 2733

SECRETARY: F.A. Widdows (Executive Director)

SUBDIVISIONS
Divisions in Qld., N.S.W., Vic., W.A., S.A., N.T. and Tas.
Special Interest Groups shown under Affiliations

AFFILIATIONS
Australian Equine Veterinary Association
Australian Small Animal Veterinary Association
Australian Veterinary Poultry Association
Veterinary Teachers and Research Workers
Australian Veterinarians in Industry
Australian Association of Cattle Veterinarians
Association of Veterinary Surgeons in Public Health
World Veterinary Association

HISTORY: Founded in 1921

PURPOSE: To promote and advance the veterinary and allied sciences and to maintain the status, honour and interests of the veterinary profession.

ACTIVITIES: Federal Annual General Meeting and Conference; regional divisional and special interest group meetings.

PUBLICATIONS
Australian Veterinary Journal
Australian Veterinary Bulletin
Proceedings of the divisional and Annual General meetings.

LIBRARY: Max Henry Memorial Library

AWARDS
Gilruth Prize
Practitioner of the Year Award
Fellowships
Prizes to students

MEMBERSHIP: 2107 (ordinary, fellows, husband-wife, overseas, life fellows, life members, honorary members, honorary life associate members, reduced subscriptions for recent graduates, waved fees)

170 Australian Water and Wastewater Association
P.O. Box A232, Sydney South, N.S.W. 2000
Telephone: (02) 269 6110

SECRETARY: P. Hughes

SUBDIVISIONS
N.S.W. - P. Mitchell (Branch Secretary), C
- Envirotech Australia Pty. Ltd., P.O. Box 220, Artarmon, N.S.W. 2064
Qld. - A. Pettigrew (Branch Secretary), P.O. Box 129, Brisbane Markets, Qld. 4106
Vic. - R. Povey (Branch Secretary), State Rivers and Water Supply Commission, 590 Orrong Road, Armadale, Vic. 3143
S.A. - A. Glatz (Branch Secretary), Engineering and Water Supply Department, Victoria Square, Adelaide, S.A. 5000
W.A. - R. Fimmel (Branch Secretary), A.W.W.A., P.O. Box 356, West Perth, W.A. 6005
N.T. - N.R. Allen (Branch Secretary), 634 Johns Place, Nightcliff, N.T. 5792
A.C.T. - D. Butters (Branch Secretary), C
- Department of Housing and Construction, Phillip, A.C.T. 2606
Tas. - P.E. Spratt, Fowler, England and Newtown, 132 Davey Street, Hobart, Tas. 7000

AFFILIATIONS
Water Pollution Control Federation
International Association of Water Pollution Research
International Water Supply Association

HISTORY: Founded in 1962

PURPOSE: To investigate and promote knowledge of -
(i) Water resources and their control and management, water quality standards and methods of examination. Collection, transmission, treatment and distribution of surface and underground water supplies;
(ii) the nature, collection, treatment, disposal and re-use of waste waters;
(iii) the design, construction, operation and management of water and wastewater treatment works;
(iv) the study, promotion and encouragement of pollution control of receiving waters.
To protect and improve the environment by a better understanding of the principles of water quality, treatment, water re-use ecology and pollution control; to encourage research; to facilitate the interchange of technical knowledge among its members and other interested persons and organisations by means of meetings and the publication of technical papers; to establish committees to examine and report upon specific subjects in the above fields; to form affiliations with institutes or associations whose objects are similar to those of the Association; to instruct and train members or other persons interested in the objects of the Association.

INTERESTS: Science and engineering of water industry.

ACTIVITIES: Federal Conventions and Summer Schools (biennial, each held on alternate years; Branch Technical Meetings; Regional Conferences (annual); visits to technical installations and social events.

PUBLICATIONS
Water (quarterly)
Summer School Notes

AWARDS
Thistlewaite Memorial Prize

MEMBERSHIP: 1500 (members, associates, students, sustaining members, honorary life members).

171   Australian Welding Research Association
118 Alfred Street, Milsons Point, N.S.W. 2061.
Telephone: (02) 922.3711

SECRETARY: Dr. A. Vetters

HISTORY: Founded in 1964

PURPOSE: To provide expert scientific and technical service to industry in welding and allied matters. AWRA uses research as a basis for these services to its members.

ACTIVITIES: Approx. four Conferences or Symposia held each year on specific topics

PUBLICATIONS
Australian Welding Research
AWRA Technical Notes
Proceedings of various Symposia conducted by AWRA.

LIBRARY: Comprehensive technical library for member's use.

AWARDS
Research contracts with total value approx. $60,000 are issued each year.

MEMBERSHIP: 142 (ordinary, associate, nominate members)

172   Australian Zinc Development Association
95 Collins Street, Melbourne, Vic. 3000
Telephone: (03) 63 0491

SECRETARY: J.H. McAuliffe

SUBDIVISIONS
Galvanizers Association of Australia
Zinc Die Casting Technologists Group

HISTORY: Founded in 1962.

PURPOSE: To disseminate technical or educational information on the uses and industrial applications of zinc and zinc products, technical support for industry and to encourage the latest technology.

ACTIVITIES: Technical symposia held regularly in Australian and New Zealand cities for groups up to 650 people. In-plant seminars and consultations in zinc coatings and zinc diecastings.

PUBLICATIONS
A wide range of technical manuals, reference works and technical-promotional publications on all major industrial applications of zinc. Circulation of bi-monthly Zinc Abstracts, a review of world technical literature on zinc. Full text of articles abstracted supplied free on request.

LIBRARY: Extensive zinc technical library facilities.

MEMBERSHIP: 6 member companies engaged in the mining and smelting of zinc.

173   Aviation Medicine Society of Australia and New Zealand
998 Mt. Alexander Road, Essendon, Vic. 3040

SECRETARY: Dr. G.J. Dennerstein

HISTORY: Founded in 1949

PURPOSE: To cultivate and promote aviation medicine and related sciences by holding periodical meetings of members; collection and dissemination of scientific knowledge and the publication of articles related to aviation medicine and of the scientific proceedings of meetings; conducting scientific essay or other appropriate competitions open to medical undergraduates; conference, co-operation or affiliation with bodies having similar objects within Australia or elsewhere; to provide an authoritative body of opinion on aviation medicine.

ACTIVITIES: Annual conference with more frequent Scientific Meetings.

PUBLICATIONS
Newsletter (quarterly)

MEMBERSHIP: 354 (foundation, ordinary, honorary, associate members)

174   Ballarat Astronomical Society

Ballarat Municipal Observatory, cnr. Magpie and Cobelen Streets, Mt. Pleasant, Ballarat, Vic.
(P.O. Box 284, Ballarat 3350)
Telephone: (053) 32 7967

SECRETARY: R. Duffy

HISTORY: Founded in 1957. Municipal Observatory founded in 1884.

PURPOSE: To promote discussion and observation of an amateur nature; to encourage the study and practice of astronomy, and to disseminate knowledge of the science.

INTERESTS: Telescope making, radio astronomy, astrophotography.

ACTIVITIES: Monthly General Meetings.

PUBLICATIONS
Oddie-Baker (monthly)

LIBRARY: Small library (1300 volumes)

MEMBERSHIP: 50 (adult, family, junior)

175   Bird Observers Club

BOC Centre, 183 Springvale Road, Nunawading, Vic.
(G.P.O.Box 2167T, Melbourne, 3001)
Telephone: (03) 877 5342

SECRETARY: Mrs. E.M. McCulloch

HISTORY: Founded in 1905 and has grown into an Australia wide society with a social and ornithological content.

PURPOSE: To further the study and protection of Australian birds; to act as a source of information and informed opinion on such matters.

INTERESTS: Ornithological studies; habitat improvement; conservation; popularization of bird studies.

ACTIVITIES: General meetings (monthly); study meetings (winter monthly).

PUBLICATIONS
Bird Observer(monthly newsletter)
Australian Bird Watcher (quarterly)
Field guides to groups of bird species.

LIBRARY: Materials available by post and on personal application.

MEMBERSHIP: 2600

176   British Astronomical Society, N.S.W. Branch

Sydney Observatory, Observatory Park, Sydney, N.S.W. 2000
Telephone: (02) 241 2478

SECRETARY: S.J. Elwin

HISTORY: Founded in 1893.

PURPOSE: To promote the science of astronomy especially among amateur observers.

INTERESTS: Variable stars, occultations, solar and planetary observations.

ACTIVITIES: Monthly (10 per year) at Sydney Observatory.

PUBLICATIONS
Bulletin (10 issues per year)

LIBRARY: Books and slides dealing with astronomy.

MEMBERSHIP: 150 (member, junior member, associate)

177   British Society of Rheology; Australian Branch
Materials Research Laboratory, P.O. Box 50, Ascot Vale, Vic. 3032

SECRETARY: J.G. Williams

HISTORY: The Australian Branch was formed in 1960 in Melbourne. It was then known as the Victorian Branch.

PURPOSE: To promote scientific enquiry and the diffusion of knowledge connected with the advancement of pure and applied rheology, defined as the science of the deformation and flow of matter.

ACTIVITIES: Meetings, workshops, and lecture courses are held from time to time.

MEMBERSHIP: 40 (ordinary)

178   Building Science Forum of Australia
New South Wales Division, Suite 38, 3rd Floor, 72 Pitt Street, Sydney, N.S.W. 2000
Telephone: (02) 233 5691

SECRETARY: K.S. Gordon

SUBDIVISIONS
Building Science Forum of Australia, South Australian Division (care of - T. Denton, 55 Jerningham Street, North Adelaide, S.A. 5006).

HISTORY: Founded in 1963.

PURPOSE: To improve communication and co-ordination within the Australian building industry; to make approaches to statutory and other authorities over ordinances which greatly affect the industry.

INTERESTS: Building science; building economics.

ACTIVITIES: Conferences and seminars conducted from time to time. Also evening lectures on topical subjects and annual general meeting.

AWARDS
Annual bronze medallion for best book published in Australia which deals with building, construction, architecture or a related subject.

MEMBERSHIP: Student, ordinary, corporate and sustaining members.

179 Bundaberg Astronomical Society
Goodwood Road, Alloway, Qld.
(P.O. Box 586, Bundaberg 4670)
Telephone: (071) 71 2888

SECRETARY: Mrs. J. Dunn

HISTORY: Founded in 1966.

PURPOSE: To encourage a popular interest in astronomy; to assist and give advice in the construction of telescopes; to organise observing groups for the purpose of carrying out astronomical observations; to organise field nights for the public and secondary students as a means of fostering interest in astronomy.

ACTIVITIES: General meetings held monthly.

PUBLICATIONS
Alloway Observer (bimonthly)

LIBRARY: A comprehensive library on astronomy and allied sciences.

MEMBERSHIP: 46 (full, life, associate, honorary)

180 Canberra Astronomical Society
care of- Griffin Centre, Bunda Street, Canberra, A.C.T. 2601

SECRETARY: P. Delaney

HISTORY: Founded in 1972.

PURPOSE: To promote interest in astronomical research and the practice of astronomy for members and the public.

INTERESTS: Occultations, variable stars, thin lunar crescents, observation in general.

ACTIVITIES: Monthly meetings.

PUBLICATIONS
Southern Cross (monthly bulletin)
Ephemeris (annual)
Technical papers (from members)

LIBRARY: An expanding collection of astronomy texts, recent journals and star charts.

MEMBERSHIP: 70 (full adult, student concessional, country)

181 Canberra Gem Society Inc.
Griffith Centre, Bunda Street, Canberra City, A.C.T. 2601.

HISTORY: Founded in 1963, originally worked through the Geology Department of the Australian National University.

PURPOSE: To promote interest and participation in lapidary, gemological and associated arts; to maintain a workshop wherin members may learn and practice such arts; to promote the conservation of Australia's geological resources.

INTERESTS: Gemmology, geology, lapidary, jewellery, enamelling.

ACTIVITIES: Monthly meetings, workshop sessions, instruction courses, jewellery classes, collection outings.

PUBLICATIONS
Canberra Gem Society Newsletter (monthly)

LIBRARY: Library maintained

MEMBERSHIP: 320 (ordinary, junior, country, life members)

182   Cardiac Society of Australia and New Zealand
365 Crown Street, Surrey Hills N.S.W.
(P.O. Box 84, Darlinghurst, 2010.)
Telephone: (02) 31 7112

SECRETARY: Dr. P.G. Caspari (Hon. Secretary)

SUBDIVISIONS
Branches in New South Wales, Victoria, South Australia, Queensland, Western Australia, Tasmania
and New Zealand.

HISTORY: Founded in 1952 as the Australasian Cardiac Society. In 1957 the name was changed to the
present title.

PURPOSE: Advancement of knowledge of the disease of the heart, encourage contact between
researchers interested in cardiology or allied subjects.

ACTIVITIES: Annual Scientific meeting.

PUBLICATIONS
Proceedings published in Australian and New Zealand Journal of Medicine

AWARDS
R.T. Hall Prize (annually).
R.T. Hall Lecture (annually)
Hempson Maddox Lecture (annually)

MEMBERSHIP: approximately 440 (members, life, associate, corresponding, honorary members).

183   Cement and Concrete Association of Australia
147 Walker Street, North Sydney, N.S.W. 2060.
Telephone: (02) 92 0316

SECRETARY: Mr. R.W. Maze (Executive Officer)

SUBDIVISIONS
N.S.W. Branch - Mr. P.I. Mahaffey (Regional Engineer), 100 Walker Street, North Sydney, N.S.W.
2060
Vic. Branch - Mr. K.D. Campbell (Regional Engineer), 60 Albert Road, South Melbourne, Vic. 3205
S.A. Branch - Mr. D.J. Amey (Regional Engineer), 254 Melbourne Street, North Adelaide, S.A. 5006
Qld. Branch - Mr. I.H. Orchard (Regional Engineer), 9th Floor, M.I.M. Building, 160 Ann Street,
Brisbane, Qld. 4000
W.A. Branch - Mr. D.R. Buchanan (Regional Engineer), 43 Ventnor Avenue, West Perth, W.A. 6005
Tas. Branch - Mr. S.E. Gill (Regional Engineer), Room 601, C.M.L. Building, 18 Elizabeth Street,
Hobart, Tas. 7000

HISTORY: Founded in 1928 as the Australian Cement Manufacturers' Association. Present name
adopted in 1946.

PURPOSE: To provide a technical service to users of cement and to extend and improve the use of the
material.

INTERESTS: Support given to research; technical service provided.

PUBLICATIONS
Constructional Review (quarterly)

LIBRARY: Reference libraries maintained.

MEMBERSHIP: 15 member companies

184   Chartered Institute of Transport

Australian Council, Unit 3, 10 Anderson Street, Templestowe, Vic. 3106
Telephone: (03) 846 2797

SECRETARY: H.J. Lawrence

SUBDIVISIONS
Sections in N.S.W., Vic., S.A., W.A., Qld., Tas., A.C.T. and northern N.S.W.

HISTORY: Founded in London in 1919. N.S.W. Section established 1935. Australian Council established in Melbourne in 1972.

PURPOSE: Promotion of traffic science and the art of transport.

ACTIVITIES: Luncheons; evening meetings, seminars, conferences.

PUBLICATIONS
Australian Transport (bi-monthly)

MEMBERSHIP: 1800 (fellows, members, licientiates, associates, students).

185   Clean Air Society of Australia and New Zealand

P.O. Box 191, Eastwood, N.S.W. 2122
Telephone: (02) 2 0557 extn 2680

SECRETARY: R. Manuell

SUBDIVISIONS
N.S.W. - Mr. J. McLeod, Secretary, Box 4036, G.P.O., Sydney, N.S.W. 2001.
Vic. - Mr. W. Hicks, Secretary, PRA Ltd, Box 40, Altona, Vic. 3018.
Qld. - Mr. B. Thiele, Secretary, Division of Air Pollution Control, 484 Adelaide Street, Brisbane, Qld. 4000.
S.A. - Mr. G. Sweetapple, Secretary, Box 65, Rundle Street P.O., Adelaide, S.A. 5000.
W.A. - Mr. D. Sykes, Secretary, Department of Health, Box 134, G.P.O., Perth, W.A. 6001.
Tas. - Mr. T. O'Brien, Secretary, Department of Environment, 161 Davey Street, Hobart, Tas. 7000.
A.C.T. - Mr. T. McKay, Secretary, Department of Environment, Housing and Community Development, P.O. Box 1890, Canberra City, A.C.T. 2601.
New Zealand - Mr. N. Thom, Secretary, P.O. Box 56-145, Dominion Road, Auckland, New Zealand.

HISTORY: Founded in 1966.

PURPOSE: To advance the knowledge and practical experience of air pollution and air pollution control in Australasia; to provide an organisation which will gather, collate and distribute this experience and knowledge to its members and the general community; to promote scientific discussions of and research into the problems of air pollution and air pollution control; to maintain contact and establish liaison with organisations with similar interests in other countries; to provide scholarships, exhibitions, bursaries and funds for the purpose of promoting education in the science and practice of air pollution control; to make representations to the government regarding the carrying out of the objects of the Society.

ACTIVITIES: International conferences (triennially); meetings held by each Branch at regular intervals, and occasional Symposia on specific topics such as smog, analytical techniques etc.

PUBLICATIONS
Clean Air (quarterly)
Proceedings of symposia and international conferences.

AWARDS
Clean Air Medal (occasional)
Regular contributions to prizes and scholarships at selected Australian and New Zealand universities.

MEMBERSHIP: 700 (individual, organizational, sustaining members)

186   Combustion Institute (Australian Section)

Aeronautical Research Laboratories, Box 4331 G.P.O., Melbourne, Vic. 3001.
Telephone: (03) 64 0251 extn 404

SECRETARY: R.E. Parvia (Secretary); D.R. Warren (Chairman)

HISTORY: Parent body founded in 1954, Australian Section in 1956.

PURPOSE: To promote the science of combustion and its applications.

INTERESTS: Combustion processes and their practical applications.

ACTIVITIES: International symposia (biennially); lectures, courses and symposia in Australia.

PUBLICATIONS
Abstracts and proceedings of local meetings.

AWARDS
Travel fund for grants to members attending overseas symposia, or for invited specialists coming to Australia.

MEMBERSHIP: 75 (members)

187   Commercial Apiarists' Association of New South Wales

88 South Street, Granville, N.S.W.
(P.O. Box 183, Granville 2142).
Telephone: (02) 637 8218

SECRETARY: C.W. McIntyre

SUBDIVISIONS
Tamworth, Bathurst, Inverell, Southern Tablelands (Queanbeyan), Dubbo-Mudgee, North Coast (Grafton), Sydney and Metropolitan.

HISTORY: Founded in 1932.

PURPOSE: To promote the interests and welfare of the beekeepers of New South Wales.

ACTIVITIES: Annual conference; field days; branch meetings; executive council meetings.

PUBLICATIONS
CAA News (circular to members)

MEMBERSHIP: 1050 (ordinary and associate members)

188   Concrete Institute of Australia

147 Walker Street, North Sydney, N.S.W. 2060
Telephone: (02) 92 0316

SECRETARY: K.J. Cavanagh

SUBDIVISIONS
N.S.W. Branch - Mr. P.I. Mahaffey (Secretary), 100 Walker Street, North Sydney, N.S.W. 2060
Vic. Branch - Mr. K.D. Campbell (Secretary), 60 Albert Road, South Melbourne, Vic. 3205
S.A. Branch - Mr. D.J. Amey (Secretary), 254 Melbourne Street, North Adelaide, S.A. 5006
Qld. Branch - Mr. I.H. Orchard (Secretary), 9th Floor, M.I.M. Building, 160 Ann Street, Brisbane, Qld. 4000
W.A. Branch - Mr. D.R. Buchanan (Secretary), 43 Ventnor Avenue, West Perth, W.A. 6005
Tas. Branch - Mr. S.E. Gill (Secretary), Room 601, C.M.L. Building, 18 Elizabeth Street, Hobart, Tas. 7000

HISTORY: Founded in 1963 as the Australian Prestressed Concrete Group. Name changed to Concrete Institute of Australia in 1969.

PURPOSE: The advancement of concrete technology and practice.

ACTIVITIES: Biannial conference, symposia, seminars and site visits.

PUBLICATIONS
Data sheets, technical handbooks, newsletters, technical papers.

MEMBERSHIP: 895 (sustaining, individual, student, honorary members).

189 Conservation Council of S.A. Inc.
310 Angas Street, Adelaide, S.A.
(G.P.O. Box 2403, Adelaide 5001)
Telephone: (08) 223 5155

SECRETARY: D.A. Cole

AFFILIATIONS
Australian Conservation Foundation Incorporated
International Union for Conservation in Nature

HISTORY: Founded in 1971.

PURPOSE: To provide for liaison and co-ordination in working between individual conservation bodies
in S.A. for the common aims of: maintenance of the quality of the environment, particularly the
natural environment, and the preservation of the entegrity of ecological systems; to promote the wise
use in the long term of all natural resources and responsible stewardship over them; to promote
scientific research into the existence and dynamics of all living and inanimate elements in the
environment and their ecological inter-relationships; to investigate threats to the survival of any species
and-or any natural communities; to oppose the pollution or degradation of the environment; to
encourage the spread of knowledge relating to all or any of the foregoing including the provision of
assistance to primary and secondary schools and tertiary institutions; to undertake such other
conservation activities as the Council shall from time to time adopt; to establish and administer a
Conservation Centre in furtherance of the objects of the Council.

ACTIVITIES: Quarterly Council meetings.

PUBLICATIONS
Red Gum (quarterly)
News sheet (fortnightly)

LIBRARY: Over 1000 books, monographs on environmental matters.

MEMBERSHIP: 20 member bodies, 11 associate organizations

190 Conservation Council of Western Australia Inc.
537 Wellington Street, Perth, W.A. 6000
Telephone: (092) 21 4507

SECRETARY: Mrs. M. Madden

SUBDIVISIONS
30 different Conservation Groups

HISTORY: Founded in 1967.

PURPOSE: To protect the environment.

ACTIVITIES: Council meets monthly.

PUBLICATIONS
Annual Report, submissions

MEMBERSHIP: 30 Delegate Bodies

191 Contact Lens Society of Australia

Suite 818, Australia Square Tower, George Street, Sydney, N.S.W. 2000.
Telephone: (02) 27 3997

SECRETARY: K.W. Bell

SUBDIVISIONS
State chapters in Qld, N.S.W., Vic., Tas., S.A., W.A., A.C.T.

HISTORY: Founded in 1962.

PURPOSE: To promote scientific research in the field of contact lens work and to encourage the interchange of ideas and experiences amongst persons interested in or engaged in the prescribing and fitting of contact lenses.

ACTIVITIES: Annual conference and general meeting. State chapters organise regular meetings. International Contact Lens Congress held every three years.

AWARDS
Contact Lens Society of Australia Research Award (annually)

MEMBERSHIP: 236 (ordinary, honorary, life members)

192 Council of Australian Food Technology Associations Inc.

44 Miller Street, North Sydney, N.S.W. 2060
Telephone: (02) 922 3114

SECRETARY: J.I. Martyn (National Executive Director)

SUBDIVISIONS
Food Technology Associations of -
New South Wales - 60 York Street, Sydney, 2000. Secretary, S.M. Adams (02) 290 0700.
Victoria - 370 St. Kilda Road, Melbourne, 3004. Secretary, H. Lawrence (03) 698 4111.
Queensland - 375 Wickham Terrace, Brisbane, 4000. Secretary, Miss C.M. Llewellyn (07) 221 1699.
South Australia - 12 Pirie Street, Adelaide, 5000. Secretary, A.K. Sellick (08) 87 4691.
Western Australia - 212-220 Adelaide Terrace, Perth, 6000. Secretary, R.U. Capper (092) 25 8277.
Tasmania - 191 Liverpool Street, Hobart, 7000. Secretary, K. Johnston (002) 34 5933.

AFFILIATIONS
Australian Canners Association
Federated Wholesale Spirit Merchants Association of Australia
Australian Council of Soft Drink Manufacturers
Australian Associated Brewers
Meat and Allied Trades Federation of Australia
Australian Tin Information Centre
Flavour and Perfume Compound Manufacturers Association
Federal Wine and Brandy Producers Council of Australia Inc.
Cold Storage Association of Australia
Australian Chilled Fruit Juice Association
Australian Poultry Industries Association
Ice Cream Manufacturers Federation of Australia
NARGA Australia Ltd
Grocery Manufacturers of Australia Ltd
Confectionery Manufacturers of Australia Ltd
National Packaging Association of Australia
National Meat Canners Association
Plastics Institute of Australia Inc.
Australian Dairy Industry Council
Food Industry Council of Australia
Australian Tin Information Centre, Gold Fields House, Sydney Cove, N.S.W. 2000)

HISTORY: Founded in 1949.

PURPOSE: Representing and co-ordinating State Food Technology Associations and kindred associations to promote standards and technical aspects for the food processing and servicing industries.

INTERESTS: Membership of the Food Standards Committee, the Food Additives Sub-committee, the Food Science and Technology Sub-committee and Food Microbiology Sub-committee of the National Health and Medical Research Council. Involvement in work of Codex Alimentarius Commission, Food Standards, Regulations, Technology.

ACTIVITIES: Executive and Technical Standing Committee meetings (monthly). Annual conference in July.

PUBLICATIONS
Food Technology in Australia (monthly)
Annual Report

LIBRARY: Located at 44 Miller Street, North Sydney

AWARDS
Education grants for selected students for tertiary studies in food technology, by food technology associations.

MEMBERSHIP: 443 food manufacturing and servicing companies (membership all at State Food Technology Association level)

193   CSIRO Officers' Association
    9 Queens Road, Melbourne, Vic. 3004
    Telephone: (03) 26 3361, 26 2461

SECRETARY: Mrs D. F. Jenner (General Secretary)

SUBDIVISIONS
Branches in A.C.T. and all states.

HISTORY: Founded in 1943

PURPOSE: To protect and-or improve the status and welfare of Officers of CSIRO and holders of CSIRO Studentships.

INTERESTS: Terms and Conditions of Employment; Arbitration activity; Superannuation; Seminars of Staff Relations; Human Factor Courses.

ACTIVITIES: Council meets approx. 4 times per year; Branch Committee meetings as required; various Council Committees meet as required.

PUBLICATIONS
CSIROOA Bulletin

AWARDS
David Rivett Medal Award

MEMBERSHIP: 2256 (full, honorary life, retired members)

194   David G. Stead Memorial Wildlife Research Foundation of Australia
    'Wirrimbirra' Sanctuary, Hume Highway, Bargo, N.S.W.
    (Box 4840 G.P.O., Sydney 2001.)
    Telephone: Sydney- (02) 637 3033; Bargo (046) 84 1112

SECRETARY: Miss K. Groat

HISTORY: Founded in 1963.

PURPOSE: To encourage interest in conservation of natural resources by the establishment of sanctuaries such as Wirrimbirra which now includes an operating Field Studies Public School where classes are conducted regularly at all levels; to maintain plantations of indigenous flora from a wide variety of habitats throughout the continent to establish their potential as cultivars; to operate a plant nursery to study cultivation techniques for Australian native plants and encourage the use of these in private gardens and public places; to maintain a sample of typical dry sclerophyll forest and associated waterways and heathland in its natural condition; to provide facilities for continued research too achieve the above objectives.

INTERESTS: Organization of field studies centre; propagation of Australian native plants.

ACTIVITIES: Annual general meeting and other meetings.

PUBLICATIONS
Wildlife Research News (quarterly)
Your Australian Garden Series
200 Australian Plants for Gardens
200 Wattles for Gardens
150 Australian Plants for Gardens (54 page special publication)

LIBRARY: Natural history and environmental studies reference library housed at Wirriumbirra.

MEMBERSHIP: 350 (individual, corporate and junior members)

195   Diecasting Institute of Australia
care of- Metal Trades Industry Association, MTIA House, 214 Northbourne Avenue, Canberra, A.C.T.
(P.O. Box 817, Canberra City 2601)
Telephone: (062) 49 6360, 49 6364

SECRETARY: L.W. Purnell (National Secretary)

SUBDIVISIONS
Victoria - E. Cantwell (State Secretary), 165 Eastern Road, South Melbourne, Vic. 3205
N.S.W. - D. Whiting (State Secretary), MTIA House, 105 Walker Street, North Sydney, N.S.W. 2060

HISTORY: Originally founded in 1954 as Zinc Alloy Die Casters Association of Australia. Name changed to present title in March 1972.

PURPOSE: To represent the interests of the industry at Federal and State levels; to promote high quality diecastings; to provide assistance and advice on safety, standards and research through specialist sub-committees; and to monitor conditions in industry by means of a confidential survey of member companies.

ACTIVITIES: State meetings held bi-monthly; National Council meetings held quarterly; Annual Conference.

PUBLICATIONS
Zinc Caster
The Zinc Caster (Colour educational film)

AWARDS
Diecasting of the Year Awards (for both aluminium and zinc)
Safety Competition

MEMBERSHIP: 58 member companies (licensed, unlicensed, overseas, associate membership)

196   Ecological Society of Australia, Incorporated
P.O. Box 1564, Canberra City, A.C.T. 2601

SECRETARY: D.A. Maelzer

SUBDIVISIONS
Regional groupings are centred in all state capitals and Canberra.

HISTORY: Founded in 1960

PURPOSE: To promote the scientific study of plants and animals in relation to their environment and to facilitate the exchange of ideas amongst ecologists; to promote the application of ecological principles to the development, utilization and conservation of Australian natural resources; to advise governmental and other agencies in matters where application of ecological principals may be of assistance; to foster the preservation and sound management of natural areas for scientific and recreational purposes; to promote publication of results of ecological research.

ACTIVITIES: Biennial Symposium; annual meeting; general meeting in conjuction with ANZAAS.

PUBLICATIONS
Proceedings of the Ecological Society of Australia.
Bulletin of the Ecological Society of Australia
Memoire of the Ecological Society of Australia

MEMBERSHIP: 550 (full members, student members)

197   Electricity Supply Association of Australia
V.C.A. Building, 1 Exhibition Street, Melbourne, Vic.
(G.P.O. Box 1823Q, Melbourne, 3001.)
Telephone: (03) 63 5140

SECRETARY: J. Purves

HISTORY: Founded in 1918.

PURPOSE: The furtherance of the development, operation and management of the electricity supply industry in the public and national interest.

INTERESTS: Generation, transmission and distribution of electricity with its associated administrative, financial, personnel and environmental fields.

ACTIVITIES: Conferences and committee meetings held regularly, covering all states and Australian government areas.

PUBLICATIONS
Annual statistics, technical and safety publications.

AWARDS
C.G.H. McDonald Memorial Prize
E.S. Cornwall Memorial Prize (contributor)
The Electrical Research Board is financed by members of the association

MEMBERSHIP: 70 (public electricity supply organizations)

198   Electricity Supply Engineers' Association of N.S.W.
93 Bynya Road, Palm Beach, N.S.W. 2108
Telephone: (02) 919 5020

SECRETARY: H.J. Toepfer

AFFILIATIONS
Australian Liaison Committee of CIRED (International Conference on Electricity Distribution)

HISTORY: Founded in 1924.

PURPOSE: To do all such acts and things as the Association may consider of benefit to the electricity supply industry, including inter alia: The free exchange of technical, commercial and administrative information relating to the management of electricity supply undertakings, by conference, correspondence and other means; to bring about a closer co-operation between Electricity Supply Engineers and between Electricity Supply Engineers and Statutory Electricity Authorities; to promote the science and practices relating to the economic development of public supply of electricity and its utilisation; to encourage preparation of technical papers by members on application of engineering advances; to encourage applied research and development; to advance the engineering profession and to do all such things as are conducive or incidental to the objects of the Association.

ACTIVITIES: Monthly Board of Management Meetings, Annual Conference.

PUBLICATIONS
Monthly Bulletin
Proceedings of the Annual Conference

AWARDS
Conway Prize (annual)
Electricity Supply Engineers' Association of N.S.W. Prizes (annual)
Award of Merit (annual)

MEMBERSHIP: 280 (honorary, life, full associate)

199   Endocrine Society of Australia
Endocrine Unit, Royal Adelaide Hospital, Adelaide, S.A. 5000

SECRETARY: Dr. P. Harding

SUBDIVISIONS
N.S.W. Branch - Prof. S. Posen, Sydney Hospital
Vic. Branch - Dr. H.G. Burger, Prince Henry's Hospital
Qld. Branch - Dr. R.D. Gordon, Greenslopes Repatriation Hospital
A.C.T. Branch - Dr. C. Eastman, Woden Valley Hospital
W.A. Branch - Dr. D. Gutheridge, Sir Charles Gairdner Hospital

AFFILIATIONS
Endocrine Society of New Zealand
International Society of Endocrinology

HISTORY: Founded in 1958.

PURPOSE: The advancement of knowledge in endocrinology and metabolism.

INTERESTS: Endocrinology and metabolism of thyroid, adrenal, gonadal, hypothalamic, pituitary, pancreas (insulin), gut and reproductive hormones.

ACTIVITIES: Annual scientific and annual general meeting in August each year; seminar meetings in February each year.

PUBLICATIONS
Proceedings of the Endocrine Society of Australia (annual, abstracts of papers presented at annual meeting and seminar meeting)

MEMBERSHIP: 419 (ordinary, honorary life, sustaining members)

200   Entomological Society of Queensland
Entomology Department, University of Queensland, St. Lucia, Qld. 4067

SECRETARY: B. Cantrell

HISTORY: Founded on 14th June 1923

PURPOSE: The furtherance of pure and applied entomological science.

ACTIVITIES: Regular monthly meetings(nine times yearly).

PUBLICATIONS
News Bulletin (approximately nine times yearly).

AWARDS
Annual bursary awards as part of Queensland Science Teachers'Association Science Contest.

MEMBERSHIP: 335 (country, ordinary, associate members).

201 Environment Studies Association of Victoria
324 William Street, Melbourne, Vic 3000
Telephone: (03) 329 5377

SECRETARY: R.D. Piesse (Director)

HISTORY: Founded in 1972

PURPOSE: To encourage the understanding of the total environment through teaching techniques of field study on expertly led courses, to develop environment study centres, to publish resource materials and to act as a 'clearing house' and source of advice on environmental education.

INTERESTS: The Association is currently involved in a project to develop the property 'Glenewart' (owned by the Victorian Conservation Trust) as a land use demonstration area and environmental studies centre, near Launching Place.

PUBLICATIONS
Monthly newsletter
Reports of Courses
Annual Course Calender

LIBRARY: Library maintained on environmental education, especially on outdoor study aspects

MEMBERSHIP: 560 (ordinary, life, group, member body)

202 Ergonomics Society of Australia and New Zealand Inc.
Defence Engineering Analysis, Department of Defence, Russell Offices, Canberra, A.C.T. 2600

SECRETARY: J.H. Adams

SUBDIVISIONS
Branches in N.S.W., Vic., S.A., A.C.T., and Qld.

AFFILIATIONS
Australian and New Zealand Association for the Advancement of Science Incorporated
International Ergonomics Association

HISTORY: First Ergonomics Conference held in Australia in 1964. Society was formally established in 1967.

PURPOSE: To promote learning in, and stimulate research into, the relationship between man and his occupation, equipment and environment; to advance education in and promote the use of anatomical, physiological, psychological and engineering knowledge applied to the practical problems arising from this relationship.

ACTIVITIES: Annual Conference; branch meetings.

PUBLICATIONS
Ergonomics Society of Australia and New Zealand Newsletter (issued only to Society members)

MEMBERSHIP: 254 (fellows, members, associate members, affiliated organizations)

203 Federal Council of Australian Apiarists' Associations
88 South Street, Granville, N.S.W.
(P.O. Box 183, Granville 2142.)
Telephone: (02) 637 8218

SECRETARY: C.W. McIntyre

AFFILIATIONS
Commercial Apiarists' Association of New South Wales
Victorian Apiarists' Association
South Australian Apiarists' Association
Farmers' Union of Western Australia(Beekeepers' Section)
Queensland Beekeepers' Association
Tasmanian Beekeepers' Association

HISTORY: Founded in 1934

PURPOSE: To provide a means whereby Australian apiarists may be represented through a common organization; to promote the welfare of the industry.

INTERESTS: All those things affecting the welfare of the honey industry and the individuals comprising it.

ACTIVITIES: Annual meeting of delegates from member associations. Special meetings if required.

PUBLICATIONS
Internal circulars only.

MEMBERSHIP: 2200 (members belong to six state associations)

204   Field Naturalists' Club of Victoria
National Herbarium, The Domain, South Yarra, Vic. 3141.
Telephone: (03) 92 8579

SECRETARY: R.H. Riordan (Honorary Secretary)

SUBDIVISIONS
Junior clubs at Hawthorn, Preston, Montmorency, Black Rock.
Botany, marine biology, microscopy, geology, mammal survey and field survey groups.

AFFILIATIONS
29 affiliate groups throughout Victoria.

HISTORY: Founded in 1880; Wilson's Promontary Reserve Movement established in 1904; Wyperfeld National Park reserved in 1921, Sperm Whale Head reserved in 1927; National Monuments and Parks Movement inaugarated in 1936; areas at Mallacoota, Cumberland and Wyperfeld reserved in 1937.

PURPOSE: Promotion of the study of natural history; preservation of flora and fauna indigenous to Australia, Papua New Guinea and New Zealand, particularly to Victoria; to collect and disseminate information.

PUBLICATIONS
Victorian Naturalist (monthly)

AWARDS
Australian Natural History Medallion

MEMBERSHIP: approximately 1000 (ordinary, country, life, junior members)

205   Field Naturalists' Society of South Australia Inc.
Box 1594, G.P.O., Adelaide, 5001.
Telephone: (08) 388 5411

SECRETARY: B.J. Warren

SUBDIVISIONS
Botany Club, Mammal Club, Herpetology Group, Conservation Committee, Junior Naturalists' Clubs
One branch in Adelaide and another at Tea Tree Gully

AFFILIATIONS
Northern Naturalists' Society
Murray Bridge Field Naturalists' Club
Kangaroo Island Flora and Fauna Club
Conservation Council of S.A. Inc.
Adelaide Bush Walkers' Club
National Trust of Australia (S.A. Branch)
Naracoorte-Lucindale Field Naturalists' Club
Millicent Field Naturalists' Club

HISTORY: Founded in 1883 as Field Naturalists' Section of Royal Society of South Australia. Incorporated in 1959 as independent Society under present title.

PURPOSE: To promote the practical study of natural history by affording opportunities for meeting and working together.

INTERESTS: Both the Mammal Club and Herpetology Group undertake surveys of National Parks and Conservation Parks throughout the whole state. These clubs have been instrumental in locating rare species and in several instances undescribed species of mammals and reptiles. The Botany Club undertakes botanical surveys both in Conservation Parks and other areas which are potentially suitable for reservation. Some occasional surveys of areas are made on behalf of local Councils (both city and country), and the preservation of roadside vegetation continues to be an interest of this club. Speakers are supplied to meetings and to interested Primary and High Schools. The Society is represented both on the Council of the National Trust (S.A. Branch) and the Conservation Council of South Australia. The Society has four properties as follows:
Manning Reserve at McLaren Flat (Mount Lofty Ranges), 111 acres; white sand scrub comprising of sclerophyll community of *Eucalyptus fasciculosa - Banksia ornata - Xanthorrhoea semiplana* and numerous sclerophyll undershrubs.
Forest Range (Mount Lofty Ranges), higher rainfall (circ. 45 inches per annum) sclerophyll forest, 37 acres; comprising *Eucalyptus obliqua - Exocarpos cupressiformis* and many undershrubs typical of the higher Mt. Lofty Ranges.
Lirabenda Reserve at Mylor (Mount Lofty Ranges), 17 acres and house occupied by a tennant; higher rainfall area (circ. 45 inches), with vegetation similar to Forest Range property.
Carpenter's Rocks (Lower South East of S.A. near Mount Gambier) 132 acres; recently acquired by the Society, native well (small limestone sinkhole) dry sclerophyll scrub - *Eucalyptus huberana - Eucalyptus obliqua - Melaleuca lancoelata - Grevillea ilicifolia*.

PUBLICATIONS
South Australian Naturalist (quarterly)
Special publications issued occasionally.

LIBRARY: Reference library maintained.

MEMBERSHIP: approximately 600 (life, general. junior, family members)

206   Food Technology Association of New South Wales
60 York Street, Sydney, N.S.W.
(Box 3968, G.P.O., Sydney, 2001)
Telephone: (02) 290 0700

SECRETARY: S.M. Adams

AFFILIATIONS
Council of Australian Food Technology Associations Inc.

HISTORY: Founded in 1946.

PURPOSE: To promote and advance the scientific and technical aspects of the food processing, manufacturing and distributing industries of Australia and other industries closely related thereto.

ACTIVITIES: Council meetings (monthly); annual meeting.

AWARDS
Scholarship offered annually in food technology at the University of N.S.W.; three scholarships at the Hawkesbury Agricultural College.
Donation to the Sydney Technical College Prize Fund for Food Technology.

MEMBERSHIP: 180 (corporate, associate, honorary members)

207 Food Technology Association of Tasmania

191 Liverpool Street, Hobart, Tas.
(G.P.O. Box 793H, Hobart 7001.)
Telephone: (002) 34 5933

SECRETARY: K.S. Johnston

HISTORY: Founded in 1932.

PURPOSE: To promote the scientific and technical aspects of the food processing, manufacturing and distributing industries of Australia and other closely related countries; to disseminate amongst members scientific and technical knowledge regarding food and ancillary industries; to render the maximum possible service on scientific and technical matters to members in these industries; to promote understanding between members.

208 Forest Products Association (W.A.)

103 Colin Street, West Perth, W.A.
(P.O. Box 14, West Perth 6005.)
Telephone: (092) 22 2088; 22 2089

SECRETARY: G.W.Kelly (Manager)

SUBDIVISIONS
Associated Sawmillers and Timber Merchants of W.A.
Plywood Distributors' Association of W.A.
Interstate Jarrah Export Association
Sleeper Processing Company
W.A. Hardwood Export Association
W.A. Sleeper Export Association
Also member companies of above sub-divisions.

HISTORY: Founded in 1972.

PURPOSE: To act in the common interest of timber and timber-based product companies.

ACTIVITIES: Conferences and meetings held whenever necessary.

PUBLICATIONS
National publications relating to member companies' interests.

MEMBERSHIP: 28 (ordinary, associate member companies)

209 Foundation for Australian Resources

6th Floor, 181 Elizabeth Street, Sydney, N.S.W. 2000
Telephone: (02) 26 1271

SECRETARY: J. Latimer (Executive Secretary)

HISTORY: Founded in 1975.

PURPOSE: To promote, foster, develop and assist the science of evaluation of natural, physical and human resources; to co-operate with academic and other institutions with similar interests in the furtherance of the science of resource evaluation and analysis; to recommend grants to Schools or Departments of academic or research institutions for the purchase of plant, equipment and materials, or otherwise, for the promotion of the science of resource analysis, from funds raised by the Foundation by way of fees, donations and the like; to promote research into the science of resource analysis and evaluation generally; to admit to membership of the Foundation, persons, firms, companies and associations, whether incorporated or unincorporated, and upon such terms and with such privileges as may be determined from time to time; to recommend the printing of publications and the issue thereof to members of the Foundation and others; to arrange for lectures, exhibitions and demonstrations; to acquire and turn to account, patents, patent rights or inventions, copyright designs, trade-marks or secret processes for the benefit of the Foundation in the pursuit of its objectives; to assist in arranging visits from abroad of experts in Science; to enter into any arrangement with any institution or association having objectives similar to those of the Foundation; to solicit donations, gifts and bequests to the Foundation; to do all things as are incidental or conducive to the attainment of the above objectives or any of them.

INTERESTS: Water pollution monitoring, health services, solar energy.

210   Gemmological Association of Australia
24 Wentworth Avenue, Sydney, N.S.W.
(G.P.O. Box 1532, Sydney 2001.)
Telephone: (02) 61 2831

SECRETARY: R.J. Byatt

SUBDIVISIONS
Branches in Sydney, Melbourne, Adelaide, Brisbane, Perth.

AFFILIATIONS
Gemmological Association of Great Britain

HISTORY: Founded in 1945.

PURPOSE: Furtherance of gemstone knowledge.

INTERESTS: Recognition and scientific identification of natural and synthetic gemstones.

ACTIVITIES: State Council meetings. Annual conference, usually in April, on a rotational basis in each state.

PUBLICATIONS
Australian Gemmologist (quarterly).

LIBRARY: Reference library maintained.

AWARDS
Australian prize for best practical and theory examinations.
Various state branch and jewellery trade prizes.

MEMBERSHIP: 2000 (ordinary, life, honorary life members, fellows)

211   Genetics Society of Australia
Research School of Biological Sciences, Australian National University,
P.O. Box 4, Canberra City, A.C.T. 2601
Telephone: (062) 49 4280

SECRETARY: Dr. G. L. Gabor Miklos

HISTORY: Founded in 1952.

PURPOSE: To promote the advancement of the science of genetics.

INTERESTS: Animal and plant breeding; biochemical and molecular genetics; biometrical and statistical genetics; cytogenetics; developmental genetics; ecological and population genetics; human genetics; microbial genetics.

ACTIVITIES: One general meeting per year

MEMBERSHIP: 200

212   Geography Teachers' Association of New South Wales
Science House, Gloucester Street, Sydney, N.S.W. 2000
Telephone: (02) 27 5589

SECRETARY: A. K. Milne

SUBDIVISIONS
Branches in Armidale, Wollongong, Newcastle.

AFFILIATIONS
Geographical Society of New South Wales
Australian Geography Teachers' Association

HISTORY: Founded in 1936.

PURPOSE: To improve the standard and teaching of geography in schools.

INTERESTS: Organization of lectures for teachers and students; the dissemination of information on subject matter, teaching methods and concepts; publication of material; awarding of annual prizes.

ACTIVITIES: Monthly meetings; 10 area conferences for senior students arranged throughout the state each year; teacher conferences of special topics (e.g. Annual Fieldwork Conference).

PUBLICATIONS
Geography Bulletin (quarterly)
Australian Geographer (half-yearly)
Geographical Education (annually)

LIBRARY: Library housed in Geography Department, University of Sydney.

AWARDS
Catherine D. J. Stimson Memorial Prize and Medal

MEMBERSHIP: 1450 (ordinary, student, corporate members)

213   Geological Society of Australia Inc.
39 Hunter Street, Sydney, N.S.W. 2000
Telephone: (02) 231 4696

SUBDIVISIONS
Divisions in each of the Australian states and A.C.T.

HISTORY: Founded in 1952.

PURPOSE: The advancement of the geological sciences.

ACTIVITIES: Conventions, symposia and special meetings.

PUBLICATIONS
Journal of the Geological Society of Australia (4 per annum)
Special Publications (irregular series)

AWARDS
Stillwell Award

MEMBERSHIP: 2800 (members, associates, students, company members)

214   Great Barrier Reef Committee
School of Biological Sciences, University of Sydney, Sydney, N.S.W. 2006

SECRETARY: Dr. P.F. Sale

HISTORY: Founded in 1922

PURPOSE: To promote the scientific investigation of the Great Barrier Reef.

MEMBERSHIP: 200

215 Guild of Dispensing Opticians (Australia) Limited
282 Victoria Avenue, Chatswood, N.S.W.
(P.O. Box 627, Chatswood 2067)
Telephone: (02) 412 3033

SECRETARY: L. R. Stewart

SUBDIVISIONS
Branches in S.A., Qld. and Tas.

AFFILIATIONS
Optical Dispensers and Spectacle Makers Guild of Australia
Western Australian Association of Optical Dispensers
Dispenser's Association of South Australia Inc.

HISTORY: Founded in 1955.

PURPOSE: To support and protect the character, status and interests of the members of that section of the optical trade which is engaged in the dispensing of optical prescriptions and the manufacture and fitting of spectacles.

MEMBERSHIP: 24

216 Horological Guild of Australasia
228 Pitt Street, Sydney, N.S.W. 2000
Telephone: (02) 982 8561

SECRETARY: E. W. Daly (Federal Secretary)

SUBDIVISIONS
Queensland Branch - Mrs. H.P. Wyeth (Secretary), 9 Jean Street, The Grange, Qld. 4051
Victorian Branch - R.M. Reyne (Secretary), 21 Burwood Road, Hawthorn, Vic. 3122
Tasmanian Branch - N.G. Schapira (Secretary), 5 Peddler Street, Newtown, Tas. 7008
Western Australian Branch - W.A. Liddell (Secretary), 41 Leon Road, Dalkeith, W.A. 6009
South Australian Branch - F.M. Leonard (Secretary), 18 River Valley Drive, Windsor Gardens, S.A. 5087

HISTORY: Branches formed in all states between 1945 and 1946. Federal body founded in 1951.

PURPOSE: To promote unity and honest dealing, and improvements in status and welfare of horology; to improve the practical and general knowledge of those engaged in horology.

ACTIVITIES: Monthly committee meetings; general meetings (bi-monthly); biennial conferences.

PUBLICATIONS
N.S.W. Watchmaker (N.S.W. Branch)
Watchmakers of Victoria (Vic. Branch)

LIBRARY: Reference library maintained for members.

MEMBERSHIP: 990 (fellows, craft, ordinary members)

217 Hospital Physicists' Association (Australian Regional Group)
Physical Science Department, Prince of Wales Hospital, High Street, Randwick, N.S.W. 2031
Telephone: (02) 399 0111 extn 2526

SECRETARY: L.D. Oliver (Honorary Secretary)

AFFILIATIONS
Australian Institute of Physics (Biophysics Group)

HISTORY: Parent H.P.A. (Great Britain) founded in 1943. The Australian Regional Group was formed in 1962 with a certain amount of autonomy in the Australian region.

PURPOSE: To promote the science of physics in medicine,biology and cognate subjects; to report on work in progress or recently completed in various Australian centres; to maintain good liason with scientists in other branches of physics and in associated disciplines; to organise meetings for the discussion of scientific work and also professional matters which affect Australian members only.

INTERESTS: The application of physics, mathematics and engineering to medicine and biology.

ACTIVITIES: Annual Conference of Physics in Medicine and Biology; some local meetings.

PUBLICATIONS
Australasian Bulletin of Medical Physics and Biophysics (quarterly)

MEMBERSHIP: 70 (ordinary members, associates)

218   Housing Industry Association
P.O. Box 303, Woden, A.C.T. 2606
Telephone: (062) 49 4160

SECRETARY: W.J. Kirkby-Jones (National Executive Director)

SUBDIVISIONS
Divisions in Qld., Nth Qld., N.S.W., A.C.T. - Southern N.S.W., Vic., S.A. and W.A.

HISTORY: Founded in 1966.

PURPOSE: To represent the housing industry, to provide service to members and to carry out research into housing problems in Australia.

ACTIVITIES: Annual Convention; frequent symposia; Annual meetings of members in all Divisions; monthly or quarterly meetings of Directors.

PUBLICATIONS
Divisional Newsletters
Research Publications

MEMBERSHIP: Approx. 7000 members

219   Ian Clunies Ross Memorial Foundation
191 Royal Parade, Parkville, Vic. 3052.
Telephone: (03) 347 6077, 347 6276

SECRETARY: R. Archer (Administrative Officer)

SUBDIVISIONS
Conningham Street, Glenside, S.A. 5065 (Telephone: (08) 79 7821)
20-22 Stirling Highway, Nedlands, W.A. 6009 (Telephone: (092) 86 7077)

PURPOSE: To provide and maintain a building and services at Clunies Ross House (accomodating the National Science Centre) in Parkville. This centre provides meeting facilities for 98 accredited scientific and-or technological societies, 25 of which are housed in the centre. Meeting facilities are also provided in South Australia at Australian Mineral Foundation Inc., Glenside and in Western Australia at Australian Institute of Management, Nedlands.

220   Illuminating Engineering Societies of Australia
National Council, P.O.Box 189, Blair Athol, S.A. 5085.
Telephone: (08) 297 4111

SECRETARY: N. Brown (Executive Officer)

SUBDIVISIONS
Illuminating Engineering Society of Australia (Vic.), 64 Elizabeth Street, Melbourne, Vic. 3000.
Hobart Chapter - P.G. Rich, Hydroelectric Commission, 16 Elizabeth Street, Hobart, Tas. 7000.
Launceston Chapter - G.T. Loyd, 97 Vermont Street, Launceston, Tas. 7250.
Illuminating Engineering Society of Australia (N.S.W.), Box 4628 G.P.O., Sydney, N.S.W. 2001.
Newcastle Chapter - T.J. Smith, 7 Hunter Street, East Maitland, N.S.W. 2323.
Illuminating Engineering Society of Australia South Australia Inc., Box 1461, G.P.O., Adelaide, S.A. 5001.
Illuminating Engineering Society of Australia (W.A.),Mrs. K. C. Hyde, Lot 5, Mount Street, Darlington, W.A. 6070.
Illuminating Engineering Society of Australia (Qld.Division) P.O. Box 212, North Brisbane, Qld. 4000

HISTORY: Founded in 1930 in New South Wales and Victoria. National Council formed in 1949.

PURPOSE: To advance the art and science of natural and artificial illumination.

INTERESTS: Drafting standard codes; promotion of lighting development and research; sponsoring lighting courses; exhibitions and demonstrations of equipment; competitions for lighting installations.

ACTIVITIES: Technical meetings; annual convention and conference.

PUBLICATIONS
I.E.S. Lighting Review

LIBRARY: H.G. Fallon Library maintained by N.S.W. Society, R.J. Nott Memorial Library being formed by Vic. Society.

AWARDS
I.E.S. Awards for Meritorious Lighting

MEMBERSHIP: 885 (fellows, members, technical associates, affiliate fellows, affiliate members, associates)

221   Industrial Design Council of Australia
Estates House, 114 William Street, Melbourne, Vic. 3000
Telephone: (03) 60 1624

SECRETARY: D. Terry (National Director)

SUBDIVISIONS
N.S.W. Division - Mr. John Hold (State Director), 50 Margaret Street, Sydney, N.S.W. 2000 (Telephone: (02) 29 4273)
Vic. Division - Mr. J .Newman (State Director), 232 Victoria Parade, East Melbourne, Vic. 3002 (Telephone: (03) 419 6700)
Qld. Division - Mr. I.W. Sharp (State Director), Comalco House, 50 Ann Street, Brisbane, Qld. 4000 (Telephone: (07) 229 2677)
S.A. Division - Mr. D. Harris (State Director), Flemington Street, Frewville, S.A. 5063 (Telephone: (08) 79 1671)
W.A. Division - Mr. A.G. Batten (State Director), Superannuation Building, 32 St. Georges Terrace, Perth, W.A. 6000 (Telephone: (092) 25 7911)

HISTORY: Founded in 1957

PURPOSE: To improve the design of manufactures goods, with particular emphasis on user convenience and satisfaction.

INTERESTS: Design factors in mass-produced products, encompassing user requirements, ergonomics, aesthetics, manufacture and marketing. Implementation of design policies by public bodies.

ACTIVITIES: Lecture programmes, seminars in all states, field advisory service in all mainland states.

LIBRARY: Periodicals in the industrial design fields and the design bibliography issued by International Council of Societies of Industrial Designs .

AWARDS
Essington Lewis Award
Prince Phillip Prize for Australian Design (for best Australian Design Award winning product in previous 12 months)
Australian Design Award
Package Design Award

MEMBERSHIP: 25 (Councillors)

222   Industrial Design Institute of Australia
Employers House, 21 Burwood Road, Hawthorn, Vic. 3122
Telephone: (03) 819 1311

SECRETARY: W.P. Gillam (Federal Executive Secretary), P.K. Bayly (Honorary Federal Secretary)

SUBDIVISIONS
Branches in Vic, N.S.W., S.A., W.A. and A.C.T.

HISTORY: Incorporated as a Company limited by guarantee in 1958.

PURPOSE: To serve professional designers practising as private consultants or staff designers.

INTERESTS: Representation of professional designers; ethical conduct, standards of performance, professional practice.

PUBLICATIONS
Innova Newsletter
Recommended minimum salary scales for industrial designers.
Code of Professional Conduct.
Guide to Fees and Conditions of Engagement.

MEMBERSHIP: 350 (fellows, associates, licentiates, students)

223   Industrial Relations Society of Australia
Box 1186, G.P.O., Sydney, N.S.W. 2001.

SECRETARY: T. Moore

SUBDIVISIONS
Industrial Relations Societies of A.C.T., Qld., Tas., W.A., S.A., N.S.W. and Vic.

AFFILIATIONS
International Industrial Relations Association

HISTORY: Founded in 1964 as a federation of the state Industrial Relations Societies.

PURPOSE: To organize and foster discussion, research and education within the field of industrial relations.

INTERESTS: All aspects of employer-employee relations.

ACTIVITIES: Each state society has an annual convention. National convention every 4 years (next in 1978).

PUBLICATIONS
Journal of Industrial Relations
State newsletters and monographs.

AWARDS
Prize of $1,000 awarded to coincide with each national convention for an original work on Australian industrial relations.

MEMBERSHIP: 2500 (ordinary, student members)

224 Institute of Actuaries of Australia and New Zealand
5 Moorina Road, St. Ives, N.S.W. 2075
Telephone: (02) 44 3311

SECRETARY: A.K. Wylie

SUBDIVISIONS
Vic. - M.J. Dwyer (Secretary), T. and G. Mutual Life Society Limited, 147 Collins Street, Melbourne, Vic. 3000.
N.S.W. - A.K. Wylie (Secretary), 5 Moorina Road, St. Ives, N.S.W. 2075.

AFFILIATIONS
Institute of Actuaries (London)
Faculty of Actuaries (Edinburgh)

HISTORY: Founded in 1963 as lineal descendant of the Actuarial Society of New South Wales which was founded in 1897.

PURPOSE: To enhance the status of the actuarial profession; to make representations to governments and other bodies on affairs affecting actuarial science; to provide a forum for discussion of matters of actuarial interest.

INTERESTS: Life and general assurance; consulting practices; banking; stock exchange and investment activities; federal and state governments; universities.

ACTIVITIES: Biennial conference; monthly meetings.

PUBLICATIONS
Bulletin of the Institute of Actuaries of Australia and New Zealand (annual)
Transactions of the Institute of Actuaries of Australia and New Zealand (annual)

LIBRARY: Libraries maintained by - W. Easton, A.M.P. Society, Sydney Cove, N.S.W. 2000 and F.H. Baker, Colonial Mutual Life Assurance Society Ltd., 330 Collins Street, Melbourne, Vic. 3000.

AWARDS
G.M. Parker Fund
H.M. Jackson Memorial Fund

MEMBERSHIP: 672 (fellows, associates, students, lay members)

225 Institute of Australian Geographers
Department of Geography, University of Sydney, N.S.W. 2006.
Telephone: (02) 660 9309

SECRETARY: Dr. P.D. Tilley

HISTORY: Founded in 1959.

PURPOSE: To promote geography and geographical research in Australia and to represent Australian geographers overseas; to maintain contact with other organizations having kindred purposes

ACTIVITIES: Annual conference

PUBLICATIONS
Australian Geographical Studies

MEMBERSHIP: Approximately 300 (ordinary, associate, overseas, honorary members)

226 Institute of Automotive Mechanical Engineers
229 Great North Road, Five Dock, N.S.W.
(P.O. Box 93, Five Dock, 2046.)
Telephone: (02) 83 4711

SECRETARY: F.R. Burgess

SUBDIVISIONS
Branches in Sydney, Brisbane, Melbourne, Adelaide, Perth, Darwin, Canberra and also Malaysia, Singapore, Fiji and Papua New Guinea.
Brisbane Branch - C. Slaughter, 8 Clyde Road, Herston, Qld. 4006
Canberra Branch - A.J. Collett, P.O. Box 3, Cook, A.C.T. 2614
Melbourne Branch - A. Levins, 3rd Floor, 380 Lonsdale Street, Melbourne, Vic. 3000
Adelaide Branch - R.H. Gray, P.O. Box 368, Adelaide, S.A. 5001
Perth Branch - W.F. Harry, P.O. Box 272, Perth, W.A. 6001

HISTORY: Founded in 1936.

PURPOSE: To promote technical knowledge of all motor propelled vehicles.

INTERESTS: Automotive trade.

ACTIVITIES: National conference (annually); branch meetings (monthly)

PUBLICATIONS
Australian Automotive Engineering and Equipment

LIBRARY: Library presently being established.

AWARDS
Various awards to students of technical colleges in all states undertaking automotive engineering trade courses.

MEMBERSHIP: 7000 (members, associate members, associates, affiliates, students)

227 Institute of Diesel Engineers of Australia (Inc.)
10th Floor, 47 York Street, Sydney, N.S.W. 2000.
Telephone: (02) 29 3435

SECRETARY: C.A. Williams

SUBDIVISIONS
New South Wales Division - as above
Queensland Division - Mrs. M.A. Victorsen (Secretary), P.O. Box 79, Morningside, Qld. 4170
Victorian Division - Mr. B.W. Farrell (Secretary), 4 Barbara Avenue, Glen Waverley, Vic. 3150
Branches in Mt. Isa, Townsville, Bundaberg and Mackay

HISTORY: Founded in 1944; incorporated in 1947.

PURPOSE: To disseminate technical information and to promote education relating to diesel engines.

INTERESTS: Scientific knowledge of the mechanism of all diesel or compression ignition engines.

ACTIVITIES: Monthly branch and division meetings and-or inspections; occasional seminars.

PUBLICATIONS
I.D.E.A. (every 3 months)
Institute Journal I.D.E.A.

LIBRARY: Small library at the general office

MEMBERSHIP: 700 (members, associate members, associates, provisional associates, students, affiliate companies)

228 Institute of Electrical Inspectors
24 Holmwood Avenue, Strathfield South, S.A.
(P.O. Box 147, Summer Hill 2130)
Telephone: (02) 642 6336

SECRETARY: L.T. O'Donnell

SUBDIVISIONS
Divisions in all states of Australia

HISTORY: Founded in 1938 in N.S.W. First divisions established in 1947 (N.S.W. and Qld.). S.A. Division formed in 1950, W.A. and Tas. Divisions formed in 1952, Vic. Division formed in 1972.

PURPOSE: To secure and promote uniform administrative ordinances and inspection methods in relation to the installation and use of electrical materials and equipment.

INTERESTS: Electricity supply industry and electrical standards. Has representatives on the S.A.A. WiringRules Committee.

ACTIVITIES: Divisional meetings usually held monthly except for Tasmania (3 times per year). Divisional Annual meetings held in August. Full Institute Annual General meetings held in September, usually in division states in rotation. Discussion nights on S.A.A. Wiring Rules and lectures with guest lecturers.

PUBLICATIONS
I.E.I. Journal (monthly)

LIBRARY: Limited library facilities

AWARDS
Awards for best electrical apprentices in year in Vic., Tas., Qld. and N.S.W.

MEMBERSHIP: 1100 (corporate, associate, social, life and honorary members)

229 Institute of Foresters of Australia Inc.
P.O.Box 73, Canberra, A.C.T. 2600
Telephone: (062) 81 8343

SECRETARY: G. Croston

SUBDIVISIONS
Divisions within each state; branches in country areas within some divisions.

AFFILIATIONS
Ian Clunies Ross Memorial Foundation
Australian Conservation Foundation Incorporated

HISTORY: Founded in 1935

PURPOSE: To advance the cause of forestry and to maintain high standards of qualifications and practice.

ACTIVITIES: A general conference every 3 years; meetings of divisions and branches; field days.

PUBLICATIONS
Australian Forestry (quarterly)
I.F.A. Newsletter (quarterly, to members only)

AWARDS
N.W. Jolly Medal
A.R. Henderson Bequest
Hedges Prize

MEMBERSHIP: 1200 (fellows, members, student members, associates, honorary members)

230   Institute of Fuel (Australian Membership)
22 Monteith Street, Turramurra, N.S.W. 2074
Telephone: (02) 449 1800

SECRETARY: C.A.J. Paulson

SUBDIVISIONS
Branches in Sydney, Melbourne, Perth, Newcastle, Adelaide, Brisbane

HISTORY: Institute founded in United Kingdom in 1927. Australian membership 1952.

PURPOSE: The advancement of various branches of fuel technology by establishing appropriate standards of professional practice and encouraging the pursuit of knowledge in the areas of science, engineering and technology as applied to the preparation, treatment and utilization of sources of heat and power.

ACTIVITIES: Biennial conference and regular meetings by the various groups throughout Australia

AWARDS
Institute of Fuel Prize
C.R. Kent Lecture and Medal
Australian Industries Fuel Scholarship

MEMBERSHIP: 459 (senior fellows, fellows, members, collective members, associates, students, graduates)

231   Institute of Industrial Engineers
12 City Road, Darlington, N.S.W. 2008 (Federal Office)
Telephone: (02) 212 1163

SECRETARY: Mr. P.W. Everest (Federal Secretary)

SUBDIVISIONS
Divisions in New South Wales, Queensland, South Australia, Victoria, Western Australia.

AFFILIATIONS
Institute of Industrial Engineers (U.S.A.)
Institute of Practitioners in Work Study, Organization and Methods (U.K.)
World Confederation of Work Study
Pacific Asian Federation of Industrial Engineers

HISTORY: Founded in 1954 as the Australian Methods Engineers Association.

PURPOSE: To encourage the study of the principles and practice of industrial engineering and to set standards for membership of the profession; to collect and disseminate information in the field of industrial engineering; to represent the views of those engaged in industrial engineering, maintain ethical standards, protect the interests of members, and develop the profession in line with the needs of industry and commerce.

ACTIVITIES: Meetings, discussion groups, lectures, films, plant visits, study courses. Biennial conference.

PUBLICATIONS
Industrial Engineer

MEMBERSHIP: 1500 (fellows, honorary members, members, associates, graduates, student members, affiliates, company members)

232   Institute of Instrumentation and Control Australia
care of- F.O. Barnett and Co., 450 Little Collins Street, Melbourne, Vic. 3000
Telephone: (03) 83 8235

SECRETARY: H. N. Brann (161 Gordon Street, Balwyn, Vic 3103.)

SUBDIVISIONS
New South Wales Division - P.O.Box 366, Crows Nest, 2065
Queensland Division - 11 Overend Street, East Brisbane, 4169
South Australian Division - The Australian Mineral Foundation, Conyngham Street, Glenside, 5065
Victorian Division - P.O.Box 82, Balwyn, 3103
Western Australian Division - P.O.Box 123, Nedlands, 6009
Newcastle Branch - P.O.Box 41, Kotara Fair, Adamstown, 2067
Mackay Branch - R. Wallace, care of- A.S.M. Pty. Ltd., Pleystowe, 4740

AFFILIATIONS
International Measurement Confederation (IMEKO)

HISTORY: Australian Society of Instrument Technology formed 1943 in Victoria; in 1944 the Institute of Instrument Technology, Australia was formed in New South Wales and in 1952 a branch of the Australian Society of Instrument Technology was formed in South Australia. In 1957 the three bodies amalgamated to form the Society of Instrument Technology, Australia. The present title was adopted in 1966. Admitted to International Measurement Confederation (IMEKO) in 1975 as the appropriate Australian representative body.

PURPOSE: To promote and provide facilities for discussion, dissemination of information, technical education, research and standardisation in the science of instrument technology (i.e. instrumentation and control).

ACTIVITIES: Monthly meetings of Divisions; technical lecture series; symposia and exhibitions; sponsors lecture series, workshops, etc; international meetings with IMEKO.

PUBLICATIONS
Australian Journal of Instrumentation and Control (6 per annum)
Divisional and Branch Newsletters (usually monthly)

MEMBERSHIP: 775 (fellows, members, senior associates, graduate, students, affiliates, affiliated bodies, subscribers)

233 Institute of Marine Engineers, Australia-New Zealand Division
Clunies Ross House, 191 Royal Parade, Parkville, Vic. 3052
Telephone: (03) 347 2570

SUBDIVISIONS
Branches in Queensland, New South Wales (Sydney and Newcastle), Australian Capital Territory, South Australia, Western Australia, New Zealand (Auckland, Wellington, Christchurch)

HISTORY: Founded in 1889 in United Kingdom

PURPOSE: To promote the scientific and practical development of marine engineering; to enable marine engineers to meet and correspond and facilitate the exchange of information; to maintain and improve the status of marine engineers and the profession; to co-operate with educational bodies for the furtherance of education in marine engineering.

ACTIVITIES: Meetings, conferences.

234 Institute of Materials Handling, South Australian Division
4 Torrens Avenue, Paradise, S.A. 5075
Telephone: (08) 212 5254

SECRETARY: C.R. Wilson

AFFILIATIONS
Other Divisions in Vic., N.S.W. and W.A.

HISTORY: Founded in the U.K. in 1953.

PURPOSE: To promote materials handling as a science.

ACTIVITIES: Monthly meetings; educational and training seminars.

PUBLICATIONS
Materials Handling and Storage

LIBRARY: Being established.

AWARDS
Being established

MEMBERSHIP: 60 (fellow, member, associate, student)

235 Institute of Materials Handling, Victorian Division
79 Buckhurst Street, South Melbourne, Vic. 3205
Telephone: (03) 699 1333

SECRETARY: J. Gillies (Secretary); P. Flinn (Chairman)

SUBDIVISIONS
Divisions also in New South Wales, Western Australia and South Australia.

AFFILIATIONS
American Materials Handling Society Inc
Japanese Materials Handling Society Inc
German Materials Handling Society Inc

HISTORY: Founded in 1953 in United Kingdom.

PURPOSE: To further the science of materials handling by providing facilities to exchange knowledge, ideas and experience in various fields of materials handling; to simulate and assist educational and training facilities in materials handling.

ACTIVITIES: Monthly meetings.

PUBLICATIONS
Materials Handling and Management

LIBRARY: Small library maintained for members.

AWARDS
Awards presented annually to successful students who have completed the Materials Handling course conducted by the Victorian Education Department.

MEMBERSHIP: 192 (fellows, members, associates)

236 Institute of Materials Handling, Western Australian Division
G.P.O. Box S1476, Perth, W.A. 6001
Telephone: (092) 60 5725

SECRETARY: L.D. Smith

AFFILIATIONS
Institute of Materials Handling (Victorian Division)
Institute of Materials Handling (N.S.W. Division)
Institute of Materials Handling (S.A. Division)
Institute of Materials Handling (U.K.)
Verein Deutscher Insgeneure (Germany)
Japanese Materials Handling Society
American Materials Handling Society Inc.

HISTORY: Founded in U.K. in 1953. Western Australian Division founded in 1968.

PURPOSE: To promote the science of materials handling by providing facilities for interchange of knowledge and by assisting in furthering educational endeavors. To develop improved techniques and systems of materials handling to disseminate information to users by exhibitions and conferences.

ACTIVITIES: Monthly meetings.

MEMBERSHIP: 50 (fellow, member, associate member, graduate, student member)

237   Institute of Photographic Technology
1 Eric Street, West Preston, Vic. 3072
Telephone: (03) 35 5342

SECRETARY: I. Hayson

HISTORY: Founded in 1945

PURPOSE: To promote the wider application of scientific methods in photography.

INTERESTS: All aspects of photography and related subjects.

ACTIVITIES: General meetings held monthly.

AWARDS
Institute of Photographic Technology Annual Award (given to outstanding student in Photographic Technology Diploma Course at Royal Melbourne Institute of Technology)

MEMBERSHIP: 101 (affiliates, fellows, members, honorary members, honorary fellows)

238   Institute of Quality Assurance (Australian Federal Committee)
2A Wentworth Street, Caringbar, N.S.W. 2229
Telephone: (02) 525 5458

SECRETARY: R.B. Adams

SUBDIVISIONS
New South Wales Branch - Dr. H.S. Blanks (Honorary Secretary), School of Electrical Engineering, University of New South Wales, P.O. Box 1, Kensington 2033.
South Australian Branch - B.D.P. Cooper (Honorary Secretary), 4 Fyffe Road, Hawthorndene 5051.
Victorian Branch - D.J. Goldsmith (Honorary Secretary), 17 McIndoe Parade, Parkdale 3194.

HISTORY: Founded in 1919 in the United Kingdom as the Technical Inspection Association and incorporated in 1922 as the Institution of Engineering Inspection. Renamed in 1973 to the Institute of Quality Assurance. There are now 28 branches in the U.K. and 3 in Australia.

PURPOSE: To maintain and improve the standards of quality assurance throughout industry and to uphold the status of the quality engineer; to promote and encourage the practice of quality assurance in industry.

INTERESTS: All quality control and inspection areas.

ACTIVITIES: Monthly meetings held by state branches and an annual meeting held by the Australian Federal Committee.

PUBLICATIONS
Quality Engineer

MEMBERSHIP: 280 (fellows, members, licentiates, students, associates)

239   Institute of Refrigeration and Air-Conditioning Service Engineers (Australian Council)
P.O. Box 200, South Melbourne, Vic. 3205
Telephone: (03) 419 3417

SECRETARY: D.B. Shelton

IRASE South Australia Inc., G.P.O. Box 831G, Adelaide, S.A. 5001
IRASE Western Australia Inc., G.P.O. Box T1677, Perth, W.A. 6001
IRASE Victoria Inc., P.O. Box 200, South Melbourne, Vic. 3205

HISTORY: Founded in S.A. in 1945; in W.A. in 1946 and in Vic. in 1947. Australian Council formed in 1949.

PURPOSE: To advance the science and practice of refrigeration and air conditioning servicing and the usefulness and efficiency of persons therein. To encourage the general understanding of service engineers between one another and as a group for the benefit of the user public.

ACTIVITIES: Monthly meetings including technical lecture; Annual Meeting; Annual Conference alternating between each state division.

PUBLICATIONS
IRASE Data Manual (members only)
Celsius (monthly)

LIBRARY: Technical library.

AWARDS
IRASE Refrigeration Apprentice of the Year Award (issued in each state division)

MEMBERSHIP: 833 (senior, junior, affiliate, probationary)

240   Institute of Wood Science (Australian Branch)
P.O. Box 56, Highett, Vic. 3190
Telephone: (03) 95 0333

SECRETARY: W. G. Keating

HISTORY: Founded in United Kingdom in 1955. Australian Branch formed in 1972.

PURPOSE: To advance the scientific, technical, practical and general knowledge of persons interested in the study of wood and allied subjects.

ACTIVITIES: Annual meeting and three or four general meetings throughout the year; lectures, symposia and visits.

PUBLICATIONS
Journal of the Institute of Wood Science
Newsletter
Proceedings of meetings

MEMBERSHIP: Approximately 120 (fellows, members, associates)

241   Institution of Chemical Engineers, Australian National Committee
P.O. Box 9, Killara, N.S.W. 2071
Telephone: (02) 498 4420

SECRETARY: C.W.V. Vernon

SUBDIVISIONS
Queensland Group - Dr. P.F. Greenfield (Secretary), Department of Chemical Engineering, University of Queensland, St Lucia, Qld. 4067.
N.S.W. Group - Dr. C.J.D. Fell (Secretary), School of Chemical Engineering, University of N.S.W., P.O. Box 1, Kensington, N.S.W. 2033.
Victorian Group - Dr. R.B. Newell (Secretary), Department of Chemical Engineering, Monash University, Clayton, Vic. 3168.
S.A. Group - Mr. I.R. Williams (Secretary), care of - The Australian Mineral Foundation Inc., Conyngham St., Glenside, S.A. 5065.
W.A. Group - Mr. N.C. Philip (Secretary), 216 Broome St., Cottesloe, W.A. 6011.

HISTORY: Founded in England in 1922. In Australia, groups were established in Victoria in 1960, New South Wales in 1962, Queensland in 1967, South Australia in 1969. The Australian National Committee was established in 1967.

PURPOSE: To provide facilities for chemical engineering education, chemical engineering research and practice and associated documentation, the publication of papers and the holding of meetings on subjects of interest to chemical engineers. The Institution also is a qualifying body in that it grants certificates of competence to chemical engineers, conducts examinations and assesses training and experience.

ACTIVITIES: Regular technical meetings, symposia and national conferences.

MEMBERSHIP: Approximately 1100 (fellows, members, graduate members, student members)

242   Institution of Civil Engineers, Victorian Local Association
Clunies Ross House, 191 Royal Parade, Parkville, Vic. 3052
Telephone: (03) 347 2570

SECRETARY: N. P. Caswell (Hon. Secretary)

HISTORY: A Victorian Advisory Committee of the Institution was formed in 1890 and the Victorian Association was formally constituted in 1937. Membership was extended to residents of Tasmania in 1939 and South Australia in 1949.

PURPOSE: To promote the art and science of civil engineering by maintaining contact between members in Victoria, South Australia and Tasmania and the Institution headquarters in London, and by local meetings and visits for members.

ACTIVITIES: Site visits and meetings

AWARDS
Fred Green Memorial Prize (3 prizes annually)

MEMBERSHIP: 400 (fellows, members, honorary fellows, companion, student members)

243   Institution of Electrical Engineers, N.S.W. Overseas Committee
Box 701, G.P.O., Sydney, N.S.W. 2001
Telephone: (02) 239 6781

SECRETARY: T.K. Litchfield (Electricity Commission of N.S.W., 1 Castlereagh Street, Sydney, N.S.W.)

SUBDIVISIONS
The I.E.E. (U.K.) is divided into four divisions:- Control and Automation; Electronics; Power; Science, Educational and Management

AFFILIATIONS
Other Australian committees are operated in Vic., Qld., S.A., W.A. and Tas.

HISTORY: The parent Institution was formed in 1871 as the Society of Telegraph Engineers. In 1880 it became the Society of Telegraph Engineers and Electricians and in 1888 the Institution of Electrical Engineers. Granted Royal Charter of Incorporation in 1921.

PURPOSE: To promote the dissemination of knowledge of electrical science and technology; to act as a qualifying body; to act, as a regulating body for the profession of electrical engineering.

PUBLICATIONS
IEE NSW Newsletter

MEMBERSHIP: 740 (fellow, member, associate member, student)

244 Institution of Electrical Engineers, Tasmania
7 Benjafield Terrace, Mount Stuart, Hobart, Tas. 7000
Telephone: (002) 28 2750

SECRETARY: S. Taylor (Overseas Representative of the Council for Tasmania)

MEMBERSHIP: 60

245 Institution of Electrical Engineers, Victorian Organization
Clunies Ross House, 191 Royal Parade, Parkville, Vic. 3052
Telephone: (03) 347 2570

SUBDIVISIONS
Other Australian groups in New South Wales, Queensland, South Australia, Tasmania, Western
Australia and throughout the British Commonwealth.
Electronics, Power, Science and General Divisions.

HISTORY: Parent Institution founded in 1871 as Society of Telegraph Engineers; 1880 Society of
Telegraph Engineers and Electronics; 1888 Institution of Electrical Engineers; 1921 Royal Charter.

PURPOSE: To promote the general advancement of electrical science and engineering and their
applications; to facilitate the exchange of information and ideas on these subjects by means of
meetings, exhibitions, publications, the establishment of libraries; and to give financial assistance for
the promotion of invention and research.

MEMBERSHIP: 412 (honorary fellows, fellows, companions, members, associate members, associates,
students)

246 Institution of Engineers, Australia
National Headquarters, 11 National Circuit, Barton, A.C.T. 2600
Telephone: (062) 73 3633

SECRETARY: E.D. Storr

SUBDIVISIONS
Australian Capital Territory Division - National Circuit, Barton, 2600
New South Wales Division - 118 Alfred Street, Milsons Point, 2061
Newcastle Division - 27 King Street, Newcastle, 2300
Victorian Division - 191 Royal Parade, Parkville, 3052
Queensland Division - 447 Upper Edward Street, Brisbane, 4000
South Australian Division - 11 Bagot Street, North Adelaide, 5006
Western Australian Division - 10 Hooper Street, West Perth, 6005
Divisions are sub-divided geographically into groups and technically into branches.
Colleges of Civil Engineers, Chemical Engineers, Electrical Engineers, Mechanical Engineers and a
General College of Engineering based at National Headquarters and supported by specialist National
Committees, Task Forces etc.

AFFILIATIONS
Australian Geomechanics Society (Technical unit of Institution in co-operation with the Australasian
Institute of Mining and Metallurgy

HISTORY: Founded in 1919 by the amalgamation of 12 engineering societies. Royal charter granted in
1938.

PURPOSE: To promote and advance the science and practice of engineering in all its branches and to
facilitate the exchange of information and ideas in relation thereto.

INTERESTS: Organises meetings where papers may by presented; sponsors joint seminars of conferences
with other learned societies; organization of courses relevant to engineering.

ACTIVITIES: Annual Engineering Conference; regular national Symposia and Conferences on particular
topics;general Divisional and specialised Branch, Section and group meetings; joint seminars and
conferences;educational courses organized by Divisions.

PUBLICATIONS
Engineers Australia
Civil Engineering Transactions
Chemical Engineering Transactions
Australian Geomechanics Journal
Electrical Engineering Transactions
Divisional Bulletins (monthly)

LIBRARY: Engineering library maintained at the National Headquarters

AWARDS
Peter Nicol Russell Memorial Medal
Numerous specialist awards on both national and local basis.
Sydney Division Prize for Graduates and Students

MEMBERSHIP: 30 000 (honorary fellows, fellows, members, graduates, students, associates)

247 Institution of Gas Engineers (Australia)
10 Elston Avenue, Denistone, N.S.W. 2114
Telephone: (02) 85 6902

SECRETARY: J.F. Hubbard

HISTORY: Founded in 1920 as the Gas Manager's Association of New South Wales

PURPOSE: To encourage the assembly of persons engaged in the promotion of the gas industry in all phases or any phase; to provide for the dissemination of knowledge by fostering the preparation of papers and such addresses to be delivered at meetings of members and others; to assist by federation or otherwise kindred organisations in the promotion of the gas industry and the institution.

ACTIVITIES: Annual Conference and General Meeting; support and attendance at Local Government conferencesand activities.

MEMBERSHIP: 208 (members, associate members)

248 Institution of Mechanical Engineers (Australian Branch)
Room 503, 191 Royal Parade, Parkville, Vic. 3052
Telephone: (03) 347 2570

SECRETARY: Mrs. M. Daunt

SUBDIVISIONS
Northern sub-branch, Southern sub-branch, Western Australian panel, South Australian panel, Queensland panel.

AFFILIATIONS
Council of Engineering Institutions (London)

HISTORY: Parent institution founded in United Kingdom in 1847; Australian branch in 1960.

PURPOSE: To act as the qualifying body for the profession; to publish papers and to organize meetings.

INTERESTS: Mechanical engineering including railways and automobiles.

ACTIVITIES: Approximately eight meetings per year in each Australian capital city.

PUBLICATIONS
Mechanical Engineering News (monthly)
Chartered Mechanical Engineer (monthly)
Journal of Mechanical Engineering Science (quarterly)
Papers, conference proceedings

MEMBERSHIP: Approximately 1700 (corporate members, including fellows and members; non-corporate members including companions, associates, graduates and students)

249 Institution of Metallurgists (Australian Region)
Materials Research Laboratories, P.O. Box 50, Ascot Vale, Vic. 3032
Telephone: (03) 31 7222 (extn 1556)

SECRETARY: Dr. C.W. Weaver

AFFILIATIONS
Australian Institute of Metals
Metals Society, London

HISTORY: Founded in London in 1945. Australian Region formed in 1965.

PURPOSE: To promote, encourage, advance and co-ordinate the study and science of metallurgy in all its aspects. A professional qualifying body for metallurgists and materials technologists world-wide.

PUBLICATIONS
Metallurgist and Materials Technologist

250 Institution of Production Engineers, Australian Council
Clunies Ross House, 191 Royal Parade, Parkville, Vic. 3052
Telephone: (03) 347 2570

SUBDIVISIONS
Southern Section based in Melbourne (Clunies Ross House, 191 Royal Parade, Parkville, Vic. 3052, (Telephone: (03) 347 2570) with Branches in Adelaide and Perth.
Northern Section based in Sydney (P.O. Box 269, Riverwood, N.S.W. 2210, (Telephone: (02) 53 5020) with a Branch in Brisbane.
Specialist divisions operate in selected topics such as Numerical Control, Metrication andGroup Technology.

HISTORY: Sydney Section of the British Institution of Production Engineers inaugurated in 1937. Melbourne Section formed in 1942 and Adelaide in 1950. Australian Sub-Council formed in 1945 and became Australian Council in 1954. Incorporated by Royal Charter and a member of the Council of Engineering Institutions (U.K.).

PURPOSE: The dissemination of information on production engineering, management and professional education.

ACTIVITIES: Monthly meetings

PUBLICATIONS
Production Engineer (U.K. publication)
Australian Machinery and Production Engineering (section contained therein)
BNCS News (U.K.publication)

AWARDS
James N. Kirby Memorial Award and lecture
Jack Finlay National Award and Medal
Ian McLennan Prize
Section and Branch prizes

MEMBERSHIP: Approx.900 (fellows, members (chartered engineer grades), associate members, graduates, students, affiliated organizations)

251 Institution of Radio and Electronics Engineers Australia
Science House, 157 Gloucester Street, Sydney, N.S.W. 2000
Telephone: (02) 27 1039

SECRETARY: K.L. Finney (General Secretary)

SUBDIVISIONS

Adelaide Division - Mr. N.W. Patterson (Chairman), 9 Spruce Crescent, Lower Mitcham, S.A. 5060.
Brisbane Division - Mr. S.R. Grantham (Chairman), 26 Bowman Street, Hendra, Qld. 4011.
Townsville - Dr. J.A. Richards, Electrical Engineering Dept., James Cook University, Townsville, Qld. 4811.
Canberra Division - Mr. J.C. Jennison (Chairman), 14 Downs Place, Hughes, A.C.T. 2605.
Hobart Division - Mr. S. Reckmann (Secretary), Box 371D, G.P.O., Hobart, Tas. 7001.
Melbourne Division - Mr. S.J. Rubenstein (Chairman), Clunies Ross House, 191 Royal Parade, Parkville, Vic. 3052.
Perth Division - Mr. G.M. Thompson (Chairman), 12 West Coast Highway, City Beach, W.A. 6015.
Sydney Division - Mr. H.E. Norrie (Secretary), 10 Womerah Street, Turramurra, N.S.W. 2074.
Singapore Chapter - Mr. Brian Lee (Chairman), 16 Lynwood Grove, Singapore 13, Republic of Singapore (founded April 1976)

HISTORY: Founded in 1924

PURPOSE: To promote the science of electronics engineering in all its branches, and the usefulness and efficiency of persons engaged therein.

ACTIVITIES: Regular meetings of all divisions; biennial conference and exhibition; occasional symposia, colloquia, seminars.

PUBLICATIONS
Monitor - Proceedings of the Institution of Radio and Electronics Engineers Australia (monthly)

LIBRARY: Reference library maintained at head office.

AWARDS
Dunrossil Memorial Lecture
20 annual prizes

MEMBERSHIP: 2,443 (corporate, graduate, non-corporate members)

252 Institution of Surveyors, Australia
George Patterson House, 252 George Street, Sydney, N.S.W.
(Box 4793, G.P.O. Sydney 2001)
Telephone: (02) 241 1775

SECRETARY: A. Wood

SUBDIVISIONS
New South Wales Division - 65 York Street, Sydney 2000
Victoria Division - National Science Centre, 191 Royal Parade, Parkville 3052
Queensland Division - Morris Towers, Wickham Terrace, Brisbane 4000
Western Australia Division - 1315 Hay Street, West Perth 6005
South Australia Division - AMF Building, Conyngham Street, Glenside, 5065
Canberra Division - P.O. Box 194, Civic Square, Canberra 2608
Tasmanian Division - Box 12A G.P.O. Hobart 7001
Northern Territory Division - P.O. Box 3328, Darwin 5794

AFFILIATIONS
Royal Institution of Chartered Surveyors
Commonwealth Association of Surveying and Land Economy
American Congress of Surveying and Mapping
International Federation of Surveyors

HISTORY: Founded in 1952 by the amalgamation of existing state societies, which became divisions of the Institution. The oldest of these societies was the Victorian Institute of Surveyors, established in 1874.

PURPOSE: To promote the science and practice of surveying, raise its character and safeguard its interests and those engaged therein; to encourage the study of surveying.

INTERESTS: All branches of surveying including geodetic, topographic, aerial, hydrographic, cadastral, engineering, mining and geological surveying.

ACTIVITIES: Annual Australian Survey Congress hosted by various divisions in rotation; Annual Meeting following Congress; Annual and regular general meetings held by divisions.

PUBLICATIONS
Australian Surveyor (quarterly)
Divisions publish monthly or quarterly bulletins.

AWARDS
Medal of the Institution of Surveyors, Australia
Gold Medal of the Institution of Surveyors, Australia
R.D. Steele Prize

MEMBERSHIP: 2923 (honorary fellows, fellows, members, associates, students)

253 International Association on Water Pollution Research. Australian National Committee
P.O. Box A53, Sydney South, N.S.W. 2000
Telephone: (02) 269 5383

SECRETARY: Dr. M.J. Flynn

SUBDIVISIONS
Branches are located in most of the major countries of the world

AFFILIATIONS
Australian Water and Wastewater Association

HISTORY: Founded in 1960.

PURPOSE: To contribute most effectively to the advancement of scientific, ecological, engineering, legal and administrative research in water pollution abatement and control; to promote maximum exchange of information on water pollution research and water quality protection, and the practical application of research in engineering design, construction, operation, control and management of waste water collection systems, of purification and reclamation plants and river, lake, estuary and coastal water quality management problems; to encourage communication and a better understanding among scientists, engineers and administrators engaged in the solution of water pollution problems; to organise and sponsor international meetings and conferences where reports on important research and its application in water pollution control may be presented; to co-operate with other organisations in the environmental pollution fields.

ACTIVITIES: International Conference held biennially. Regional Meetings held in various countries every 6 months.

PUBLICATIONS
Water Research (monthly)
Progress in Water Technology (2 monthly)

MEMBERSHIP: 2000 (sustaining member, associate member, individual, student)

254 International Institute of Refrigeration. Australian National Committee
CSIRO Division of Mechanical Engineering, Graham Road, Highett, Vic.
(P.O. Box 26, Highett 3190)
Telephone: (03) 95 0333

SECRETARY: F.G. Hogg

HISTORY: Founded in 1968. (Parent organization founded in 1908 under an international agreement).

PURPOSE: To provide a link between the IIR and Australian centres of interest in relation to IIR scientific and technical activities.

INTERESTS: Theory and practice of refrigeration in all its applications, including air conditioning.

ACTIVITIES: Australian Committee - at irregular intervals. IIR - some meetings of Scientific Commissions each year, a large International Congress every four years.

PUBLICATIONS
IIR - Proceedings of Commission meetings and Congresses, a 2-monthly Bulletin, Working Party reports

LIBRARY: At IIR headquarters in Paris.

AWARDS
Awards by IIR for outstanding papers presented at meetings and Congresses.

MEMBERSHIP: Aust. Committee - 14. IIR - 900 plus 55 member countries [associate member (company), associate member (individual)].

255 International Solar Energy Society, Australian and New Zealand Section
CSIRO Division of Mechanical Engineering, Graham Road, Highett, Vic.
(P.O. Box 26, Highett 3190.)
Telephone: (03) 95 0333

SECRETARY: F.G. Hogg

SUBDIVISIONS
Local Committees in N.S.W., Vic., Qld., S.A. and W.A.

AFFILIATIONS
World Headquarters, P.O. Box 52, Parkville 3052

HISTORY: Founded in 1962 as a branch of the Association for Applied Solar Energy. Name changed in 1963 and 1971, when the parent body reformed first as the Solar Energy Society and then as the International Solar Energy Society.

PURPOSE: To encourage solar energy research and development and advance the utilization of solar energy.

INTERESTS: Solar energy

ACTIVITIES: Several meetings each year in most states. The parent society organises international conferences every 2 years.

PUBLICATIONS
Solar Energy Progress in Australia and New Zealand (annual)
Solar Energy (produced by parent society quarterly)
Sunworld (quarterly magazine)

MEMBERSHIP: Approximately 600 (individual, student, collective members)

256 Inventors' Association of Australia Limited
98 Ramsgate Road, Sans Souci, N.S.W.
(P.O. Box 32, Ramsgate 2217)
Telephone: (02) 529 8135

SUBDIVISIONS
Branches in Queensland, Victoria, South Australia, Western Australia and Tasmania

HISTORY: Founded in 1958.

PURPOSE: To discuss problems, solutions and make organized representation to improve the prospects and opportunities of inventors; to enrol firms as associate members and so act as liason between inventor with invention and manufacturer looking for new products.

ACTIVITIES: Monthly meetings in most states; provision of advice and services to members.

PUBLICATIONS
Inventus (5 per annum)
3 branch publications

MEMBERSHIP: Approximately 2000 (active inventors, associate and honorary members)

257   James Cook Astronomical Society
Green Point Community Centre, Cnr Green Point and Caravan Heads
Roads, Oyster Bay, N.S.W.
(P.O. Box 31, Sutherland, 2232)
Telephone: (02) 522 9878

SECRETARY: D. Parkes (86 Garnet Street, Miranda, N.S.W.)

HISTORY: Founded in 1963.

PURPOSE: To actively further the interests of astronomy not only amongst the members of the Society
but also the general public.

ACTIVITIES: Monthly lectures, talks or demonstrations from either member or guest speakers.

PUBLICATIONS
Southern Observer (quarterly)

MEMBERSHIP: 37 (full adult, junior members)

258   Latrobe Valley Astronomical Society
20 Hillside, Yallourn, Vic. 3838
Telephone: (051) 62 2015

SECRETARY: K. Bryant

HISTORY: Founded in 1954.

PURPOSE: To advance astronomical knowledge amongst members and the community.

INTERESTS: Monitoring of variable stars and current phenomena.

ACTIVITIES: Monthly meetings; demonstrations for community organizations; observations by
arrangement.

PUBLICATIONS
Newsletter (monthly)

LIBRARY: Astronomical and related periodicals and books.

MEMBERSHIP: 23 (ordinary, associate, junior)

259   Leather Guild
Howe and Company Pty. Ltd., P.O. Box 21, Preston 3072
Telephone: (03) 44 1241

SECRETARY: R.A. Speight (Chairman)

HISTORY: Founded in 1967

PURPOSE: To promote interest in leather and all facets of leather production, hides and materials used
in manufacture.

ACTIVITIES: Annual general meeting; 6 ordinary meetings throughout year.

MEMBERSHIP: 70 (full members, associate members)

260   Licensing Executives Society of Australia
The Forth and Clyde, 101 Mort Street, Balmain, N.S.W.
(P.O. Box 117, Balmain 2041
Telephone: (02) 8272133

SECRETARY: C. Marsh

SUBDIVISIONS
Melbourne Contact - J. Stonier, Care of B.H.P. Co. Ltd., 140 William Street, Melbourne, Vic. 3000.
Canberra Contact - R. Autard, CSIRO, Limestone Avenue, Campbell, A.C.T. 2602.

AFFILIATIONS
Licensing Executives Society International

HISTORY: LES Australia held its inaugural meeting in 1974. LES International grew out of LES
U.S.A. which was founded in 1965.

PURPOSE: The fostering of high standards and improved skills and techniques in the buying, selling
and licensing of technology, including industrial property.

INTERESTS: The licensing of patents, trade marks, designs, copyrights and know how and the associated
problems arising in fields of technology, law and accounting.

ACTIVITIES: Annual meeting, usually of two days duration, regular lunchtime or evening meetings in
Sydney, Melbourne, Adelaide and Canberra.

PUBLICATIONS
Transcripts of meetings and conferences available from secretary.

MEMBERSHIP: 120 (active, academic, honorary members)

261   Linnean Society of New South Wales
Science Centre, 35 Clarence Street, Sydney, N.S.W. 2000
Telephone: (02) 29 7747

SECRETARY: A.M. Ginges

HISTORY: Founded in 1874

PURPOSE: To promote the cultivation and study of the science of natural history in all its branches.

INTERESTS: Biological and earth sciences; microbiology; biochemistry.

ACTIVITIES: Approximately 7 meetings per year.

PUBLICATIONS
Proceedings of the Linnean Society of New South Wales

LIBRARY: Approximately 190,000 volumes

AWARDS
Linnean Macleay Fellowship
Linnean Macleay Lectureship in Microbiology (University of Sydney)

MEMBERSHIP: 305 (ordinary, corresponding, honorary members)

262   Malacological Society of Australia
G.P.O. Box 1277L, Melbourne, Vic. 3001.

SUBDIVISIONS
Vic. Mrs. E. Tenner, Secretary, 9 Foch Street, Reservoir, Vic. 3073.
N.S.W. - Dr. W. Ponder, Secretary, care of - Australian Museum, College Street, Sydney, N.S.W.
2000.
Qld. - Mrs. P. Sinclair, Secretary, 29 Prince Edward Parade, Redcliffe, Qld. 4020.

HISTORY: Founded in 1956 as a transformation of the former Malacological Club of Victoria (founded 1953).

PURPOSE: To promote and stimulate interest in the study of molluscs and their conservation.

ACTIVITIES: Monthly meetings of branches

PUBLICATIONS
Australian Shell News (quarterly)
Journal of the Macalogical Society of Australia (annually)

MEMBERSHIP: Approximately 700 (full, junior, corporate members)

263   Management Services Group of Victoria
Staff Development Centre, 128 Exhibition Street, Melbourne, Vic. 3000
Telephone: (03) 651 6889

SECRETARY: T.J. Carr

HISTORY: Founded in 1953

PURPOSE: To promote the interchange of information concerning the full range of management services and to keep members informed of advancements in management concepts and techniques; to bring people of similar interests together for discussion and to provide avenues for contact between people in different organizations.

INTERESTS: Organization and methods, clerical work study, industrial engineering, personnel administration, staff development, operations research, office machines and aids, automatic data processing.

ACTIVITIES: Monthly meetings of Committee of Management; monthly general meetings; seminars on special topics.

MEMBERSHIP: Corporate membership with an indeterminate number of individual members from 103 State, Australian government departments, semi-government, private industry and commerce, management consultants and educational bodies.

264   Marine Aquarium Research Institute of Australia
P.O. Box 10, Carlton, N.S.W. 2218
Telephone: (02) 665 1821, 48 5810

SECRETARY: T.J. Hogan

SUBDIVISIONS
N.S.W. Branches:- Sydney - P.O. Box 279, Coogee, 2034; Wollongong - 17 Inaga Avenue, West Wollongong 2500; Newcastle - P.O. Box 73, Morrissett 2264
Qld. Branches:- Cairns - 20 Falls Street, Machans Beach 4871; Brisbane - 9 Joachim Street, Holland Park 4121
Vic. Branch:- Melbourne - 9 Hawkins Avenue, Box Hill North 3129
S.A. Branch:- Adelaide - 183 Gawler Place, Adelaide 5000

HISTORY: Founded in 1969.

PURPOSE: To foster and disseminate knowledge of marine organisms in a closed circuit system.

INTERESTS: All species of vertebrates, invertebrates, algae capable of being maintained in aquaria.

ACTIVITIES: National Convention (annual), Branch meetings (monthly).

MEMBERSHIP: 280

265 Medical Society of Victoria
293 Royal Parade, Parkville, Vic. 3052
Telephone: (03) 347 8722

SECRETARY: Dr. W.M.G. Leembruggen

AFFILIATIONS
Australian Medical Association

HISTORY: Founded in 1852. In 1907 agreement was reached to amalgamate with the Victorian Branch of the British Medical Association, which had been founded in 1879, and reciprocal membership rights were extended to members of both bodies. When the Victorian Branch of the B.M.A. became the Victorian Branch of the Australian Medical Association in 1962, the relationship remained unchanged. All property of the Branch is held in the name of the Society, but in all other respects the two organizations are, for practical purposes, identical, and have common aims and activities.

PURPOSE: As for Australian Medical Association

266 Medico Legal Society of New South Wales
Care of- A.M.A., P.O.Box 121, St.Leonards, N.S.W. 2065
Telephone: (02) 439 8822

SECRETARY: Dr. J. Martin; D.M.J. Bennett (Secretaries)

HISTORY: Founded in 1947. The Society became dormant during the 1950's and recommenced active work in 1960.

PURPOSE: The promotion of medico legal knowledge in all its aspects. Interest over all subjects where the disciplines of law and medicine overlap including subjects relating to professional problems and subjects of general and philosophic interest.

ACTIVITIES: Meetings usually held quarterly.

PUBLICATIONS
Proceedings of the Medico Legal Society of New South Wales

MEMBERSHIP: 403 members

267 Melbourne University Engineering Students' Club
Engineering School, University of Melbourne, Parkville, Vic. 3052

HISTORY: Commenced ca 1880 as MUES Society, changed to MUESC in 1936

PURPOSE: To liase with Faculty on course content and extra-curricular activities; to promote social and intellectual contact between students, staff and engineers.

INTERESTS: All aspects of the engineering profession which may affect the student now or in the future.

ACTIVITIES: Committee meetings held fortnightly; Annual General Meeting; National Symposium.

PUBLICATIONS
Cranks and Nuts (annual)
Quo Vadis

MEMBERSHIP: 1100 (students, patrons, post-graduates, honorary, life members)

268 Melbourne University Science Students' Society
Union House, University of Melbourne, Parkville, Vic. 3052
(Box 32, Union Basement, University of Melbourne, Parkville 3052)

AFFILIATIONS
National Science Faculty Association
Society is affiliated with the Melbourne University Students' Representative Council and the National Union of Australian University Students through the N.S.F.A.

HISTORY: Founded in 1888, originally an academic society until ca. 1905 when it became a students' society.

PURPOSE: To act as representative and organization for all science students; to further staff-student co-operation: to promote the study and application of science; to further inter-faculty co-operation; to provide social functions for science students that would not otherwise be available.

ACTIVITIES: Periodical general meetings; weekly committee meetings; annual N.S.F.A. conference at a different university each year.

PUBLICATIONS
Neutrino (quarterly)

MEMBERSHIP: 2600 (full, admitted members)

269   Meteorological Society of N.S.W.
P.O. Box 105, North Ryde, N.S.W. 2113
Telephone: (02) 88 9551

SECRETARY: G.S. Hawke, School of Earth Sciences, Macquarie University, North Ryde, N.S.W. 2113

HISTORY: Founded in June 1971

PURPOSE: To bring together in one group all those interested in weather or any other branch of meteorology; to develop these interests by means of lectures, discussions and publications; to disseminate information and create a more general awareness of the role of weather in the natural environment.

ACTIVITIES: Meetings on second Wednesday of the month from Feb.to Nov.inclusive

PUBLICATIONS
Weatherfront (biannual journal)

MEMBERSHIP: 80 (full, associate, student)

270   Microfilm Association of Australia Limited
G.P.O. Box 3678, Sydney, N.S.W. 2001

SECRETARY: M. Gemenis

SUBDIVISIONS
Sydney - G. Moore (Secretary), G.P.O. Box 367B, Sydney, N.S.W. 2001 (Telephone: (02) 232 2222 ext 432)
Melbourne - I. Wilson (Secretary), G.P.O. Box 1835Q, Melbourne, Vic. 3001 (Telephone: (03) 350 1222 ext 469)
Perth - B. Davis (Secretary), G.P.O. Box S1508, Perth, W.A. 6001 (Telephone: (092) 22 5354)
Adelaide - B. Tyndale (Secretary), G.P.O. Box 1447, Adelaide, S.A. 5001 (Telephone: (08) 276 0711)

HISTORY: Superseded the Microfilm Association of Australia on 25th March, 1974

PURPOSE: To distribute freely and interchange information on the latest techniques in microforms.

ACTIVITIES: International Microfilm Conference; tutorials are arranged; monthly branch meetings

PUBLICATIONS
Micrographics Australia

MEMBERSHIP: (Private, representative, sustaining members)

271 Monash Astronautical Society
Faculty of Engineering, Monash University, Clayton, Vic. 3168
Telephone: (03) 25 4953, 97 6204

HISTORY: Founded in 1972.

PURPOSE: To promote interest in astronautics, space science and astronomy.

INTERESTS: Developments in space exploration and exploitation, Australian involvement with space, student tracking station project.

ACTIVITIES: Semi-regular space documentary film shows for the general public.

PUBLICATIONS
Capcom (bi-monthly)

LIBRARY: Small collection of recent aerospace periodicals.

MEMBERSHIP: 50

272 National Association of Testing Authorities, Australia
688 Pacific Highway, Chatswood, N.S.W. 2067
Telephone: (02) 411 4000

SECRETARY: H.F. Monaghan (Registrar)

SUBDIVISIONS
Victoria - K.N. Stanton (Deputy Registrar), National Association of Testing Authorities, Australia, Clunies Ross House, 191 Royal Parade, Parkville, Vic. 3052 (Telephone: (03) 347 1166).
Queensland - R. Wallace, Director of Technical Education, 417 Main Street, Kangaroo Point, Qld 4169 (Telephone: (07) 24 6950).
South Australia - L. R. Chester, 12 Tennyson Avenue, Tranmere, S.A. 5073 (Telephone: (08) 262 1432).
Western Australia - R.W. Taylor, Managing Director, Engineering X-ray Laboratories Pty. Ltd., 259 Star Street, Welshpool, W.A. 6106 (Telephone: (092) 61 9082).
Tasmania - D.J. Clark (State Secretary), National Association of Testing Authorities, Australia, G.P.O. Box 461E, Hobart, 7001 (Telephone: (002) 23 7537).

PURPOSE: To organise a national testing service to meet the needs of government, industry and commerce by the registration, on a voluntary basis, of testing laboratories throughout Australia and its territories.

INTERESTS: Acoustic and vibration measurement; biological, chemical and electrical testing; heat and temperature measurement; mechanical testing; metrology; non-destructive testing; optics and photometry.

ACTIVITIES: Conferences, symposia and workshops are organised on specific topics as required. Annual general meeting in October of each year.

PUBLICATIONS
NATA Register of Laboratories
NATA Directory
NATA News
Requirements for registration booklets

LIBRARY: Comprehensive holding of specifications issued by Standards Association of Australia, British Standards Institution and the American Society for Testing and Materials.

MEMBERSHIP: 1003 testing authorities

273 National Capital Agricultural Society
Flemington Road, Lyneham, A.C.T.
(P.O. Box 404, Dickson 2602)
Telephone: (062) 41 2478, 41 2480

SECRETARY: R.R. Rochford

HISTORY: First Agricultural Show held in 1908, and the N.A.C.S. was formed in 1930.

PURPOSE: To promote, foster and encourage the development of the agricultural, pastoral and horticultural industries, and other industries in Australia, and in particular in the A.C.T.

ACTIVITIES: Council meetings held monthly. Annual Canberra National Show, Canberra National Wine Show, N.C.A.S. Championship Cat Shows, Sheep Shearing Competition.

PUBLICATIONS
Cats (quarterly)
Prize schedules, section catalogues

MEMBERSHIP: 650 (life, honorary life, associate - adult annual, junior)

274 National Heart Foundation of Australia
55 Townsend Street, Phillip, A.C.T.
(P.O.Box 2, Woden, 2606)
Telephone: (062) 82 2144

SECRETARY: R.L. Paramor

SUBDIVISIONS
New South Wales Division, 365 Crown Street, Sydney, 2000
Victoria Division, Royal Parade, Parkville, 3052
Queensland Division, Princess Alexandra Hospital, Ipswich Road, Woolloongabba, 4012
Western Australia Division, 56 Havelock Street, West Perth, 6005
South Australia Division, 135 Hutt Street, Adelaide, 5000
Tasmania Division, Royal Hobart Hospital, Hobart, 7000
A.C.T. Division, 5 Liversidge Street, Acton, 2601.

HISTORY: Founded in 1959 as a private non-profit organization comprising the National Heart Foundation of Australia as the national headquarters and governing body of a federation of separately incorporated State Member Foundations (or State Divisions).

PURPOSE: To raise and apply funds for the purpose of combating death and suffering caused by cardiovascular diseases. The funds are especially directed to research into the causes, prevention and treatment of cardiovascular disease; into the education of the community and the medical profession in various aspects of the cardiovascular diseases; and in the rehabilitation of heart sufferers.

ACTIVITIES: Meetings of the various boards and committees; international conferences at three-yearly intervals; other scientific meetings for particular purposes more frequently.

PUBLICATIONS
National Heart News
Notes on Cardiovascular Disease
Annual Report; Research in Progress (annual)

LIBRARY: Small libraries maintained in national and state offices.

AWARDS
Warren McDonald International Fellowship
Research fellowships; grants-in-aid for research; vacation scholarships.

MEMBERSHIP: State Member Foundations, members at large, the persons for the time being comprising theBoard and a member of the Cardiac Society of Australia and New Zealand.

275 National Safety Council of Australia
343 Little Collins Street, Melbourne, Vic. 3000
Telephone: (03) 67 7278

SUBDIVISIONS
Queensland Division - M. Adams, 445 Upper Edward Street, P.O. Box 103, North Brisbane, 4000 (telephone (072) 218355)
New South Wales Division - W.B. McCosker, 491 Kent Street, Sydney, 2000 (telephone (02) 61 8136)
Victorian Division - F.Y. Turley, 191 Royal Parade, Parkville, 3052 (telephone (03) 347 2144)
South Austrralian Division - R.G. Fenwick, 105 Port Road, Bowden, 5007 (telephone (08) 46 4023)
Tasmania Division - A.C. Syrett, 31 Goulbern Street, Hobart, 7000 (telephone (002) 34 4091)
Western Australia - N.S.C. of W.A., Inc., J. B. Boulton, Sancliffe Street, P.O. BOX 42,Mt. Lawley, 6050 (telephone (092) 72 1666).
Industrial Foundation for Accident Prevention, A.D.Galton-Fenzi, McCabe Street, P.O. Box 28, Mosman Park, 6012 (telephone (092) 25 1344)

HISTORY: Founded in 1928, in Victoria; in 1959 it was reorganised and new Articles of Association were adopted in 1961, to place the Council on a more truly federal basis. The Council is now registered in Canberra, with Divisions established in all States.

PURPOSE: To devise and encourage adoption of safety measures of all kinds; to promote discussion of all matters relating to safety measures; to conduct an educational campaign among the people of Australia to stimulate adoption and observance of safety measures and to consider, initiate and support improvements in the laws of the Australian, State and local governing bodies, calculated to prevent accidents.

ACTIVITIES: Federal Council, Executive and State Managers' Meetings. Participation in Australian and State Government organised Industrial Safety Conferences.

PUBLICATIONS
Australian Safety News (bi-monthly)
Australian Family Safety (quarterly)
Annual Reports, booklets, leaflets, posters, educational material.

LIBRARY: Reference library maintained.

MEMBERSHIP: 2939 (Industrial Safety Service, associate members)

276 Natural Resources Conservation League of Victoria
593-615 Springvale Road, Springvale South, Vic.
(P.O. Box 104, Springvale 3171)
Telephone: (03) 546 9086, 546 4740

SECRETARY: E.U.C. Adamson

AFFILIATIONS
Junior Tree Lover's League
Soil and Water Conservation Society of Victoria

HISTORY: Founded in 1944 as 'Save the Forests' Campaign and incorporated as N.R.C.L. in 1951.

PURPOSE: To enlist public co-operation in conservation of natural resources.

ACTIVITIES: Forums and environmental field study days.

PUBLICATIONS
Victoria's Resources (quarterly)
Man, the Earth and Tomorrow (out of print)
Miscellaneous occasional publications

MEMBERSHIP: Approx 4000 (Complete membership representing organizations, individual full members, farm members,associates, associate school organizations)

277   Nature Conservation Council of New South Wales
399 Pitt Street, Sydney, N.S.W. 2000
Telephone: (02) 233 5388

SECRETARY: J.K. Hibberd (Executive Secretary)

AFFILIATIONS
50 affiliated organizations which must be interested in the conservation of nature and natural resources.

HISTORY: Founded in 1955

PURPOSE: To promote the cause of conservation throughout N.S.W.

INTERESTS: Conservation and the environment; land use and resource utilization; environmental education; conservation and ecological research.

ACTIVITIES: Annual conference in September or October. Special conferences as required. Executive meets monthly to implement follow up from conferences, and to act upon urgent matters as arise.

PUBLICATIONS
Annual Report. Irregular bulletins to member bodies.

MEMBERSHIP: 53 (full, associate, supporting members); total individual membership of these bodies approx. 100,000.

278   Nature Conservation Society of South Australia (Inc.)
Box 751, G.P.O., Adelaide, S.A. 5001
Telephone: (08) 223 5155

SECRETARY: D. W. Moyle

SUBDIVISIONS
Eyre Peninsula Branch
Land Use Sub-committee and various ad hoc groups.

HISTORY: Founded in 1962

PURPOSE: To promote wise long-term use of natural resources and especially the conservation of nativeflora and fauna, where possible in extensive wilderness areas, but also in developed areas. TheSociety believes that research and field investigations must precede recommendations for action.It conducts detailed biological studies of regions and takes an active role in environmental issues.

ACTIVITIES: Monthly general meetings, occasional public lectures, annual field survey in an actual or potential national park.

PUBLICATIONS
Quarterly newsletter, survey reports, submissions, educational materials.

LIBRARY: General conservation library containing books, periodicals, monographs and reports.

MEMBERSHIP: 320 (single, student, pensioner, family, life members)

279   New South Wales Field Ornithologists Club
90 Picnic Point Road, Picnic Point, N.S.W. 2213
Telephone: (02) 771 6185

SECRETARY: Miss J.M. Pegler

HISTORY: Founded in July 1966 as Gould League Birdwatchers. Changed to present name in July 1970.

PURPOSE: To promote the study and conservation of Australian birds and their habitat.

ACTIVITIES: Monthly meetings and field outings.

PUBLICATIONS
Australian Birds (quarterly)
Four newsletters produced annually as well as another four printed supplementary to 'Australian Birds'.

MEMBERSHIP: 327 (individual, family, junior members)

280 New South Wales Horticultural Propagation Co-operative Society Ltd.
Lot 6, Annangrove Road, Rouse Hill, N.S.W.
(P.O. Box 99, Round Corner 2154)
Telephone: (02) 628 1472

SECRETARY: K.E. Gallard

HISTORY: Formed on 27 August 1975 from the Bud Selection Co-operative Society

PURPOSE: To arrange and encourage the maintenance of sources of suitable horticultural propagation materials such as seeds, budwood, cuttings, plants, runners; to arrange the supply and distribution of such material.

ACTIVITIES: Annual Meeting.

MEMBERSHIP: 7 directors

281 New South Wales Institute for Educational Research
Alexander Mackie College of Advanced Education, Albion Avenue,
Paddington, N.S.W. 2021
Telephone: (02) 31 8068

SECRETARY: Miss J. Cust

SUBDIVISIONS
Branch in Newcastle

AFFILIATIONS
Australian Council for Educational Research

HISTORY: Education Society was established at Sydney Teachers' College in 1910. The Society was reconstituted in 1928 to form the New South Wales Institute for Educational Research.

PURPOSE: The encouragement of study, research and service in education.

ACTIVITIES: General meetings including annual general meeting.

PUBLICATIONS
N.S.W.I.E.R. Bulletin (occasional)

LIBRARY: Small library maintained for use of members.

AWARDS
Prizes awarded annually to outstanding graduates in education on basis of research thesis.

MEMBERSHIP: 169 ordinary members

282 North Queensland Naturalists Club
Box 991, Cairns, Qld. 4870.
Telephone: (070) 53 1183

SECRETARY: Mrs. D. Magarry

AFFILIATIONS
Cape York Conservation Council

HISTORY: Founded in 1932.

PURPOSE: To promote the study of natural history in all its branches; to preserve and to encourage preservation of the flora and fauna of North Queensland and its contiguous waters; to publish literature as deemed desirable; to support any organization for the furtherance of the study of natural history.

ACTIVITIES: Monthly meetings and field study days.

PUBLICATIONS
North Queensland Naturalist
Check List of Orchidaceous Plants of North Queensland
Check List of Birds of North Queensland
Edible Plants of North Queensland
Check List of Dryopodidae
Marketable Fish of the Cairns Area
Check List of Ferns

MEMBERSHIP: Approximately 120 (town, country, junior members)

283   **Nutrition Society of Australia**
care of- CSIRO Division of Animal Production, Great Western Highway, Prospect, N.S.W.
(P.O. Box 239, Blacktown 2148)
Telephone: (02) 631 8022

SECRETARY: Dr. J.L. Black

SUBDIVISIONS
Adelaide - Dr. B. Radcliffe, Secretary, Agronomy Department, Waite Agricultural Research Institute, Glen Osmond, S.A. 5064
Armidale - Dr. J.L. Corbett, Secretary, CSIRO Pastoral Research Laboratory, Private Bag, P.O. Armidale, N.S.W. 2350
Brisbane - Mrs. Y. Webb, Secretary, Department of Paramedical Studies, Queensland Institute of Technology, P.O. Box 246, North Quay, Qld. 4000
Canberra - Dr. M. Freer, Secretary, CSIRO Division of Plant Industry, P.O. Box 1600, Canberra City, A.C.T. 2601
Melbourne - Mr. G.A. Eldridge, Secretary, Institute of Agriculture, Werribee, Vic. 3030
Perth - Mr. B.J. Mackintosh, Secretary, Department of Animal Science, University of W.A., Nedlands, W.A. 6009
Sydney - Dr. J.R. Mercer, Secretary, Department of Animal Husbandry, University of Sydney, N.S.W. 2006

HISTORY: Founded in 1975.

PURPOSE: To advance the scientific study of nutrition and its applications to man and animals; to facilitate and encourage the exchange of ideas and techniques between people involved in aspects of human and animal nutrition; to become involved in public issues relating to the science of nutrition when appropriate.

ACTIVITIES: Annual Conference, Regional Group meetings.

PUBLICATIONS
Proceedings of the Nutrition Society of Australia
Newsletters (3-4 annually)

MEMBERSHIP: 400 (ordinary, corresponding, student, honorary)

284   **Oil and Colour Chemists' Association, Australia**
Walpamur Paints Pty. Ltd., P.O. Box 100, West Footscray, Vic. 3012

SECRETARY: R. Smith (Federal Secretary)

SUBDIVISIONS
Sections in New South Wales, Queensland, South Australia, Victoria, Western Australia.

AFFILIATIONS
Oil and Colour Chemists' Association (U.K.)

HISTORY: Oil and Colour Chemists' Association (U.K.) was founded in 1918. O.C.C.A. in Australia was established in 1946 and became an independent association in 1968.

PURPOSE: To further the development of the science and technology of the oil and colour industries and to facilitate the exchange of information and ideas thereon.

INTERESTS: Paints, varnishes, lacquers, printing inks.

ACTIVITIES: Regular technical meetings by each state section. Federal convention held annually in each state in turn.

PUBLICATIONS
Australian Oil and Colour Chemists' Association Proceedings and News
Raw Materials Index
Handbook of Surface Coatings

MEMBERSHIP: 900 (honorary, ordinary, associate, junior, retired)

285   Ophthalmic Research Institute of Australia
Prevention of Blindness Unit, Royal Victorian Eye and Ear Hospital, Victoria Parade, Melbourne, Vic.
Telephone: (03) 89 7916

SECRETARY: Dr. P. Hardy Smith

PURPOSE: To promote research into diseases of the eye.

INTERESTS: Ophthalmology.

ACTIVITIES: Annual General Meeting.

PUBLICATIONS
Annual Report

AWARDS
Annual grants to approved applicants from endowment funds

MEMBERSHIP: 230 (ordinary, honorary)

286   Opticians and Optometrists Association of N.S.W.
235 Elizabeth Street, Sydney, N.S.W. 2000
Telephone: (02) 26 5284

SECRETARY: Mrs. J. Welch

HISTORY: Founded in 1926

ACTIVITIES: Monthly meetings

PUBLICATIONS
N.S.W. Journal of Optometry

AWARDS
Student prize at University of N.S.W.

287   Orchid Society of N.S.W. Ltd.
121 Cardsnal Avenue, West Pennant Hills, N.S.W. 2120
Telephone: (02) 84 3061

SECRETARY: C.R. Jones

AFFILIATIONS
47 affiliated societies in N.S.W.

HISTORY: Founded in 1934

PURPOSE: To promote orchid culture in Australia.

INTERESTS: Conservation and culture of orchids

ACTIVITIES: Monthly meetings on the last Monday of every month, conferences held every two years.

PUBLICATIONS
Orchid News (monthly bulletin)

LIBRARY: Comprehensive orchid library

AWARDS
Prizes awarded at Winter and Summer Shows

MEMBERSHIP: 450 (Metropolitan, associate, country-overseas, junior)

288   Organic Gardening and Farming Society of Tasmania
G.P.O. Box 1281, Launceston, Tas. 7250
Telephone: (003) 98 2150

HISTORY: Founded in 1972.

PURPOSE: To foster interest in, research into and adoption of organic gardening and farming practices.

ACTIVITIES: Monthly branch meetings, annual conference, and an Organic Festival.

PUBLICATIONS
Organic Gardener and Farmer (quarterly)

MEMBERSHIP: 1200

289   Orthoptic Association of Australia
Orthoptic Department, Sydney Eye Hospital, Sir John Young Crescent,
Woolloomooloo, N.S.W.
(P.O. Box E47, St. James 2000)
Telephone: (02) 230 0111 ext 2217

SECRETARY: Ms. V. Gordon

SUBDIVISIONS
Branches in N.S.W. and Vic.

PURPOSE: To further and safeguard the interests of members insofar as these are in accord with those of the general public; to elevate the standard of orthoptic education among its members; to provide a channel for communication between the orthoptic profession and other bodies concerned in the education of orthoptists; to provide a medium for the exchange of views between members on scientific matters, and such ethical matters as may be defined by the Orthoptic Board of Australia; to co-operate with similar bodies overseas; to produce a scientific journal to be called the Australian Orthoptic Journal; to determine and negotiate proper financial remuneration for members.

INTERESTS: Ocular motility, specific learning difficulties, defective vision.

ACTIVITIES: Annual Scientific conference; State branches hold 3 general meetings and one A.G.M. per year; N.S.W. branch holds annually a combined scientific meeting of Orthoptists and Opthalmologists.

PUBLICATIONS
Australian Orthoptic Journal
N.S.W. branch newsletter

LIBRARY: Orthoptic Library housed within Sydney Eye Hospital Library and Library of Cumberland
College of Health Sciences, Camperdown.

AWARDS
Emmie Russell Prize
Travel fund to attend International Orthoptic Association congress held every four years

MEMBERSHIP: 140 (full, honorary, associate, fellow)

290 Packaging Industry Environment Council
370 St. Kilda Road, Melbourne, Vic.
(P.O. Box 1469N, Melbourne, 3001)
Telephone: (03) 698 4111

SECRETARY: J.D. Honeysett (Sectretary and Executive Director)

SUBDIVISIONS
Regional sub-committees in Queensland (T.J. Pitney, telephone: (07) 262 1143), Tasmania (T.A. Swift,
telephone: (002) 23 7336), New South Wales (A.J. Fletcher, telephone: (02) 439 6633) and South
Australia (W.J. Christie, telephone: (08) 268 2755).

AFFILIATIONS
National Packaging Association of Australia
Plastics Institute of Australia Inc.

HISTORY: Founded in May, 1972

PURPOSE: To ensure that the products of the packaging industry do not adversely affect the
environment.

INTERESTS: Solid waste management and conservation of resources.

ACTIVITIES: Monthly executive committee meetings.

PUBLICATIONS
Monthly newsletter, brochures.

LIBRARY: Library which contains local and overseas information on solid waste management, recovery
of resources, legislation and associated conservation matters.

MEMBERSHIP: 23 packaging manufacturing organizations.

291 Paediatric Society of Victoria
Royal Children's Hospital, Flemington Road, Parkville, Vic. 3052
Telephone: (03) 347 5522 extn 536

SECRETARY: Dr. J.M. McNamara

HISTORY: Founded in 1906

PURPOSE: To advance the knowledge of paediatrics

ACTIVITIES: Monthly meetings

MEMBERSHIP: 256 (honorary, full members)

292 Petroleum Exploration Society of Australia

Dr. J.J.A. Poll (President, PESA), Woodside Petroleum Development
Ltd., 151 Flinders Street, Melbourne Vic. 3000
Telephone: (03) 63 2421

SECRETARY: D.W. Hamilton [Secretary-Treasurer, A.N.Z. Bank, 351 Collins Street, Melbourne, Vic.
3000 (Telephone: (03) 62 0391)]

SUBDIVISIONS
Vic.-Tas. Branch - H. Messinger (Secretary), Mobil Exploration Australia Pty. Ltd., 2 City Road,
South Melbourne, Vic. 3205 (Telephone: (03) 62 0231)
N.S.W. Branch - A. Strahan (Secretary), Esso Australia Ltd., Box 4047, G.P.O., Sydney, N.S.W. 2000
(Telephone: (02) 2 0557)
Qld. Branch - R. Paten (Secretary), Mines Administration Pty Ltd., 31 Charlotte Street, Brisbane, Qld.
4000 (Telephone: (07) 221 2366)
S.A. Branch - Dr. B. Devine (Secretary), South Australian Petroleum Exploration Group, Flemington
Street, Frewville, S.A. 5063
W.A. Branch - A. Sabitay (Secretary), Wapet Pty. Ltd., 12 George Terrace, Perth, W.A. 6000
(Telephone: (092) 25 0181)

AFFILIATIONS
Australian Petroleum Exploration Association Ltd.

HISTORY: Formerly the Professional Division of the Australian Petroleum Exploration Association
(EPEA). Name changed to present title in 1975.

PURPOSE: To promote professional and technical aspects of the petroleum industry by providing a
medium for the gathering of individuals in oil and gas exploration and the petroleum industry, for the
presentation of views and the discussion of technical and professional matters relating to the petroleum
industry on a national basis; to foster and provide continuing education for the benefit of its members;
to nurture the spirit of research among its members; and to maintain a high standard of professional
conduct on the part of its members.

ACTIVITIES: Branch meetings (monthly); Federal Executive Committee meetings (quarterly); Annual
Symposium conducted with APEA Annual Scientific Conference.

PUBLICATIONS
News sheet (quarterly, for members)

AWARDS
PESA Distinguished Paper Award (for best presentation of a paper at Annual Symposium)
PESA Distinguished Lecturer (annual)

MEMBERSHIP: Approx. 750 (Distinguished, active, associate, student, overseas)

293 Pharmaceutical Association of Australia and New Zealand

109 Greenhill Road, Unley, S.A. 5061
Telephone: (08) 272 1211

SECRETARY: R. B. Clampett

AFFILIATIONS
Australian Parmaceutical Sciences Association
Women Pharmaceutical Chemists of Australia
Australian Pharmaceutical Science Association
All State and New Zealand Pharmaceutical Societies
State Pharmacy Boards of Australia and New Zealand

HISTORY: Founded in 1907

PURPOSE: The co-ordination of activities of professional pharmaceutical bodies in Australia and liason
with the Commonwealth Pharmaceutical Association.

AWARDS
$5000 Scholarship bi-annually

MEMBERSHIP: 11,250 members of affiliated bodies.

294   Pharmaceutical Society of Australia

10th Floor, Canberra House, Marcus Clarke Street, Canberra, A.C.T.
(P.O. Box 456, Canberra City 2601)
Telephone: (062) 48 6248

SECRETARY: W.P. Ryan (Executive Director)

AFFILIATIONS
Pharmaceutical Society of New South Wales
Pharmaceutical Society of the Northern Territory
Pharmaceutical Society of Queensland
Pharmaceutical Society of South Australia, Incorporated
Pharmaceutical Society of Tasmania
Pharmaceutical Society of Victoria
Commonwealth Pharmaceutical Association

HISTORY: Incorporated in the A.C.T. in February, 1977.

PURPOSE: To define, plan, develop, implement and continually review the most effective role for the
pharmacist in the provision of contemporary health care in Australia including reference to pharmacy
manpower, manpower distribution, rationalisation of pharmaceutical services and the development of
new roles which utilise the pharmacist's scientific and professional skills and expertise in all aspects of
drug therapy; to determine ethical and professional standards and responsibilities of pharmacists in the
interests of the community, and to prepare, maintain and review a Code of Professional Conduct
which defines responsible, ethical and professional practice for all pharmacists; to liaise with allied
professional groups and pharmaceutical organisations, and to publicise the views, policies and
aspirations of pharmacists nationally whilst also protecting the rights, privileges and professional status
of pharmacy; to liaise with the national government and its agencies on all matters affecting the
professional practice of pharmacy; to co- operate with teaching institutions to develop inter alia,
appropriate pharmacy training and re-training programmes; to initiate, co-ordinate and implement
continuing and other education programmes; to foster research into pharmaceutical practice and
science; to formulate, express and execute policies for the effective practice of pharmacy; to ensure
representation of pharmacists in all areas concerned with health care provision, planning and
development; to engage in publishing activities as considered desirable; to assist at State Government
level on request.

ACTIVITIES: Quarterly meetings of Council, Annual General Meeting.

AWARDS
Kodak Fellowship

MEMBERSHIP: 8500 (ordinary, senior, student, honorary distinguished members)

295   Pharmaceutical Society of New South Wales

82 Christie Street, St. Leonards, N.S.W.
(P.O. Box 62, St. Leonards 2065)
Telephone: (02) 438 1833

SECRETARY: D.B. Moorhouse (Executive Secretary)

AFFILIATIONS
Pharmaceutical Society of Australia
All state pharmaceutical societies
Federation International Pharmaceutique
Federation Asian Pharmaceutical Associations

HISTORY: Founded in 1876.

PURPOSE: To support and protect the character and status of qualified pharmacists in the interest of
the community; to advance and encourage study and research in pharmacy and all branches of science
allied thereto; to encourage and promote the continuing education of pharmacists; to consider,
originate and promote improvements in the law relating to pharmacists or to the sale and use of
poisons; to conduct training courses for dispensary assistants.

ACTIVITIES: Monthly Council meetings, special committee meetings, Continuing Education Forums and
Seminars, Training Cources, Annual Education Conferences, Drug Information Group.

PUBLICATIONS
Clinical Basis of Pharmacy (reference book)
Pharmaceutical Society of New South Wales Bulletin (monthly)
Continuing Education Cassette programmes

LIBRARY: Reference - Historical Library at society headquarters.

AWARDS
Pharmacy Research Trust Grants
Annual prize for merit in each pharmacy year at the University of Sydney

MEMBERSHIP: 3500 (full, associate, life, honorary, fellows, student)

296   Pharmaceutical Society of South Australia, Incorporated
109 Greenhill Road, Unley, S.A. 5061
Telephone: (08) 272 1211

AFFILIATIONS
Pharmaceutical Association of Australia and New Zealand
Australian state pharmaceutical societies.
Pharmaceutical societies of New Zealand, Great Britain, Singapore, Pakistan and Malawi.

HISTORY: Founded in 1885

PURPOSE: To act as a professional association for South Australian pharmacists.

ACTIVITIES: Local meetings for members.

PUBLICATIONS
Pharmaceutical Society of S.A. Quarterly Bulletin

MEMBERSHIP: 693 (fellows, ordinary, honorary, honorary life members, student associates)

297   Pharmaceutical Society of Tasmania
152 Macquarie Street, Hobart, Tas. 7000
Telephone: (002) 23 2667

SECRETARY: Mrs. R. Mead

HISTORY: Founded in 1898

PURPOSE: To act as a professional association for qualified pharmaceutical chemists in Tasmania

ACTIVITIES: Regular monthly council meetings, quarterly general meetings. Seminars at least yearly.

PUBLICATIONS
Newsletters to members (quarterly)

AWARDS
Pharmaceutical Society of Tasmania Gold Medal Award
Research fund in operation

MEMBERSHIP: 260 (full, student members)

298   Pharmaceutical Society of Victoria
381 Royal Parade, Parkville, Vic. 3052
Telephone: (03) 380 6254

SECRETARY: H.V. Feehan

HISTORY: Founded in 1857

PURPOSE: To maintain, support and promote the character, status and interests of qualified pharmacistsin the practice of their profession; to promote the study of pharmacy and other related sciences.

INTERESTS: Operation and management of the Victorian College of Pharmacy; continuing education of pharmacists; examination of legal matters relating to the practice of pharmacy; development of sessional pharmacy practice, public health services and related matters; ethics.

ACTIVITIES: Annual general meeting, monthly council meetings, professional and scientific symposia.

PUBLICATIONS
Pharmaceutical Society of Victoria News Bulletin (monthly)
Occasional papers and reports

LIBRARY: Library of the Victorian College of Pharmacy

MEMBERSHIP: 3300 (ordinary, life members, students, fellows)

299 Pharmaceutical Society of Western Australia
28A Ventnor Avenue, West Perth, W.A. 6005
Telephone: (092) 21 4082

SECRETARY: E.P. Walsh

HISTORY: Founded in 1892

PURPOSE: Promote by every means the profession of pharmacy while maintaining its legal and ethical standards and improve and enlarge the education and training of pharmacists.

INTERESTS: Laws affecting pharmacy; education and training of pharmacists; co-operation with other health professions.

ACTIVITIES: Annual meeting, periodic conferences, seminars and lectures.

PUBLICATIONS
Newsletter published approximately bi-monthly.

AWARDS
Webster Gold Medal

MEMBERSHIP: 970 members

300 Pharmacy Guild of Australia
National Secretariat, Strickland Crescent, Deakin, A.C.T.
(P.O. Box 36, Deakin 2600)
Telephone: (062) 95 0500

SECRETARY: D.M. Gibbons (Executive Director)

SUBDIVISIONS
N.S.W. Branch - W.G. Shaw (Branch Director), 79 Lithgow Street, St. Leonards, N.S.W. 2065
Vic. Branch - W. Wright (Branch Director), 35 Walsh Street, West Melbourne, Vic. 3003
Qld. Branch - M. McKinnon (Branch Director), 132 Leichhardt Street, Brisbane, Qld. 4000
S.A. Branch - E. Kleisdorff (Branch Director), 451 Pulteney Street, Adelaide, S.A. 5000
W.A. Branch - D. Thomas (Branch Director), 896 Canning Highway, Applecross, W.A. 6153
Tas. Branch - Miss C. Jones (Branch Director), 152 Macquarie Street, Hobart, Tas. 7000

HISTORY: Founded in 1928.

PURPOSE: To represent private practice pharmacists (retail) throughout Australia; to protect the interests in the industrial relations field and to provide a wide range of services of a professional, marketing and economic nature.

ACTIVITIES: International Conference to be held in Canberra, 16-20 April 1978 (not regular event), theme - *Pharmacy in 1980's*.

PUBLICATIONS
Bimonthly magazine, newsletters and bulletins
Annual National Report

MEMBERSHIP: 5200 (full, honorary, nominal)

301 Plastics Institute of Australia Inc.
157 Fitzroy Street, St. Kilda, Vic.
(P.O. Box 131, St. Kilda West 3182)
Telephone: (03) 94 8041

SECRETARY: F. Ashworth (Operations Manager)

SUBDIVISIONS
N.S.W. Section - S. Kean (Secretary), P.O. Box 82, Flemington Markets, N.S.W. 2129 (Telephone: (02) 76 0376)
Qld. Section - R.B. Lewis (Secretary), 4th Floor, Ansett Centre, 22 Turbot Street, Brisbane, Qld. 4000 (Telephone: (07) 229 5307)
S.A. Section - A. Hamlyn (Secretary), 47 South Terrace, Adelaide, S.A. 5000 (Telephone: (08) 51 9068)
Vic. Section - L. Hadaway (Secretary), 157 Fitzroy Street, St. Kilda, Vic. 3182 (Telephone: (03) 94 8041)
W.A. Section - A. Foyster (Secretary), 266 Hay Street, Subiaco, W.A. 6008 (Telephone: (092) 81 2511)
Divisions - PVC Pipes and Fittings, Poly-olefin Pipes and Fittings, Cellular Plastics, Food Packaging, Films and Bags, Fibreglass Reinforced Plastics, Vinyl Fabricators, Plastics Moulders.

HISTORY: Founded in 1944 in New South Wales.

PURPOSE: To promote the cause of the plastics and allied industries throughout the Commonwealth of Australia and its Territories by bringing together all those interested in such industries and to provide means of intercourse between persons interested, directly of indirectly, in the plastics and allied industries.

ACTIVITIES: National Convention (1 every 4 years); numerous national and state seminars; State Section Meetings (monthly); numerous meetings of state and national divisions; Major National Committees meet periodically; State Committees meet on a regular basis.

PUBLICATIONS
Plastics News (monthly)
Plastics Action (monthly, to all company members)
Know Your Plastics (revised every 3 years)
Seminar papers published on an ad hoc basis

AWARDS
John W. Derham Memorial Award (biennially)
Industry fund for specific research projects

MEMBERSHIP: 600 company members (corporate members, service members); 750 personal members (fellows, associates, individuals)

302 Port Macquarie Astronomical Society
Port Macquarie Observatory, Rotary Park, Cnr. Lord and Stewart Streets, Port Macquarie, N.S.W. 2444
Telephone: (065) 83 1933

SECRETARY: J.K. Daniel (42 Waugh Street, Port Macquarie)

AFFILIATIONS
British Astronomical Association (N.S.W. Branch)
Astronomical Society of South Australia Inc.
Astronomical Society of New South Wales

HISTORY: Founded in 1962.

PURPOSE: To promote the science of astronomy in all branches of astronomical research.

INTERESTS: Astrophotographic work (developing and printing); telescope making (mirror grinding and testing).

ACTIVITIES: Monthly meetings (general and scientific meetings on alternate months); lectures, films and viewing of moon, planets and stars for the general public.

PUBLICATIONS
Solar System and Universe Around Us (by A. York)
Clock Paradox (by A. York)

LIBRARY: A selection of books on astronomical subjects.

AWARDS
Annual award to 1st year High School students of Port Macquarie and Wauchope for achievements in mathematics and science (books on astronomy)

MEMBERSHIP: 30 (adult, junior)

303 Postgraduate Medical Foundation, University of Sydney
11 Castlereagh Street, Sydney, N.S.W.
(P.O. Box H 111, Australia Square, 2000)
Telephone: (02) 233 2666

SECRETARY: D.B. Taberner

AFFILIATIONS
Coppleson Postgraduate Medical Institute(Victor Coppleson Memorial Institute of Postgraduate Medical Studies) administered by the Postgraduate Committee in Medicine, University of Sydney

HISTORY: Founded in 1958

PURPOSE: The promotion and development of postgraduate education, study, work and research in medicine and the advancement of the art and science of medicine.

ACTIVITIES: Annual general meeting held April-May each year.

AWARDS
Allocations made for fellowships and research grants in various fields of medicine in November, and occasionally in May, each year.

MEMBERSHIP: Approximately 900 (council members, governors, members, associates and affiliate members)

304 Provincial Sewerage Authorities Association of Victoria
Rigby House, 15 Queens Road, Melbourne, Vic. 3004
Telephone: (03) 26 4421

SECRETARY: J.D. Fagan

HISTORY: Founded in 1925

PURPOSE: To protect the interests, rights and privileges of sewerage authorities; to advise, instruct and take action in relation to any legislation affecting sewerage authorities; to maintain and extend the efficiency of sewerage authority administration throughout the State of Victoria.

ACTIVITIES: One annual session, two executive committee meetings yearly.

PUBLICATIONS
Annual report.

MEMBERSHIP: 109 full members

305   Queensland Conservational Council
147 Ann Street, Brisbane, Qld.
(P.O. Box 238, North Quay, Brisbane 4000)
Telephone: (07) 221 0330, 221 0188

SECRETARY: C. Gasteen

HISTORY: Founded in 1969.

PURPOSE: To promote the reasonable use of resources and environmental concern.

ACTIVITIES: Annual General Meeting; four General Meetings; 26 Committee Meetings.

PUBLICATIONS
Future of Moreton Island
Parks and Open Spaces
Conondale Range
Sandmining Handbook
Municipal Solid Waste Treatment

LIBRARY: Open to the public; borrowing and photocopy facilities.

AWARDS
$1000 to consultant in Moreton Island
Part time research wages paid in other publications

MEMBERSHIP: 300 (associate (individuals), member bodies)

306   Queensland Institute for Educational Research
Faculty of Education, University of Queensland, St. Lucia, Qld. 4067
Telephone: (07) 370 6969

SECRETARY: R.E. Wilkes

HISTORY: Founded in 1930

PURPOSE: To promote, as far as possible in co-operation with existing institutions, the cause of research in education.

INTERESTS: Draw up programs of educational research to be undertaken by the Institute; promote discussion on educational problems; convene lectures and meetings on educational matters; issue educational information periodically and act in close co-operation with the Australian Council for Educational Research

ACTIVITIES: Regular general meetings; annual public lecture series.

PUBLICATIONS
Queensland Institute for Educational Research Journal (2 times per year)

LIBRARY: Incorporated into Library of Department of Education.

MEMBERSHIP: 200 (general, life members)

307   Queensland Naturalists' Club
Unit 3, 136 Macquarie Street, St.Lucia, Qld. 4067
Telephone: (07) 370 8116

SECRETARY: Mrs. N.K. Thornthwaite

HISTORY: Founded in 1906

PURPOSE: The study of all branches of natural history; the preservation of the flora and fauna of Queensland; the encouragement of a spirit of protection towards native birds, animals and plants.

ACTIVITIES: Monthly meetings.

PUBLICATIONS
Queensland Naturalist
Monthly newsletter

LIBRARY: Small library for use of members.

AWARDS
Junior members Project Awards.

MEMBERSHIP: 375 (joint ordinary, ordinary, joint country, country, junior members)

308 Queensland Society of Sugar Cane Technologists
Australian Sugar Producers Association Ltd., 6th Floor, Phoenix House,
333 Adelaide Street, Brisbane, Qld.
(G.P.O. Box 608, Brisbane 4001)
Telephone: (072) 31 1881

SECRETARY: R. W. Dorr

AFFILIATIONS
International Society for Sugar Cane Technologists

HISTORY: Founded in 1929

PURPOSE: The exchange of technical knowledge and administrative information of interest to the sugar
cane industry.

INTERESTS: Administrative, agricultural and manufacturing aspects of sugar industry.

ACTIVITIES: Annual conference in one of the Queensland sugar districts.

PUBLICATIONS
Proceedings of the Queensland Society of Sugar Cane Technologists (annually)

AWARDS
Seymour House and Norman Bennett Memorial Bursaries

MEMBERSHIP: 822 (life, full, associate, student, supporting, overseas members)

309 Rail Sleeper Association (Australia)
Goldfields House, Sydney Cove, N.S.W.
(P.O. Box 4192, Sydney 2001)
Telephone: (02) 27 5651

SECRETARY: J.S. Moss

HISTORY: Founded in 1976.

PURPOSE: To bring together specialists interested in the production, distribution and use of railway
sleepers and associated products in track structures and actively to encourage the optimisation of
performance, economics and use of railway sleepers; to foster collaboration between Railways, Forestry
and Suppliers together with such other entities as have or may have an interest in the objects of the
Association; to initiate, sponsor and-or co-operate with others in research, development and test work
concerned with sleeper design, manufacture and usage; to sponsor the development of realistic
standards in respect of sleepers and associated equipment and their performance in various types of
service; to disseminate information to members and others concerning the progress of research and
new developments and to provide assistance in the evaluation of performance and economics of
sleepers as part of the rail track structure; to encourage the most appropriate use of natural resources
commensurate with economics and a care for the environment.

ACTIVITIES: Conference every 3 years and 3 meetings per year.

PUBLICATIONS
Rail Track Journal

MEMBERSHIP: 83 (corporate, personal)

310   Refrigeration and Air Conditioning Contractors Association of Australia

B12 Plaza Building, Sydney Farm Produce Markets, Flemington, N.S.W.
(P.O. Box 118, Flemington Markets, N.S.W. 2129)
Telephone: (02) 764 3404, 649 1419

SECRETARY: D.J. Staniforth

SUBDIVISIONS
RACCA-Victoria, care of- E.E. Falk, 356 Collins Street, Melbourne, Vic. 3000
RACCA-Queensland, care of- H. Collinson, 447 Upper Edward Street, Brisbane, Qld. 4000
RACCA-South Australia, care of- R. Down, P.O. Box 47, Eastwood, S.A. 5063
RACCA-New South Wales, care of- D.J. Staniforth, P.O. Box 118, Flemington Markets, N.S.W. 2129
RACCA-Western Australia, care of- B. Hamilton, 23 Beckington Way, Karinup, W.A. 6018

HISTORY: Founded in 1937

PURPOSE: To advance the science of refrigeration and air conditioning; to represent the refrigeration and air conditioning contractors; to serve the public by improving systems and techniques; to preserve technical and trading integrity of the Industry; to serve and promote the interests of the membership; to advance the educational standards of refrigeration and air conditioning tradesmen and technicians; to recognise and record technical merit.

INTERESTS: Refrigeration, air conditioning, heating.

ACTIVITIES: Conference yearly in June at rotating State locations; meetings quarterly at Sydney office. N.S.W., Vic., Qld. and W.A. Associations meet monthly; S.A. Association meets quarterly.

PUBLICATIONS
Celsius (monthly)

LIBRARY: General technical and business library.

AWARDS
Allan Robert Memorial Fund (W.A.)
Prizes and awards to State Technical Colleges

MEMBERSHIP: 480 (full, associate)

311   Royal Aeronautical Society (Australian Division)

191 Royal Parade, Parkville, Vic. 3052
Telephone: (03) 347 2570

SECRETARY: B.A.J. Scoles (Honorary Secretary)

SUBDIVISIONS
Branches in Adelaide, Canberra, Melbourne, Sydney

HISTORY: Founded in 1927, then known as the Australian Branch of the Royal Aeronautical Society.

PURPOSE: To generally advance the aeronautical art, science and engineering and promote that species of knowledge which distinguishes the profession of aeronautics and astronautics.

ACTIVITIES: Each branch holds monthly lecture meetings and-or symposia.

PUBLICATIONS
Aeronautical Journal
Aeronautical Quarterly
Aerospace

AWARDS
Sir Ross and Keith Smith Memorial Lecture (every 2nd year, Adelaide Branch)
Pioneers Memorial Lecture (Canberra Branch)
Lawrence Hargreave Memorial Lecture (Melbourne Branch)
Sir Lawrence Wackett Lecture (Melbourne Branch)
Sir Charles Kingsford Smith Memorial Lecture (Sydney Branch)
Australian Division Lecture Prize of $200 awarded for the best original paper presentedat a branch lecture meeting.

MEMBERSHIP: Approx. 600 (fellows, members, associate members, students, companions)

312   Royal Agricultural and Horticultural Society of South Australia Inc.
Royal Showground, Wayville, S.A. 5034
Telephone: (08) 87 4421, 51 4951

SECRETARY: R.H. Sedsman (Director-Secretary)

AFFILIATIONS
Royal Agricultural Society of the Commonwealth

HISTORY: Founded in 1839.

PURPOSE: Promoting primary and secondary industry in South Australia; administration of stud stock societies; agricultural extension and research; improvement of Australian wines; pedigree livestock breeding; farm machinery development.

ACTIVITIES: Quarterly meetings of Council; committee meetings; regular meetings of stud stock societies.

PUBLICATIONS
Prize schedules; Catalogues and Ring Programme.

MEMBERSHIP: 6,250 (full, life, junior members)

313   Royal Agricultural Society of New South Wales
Showground, Paddington, N.S.W.
(Box 4317, G.P.O., Sydney 2001.)
Telephone: (02) 31 7781

SECRETARY: C.M.I. Pearson (Director)

PURPOSE: To promote primary, secondary and tertiary industries in N.S.W.

INTERESTS: Agriculture, stock, viticulture, horticulture, industry.

314   Royal Agricultural Society of Tasmania
Rothmans Building, Royal Showgrounds, Glenorchy, Tas. 7010.
Telephone: (002) 72 6812

SECRETARY: C.F. Trappes (Director)

SUBDIVISIONS
Activities are carried out through semi-autonous committees appointed by the Council of the Society and including thereon persons from outside Council.

HISTORY: Founded in 1862

PURPOSE: To promote the development of the agricultural, pastoral, horticultural and industrial resources of the State of Tasmania

MEMBERSHIP: 1,400 (life, associate, annual members)

315 Royal Agricultural Society of Western Australia (Inc.)
Rothmans Building, Royal Showgrounds, Claremont, W.A.
(P.O. Box 135, Claremont 6010)
Telephone: (092) 31 1933

SECRETARY: J.F. Howson (Director and Secretary of Breed Societies)

AFFILIATIONS
52 Agricultural Societies and 38 Breed Societies.

HISTORY: Founded in 1829. First Fair and Cattle Show held in Perth in 1834 and became an annual event. Royal added to the title in 1890.

PURPOSE: To promote the development of the agricultural, horticultural, viticultural and industrial resources of the state. To encourage, promote and sanction the formation of affiliated societies.

PUBLICATIONS
Prize Schedules; Catalogues and Ring Programmes

MEMBERSHIP: 3,366 (life, ordinary, junior members, widows)

316 Royal Australasian College of Physicians
145 Macquarie Street, Sydney, N.S.W. 2000
Telephone: (02) 27 3288

SECRETARY: Dr. B. Roberts

SUBDIVISIONS
New Zealand - N.Z. Committee of the Royal Australasian College of Physicians, Kelvin Chambers, 16 The Terrace, Wellington.
Victoria - Office of the Victorian State Committee, RACS Building, Spring Street, Melbourne, 3000.
Regional committees in all other States, Australian Capital Territory and South-East Asia.

HISTORY: Founded in 1938. Developed out of a non-incorporated body, the Association of Physicians of Australasia, which was of limited membership and had been formed in 1930 to foster among physicians expansion of the scientific knowledge of medicine in Australia and New Zealand.

PURPOSE: To promote a scientific approach to the problems of disease; to bring together physicians for their common benefit; to enhance their services to the nation and to promote medical research.

INTERESTS: The opinion of the College is frequently sought by government departments on questions of medical importance to the community. Since 1963 the College has appointed teams of physicians to lecture at postgraduate courses in advanced medicine in South-East Asia in association with the University of Singapore. Close relations are maintained between the College and various societies formed for the promotion of special branches of medicine.

ACTIVITIES: Two meetings yearly, the Annual Meeting and the Ordinary Meeting. Regular meetings held by regional committees.

PUBLICATIONS
Australian and New Zealand Journal of Medicine

LIBRARY: Library devoted to works on history of medicine, especially in Australia and New Zealand

AWARDS
The College makes grants from its Endowment Funds for the purposes of education and research.

MEMBERSHIP: 2,728 (fellows, members)

317 Royal Australasian College of Radiologists
45 Macquarie Street, Sydney, N.S.W. 2000
Telephone: (02) 27 7797

SECRETARY: Dr. R.J. Mulhearn (Honorary Secretary)

141

SUBDIVISIONS
Sydney, Melbourne, Hobart, Adelaide, Western Australia, Brisbane, New Zealand.
Regional committees in all other States, Australian Capital Territory and South-East Asia.

HISTORY: Founded in 1931

PURPOSE: To promote encourage and provide for the advancement of the study of the science known as radiology (diagnostic and therapeutic) and allied sciences and for the carrying out of research and experimental work in connection with these sciences and to encourage the study and improve the practice of radiology; to conduct examinations and to grant to registered Medical Practitioners diplomas, certificates or other equivalent recognition of special knowledge in radiology; to provide facilities for general conferences and discussion and for consultation amongst members and others, and for furnishing information on all matters relating to any of the said sciences and the practice thereof; to do all other things as may be incidental or may be deemed conductive to the attainment of the objects of the College.

INTERESTS: Radiodiagnosis, radiotherapy, nuclear medicine, organ imaging; physics as applied to these sciences.

ACTIVITIES: Annual General Meeting and Scientific Session

PUBLICATIONS
Australasian Radiology

AWARDS
Baker Fellowship

MEMBERSHIP: 2,728 (fellows, members)

318   Royal Australasian College of Surgeons
Spring Street, Melbourne, Vic. 3000
Telephone: (03) 662 1033

SECRETARY: R.A. Chapman

SUBDIVISIONS
Faculty of Anaesthetists

HISTORY: Founded in 1926; Faculty of Anaesthetists founded 1952.

PURPOSE: To cultivate and maintain the highest principles of surgical practice and ethics; to promote the practice of surgery under proper conditions by securing the improvement of hospitals and hospital methods; to arrange for adequate post-graduate surgical training and to conduct examinations for admission to Fellowships; to promote research in surgery.

ACTIVITIES: Annual general scientific meeting

PUBLICATIONS
Australian and New Zealand Journal of Surgery (quarterly)

LIBRARY: Gordon Craig Library maintained.

AWARDS
George Adlington Syme Oration
Sims Commonwealth Travelling Professorship
Edward Lumley Surgical Research Fellowship
Alan Newton Prize
Gordon Taylor Prize
D.J. Glissan Prize
J.P. Ryan Scholarship (in Sydney)
Michael Ryan Scholarship in Surgery
Hamilton Russell Memorial Lecture
Rupert Downes Memorial Lecture
Archibold Watson Memorial Lecture
Herbert Moran Memorial Lecture in Medical History
Renton Prize
Cecil Gray Prize
Gilbert Brown Prize

MEMBERSHIP: 2650 College fellows; 850 Fellows of the Faculty of Anaesthetists

319   Royal Australasian Ornithologists Union
119 Dryburgh Street, North Melbourne, Vic. 3051
Telephone: (03) 329 9881

SECRETARY: T.R. Garnett

SUBDIVISIONS
Regional Atlas Organisers:-
Western N.S.W. - Mr. G. Clark, 24 Adair Street, Sculling, A.C.T. 2614
Eastern N.S.W. - Mr. R. Cooper, 2 Rofe Crescent, Hornesby Heights, N.S.W. 2077
N.T. - Mr. C. Lendon, CSIRO, P.O. Box 77, Alice Springs, N.T. 5750
Qld. - Mr. C. Corben, Wildlife Research Group (Qld.), P.O. Box 867, Fortitude Valley, Qld. 4006
S.A. - Mrs. H. Laybourne-Smith, Willowdene, 121 Milan Terrace, Aldgate, S.A. 5154
Tas. - Mr. O.M. Newman, 58 Sinclair Avenue, West Moonah, Hobart, Tas. 7009
Vic. - Dr. D. Peters, 19 Rawson Court, Heathmont, Vic. 3135
W.A. - Dr. S.J. Davies, CSIRO Division of Wildlife Research, Clayton Road, Helena Valley, W.A. 6056

AFFILIATIONS
Bird clubs and field naturalist societies in most states.

HISTORY: Founded in 1901

PURPOSE: The study and conservation of Australasian birds.

INTERESTS: Bird observatories; sea bird group.

ACTIVITIES: Annual congress and field outing.

PUBLICATIONS
Emu (quarterly)
R.A.O.U. Newsletter (quarterly)
Checklist of the Birds of Australia. Part I. Non-Passerines
Interim List of Australian Songbirds

LIBRARY: Library maintained in Melbourne.

MEMBERSHIP: Approx. 1200 (fellowships, honorary members, subscribers, ordinary members)

320   Royal Australian Chemical Institute
191 Royal Parade, Parkville, Vic. 3052
Telephone: (03) 347 1577

SECRETARY: P.W. Woodhouse

SUBDIVISIONS
New South Wales - Science House Pty. Ltd., Science Centre, 35 Clarence Street, Sydney 2000 with sections in Broken Hill, Canberra, Newcastle and Wollongong.
Queensland - care of - University of Queensland, St. Lucia, 4067 with sections in North Queensland and Darling Downs. (Dr. E.C.H. Grigg, Secretary)
South Australia - care of - CSIRO Division of Human Nutrition, Kintore Avenue, Adelaide 5000. (C.B. Storer, Secretary)
Tasmania - 8 Delta Avenue, Taroona 7006. (P.J. Phipps, Secretary)
Victoria - P.O. Box 75, Parkville, 3052 (telephone 347 2560) with sections in Geelong, Gippsland and Warrnambool
Western Australia - P.O. Box 6062, Hay Street East, Perth 6000. (M.B. Costello, Secretary)
Divisions - Analytical Chemistry; Cereal Chemistry, Chemical Education; Coordination and Metal Organic Chemistry; Electrochemistry; Industrial and Engineering Chemistry; Organic Chemistry; Physical Chemistry; Polymer Chemistry; Solid State Chemistry.

HISTORY: Founded in 1917; granted Royal Charter in 1932; granted title 'Royal' in 1949.

PURPOSE: The promotion of science and practice of chemistry in all its branches and at all levels through seminars and conferences, bringing eminent scientists from all parts of the world to Australia, arranging courses in continuing education, organising surveys.

INTERESTS: All aspects of chemistry including its branches, biochemistry and chemical engineering, both theoretical and practical, pure and applied in education, research and in industry.

ACTIVITIES: Nearly 300 seminars and meetings per year, about 8 symposia and conferences, usually 2 or 3 'workshops' or intensive refresher courses per year. National convention every four years.

PUBLICATIONS
Proceedings of the Royal Australian Chemical Institute (monthly)
Monthly newsletters by each branch and newsletters at varying intervals by the Analytical, Cereal, Polymer and Solid State Divisions
Abstracts and sometimes complete proceedings of most symposia of most divisions, occasional special publications.

AWARDS
Masson Scholarship (first degree level)
Rennie Medal
H.G. Smith Medal
Leighton Medal
Breyer Medal (Electrochemistry)
Guthrie Medal (Cereal Chemistry)
Polymer Medal
Inorganic Chemistry Award
Grimwade Memorial Lecture
Wolskel Industrial Essay Award
Olle Prize
Montgomery White Lecture
Como Award
R.K. Murphy Medal (Industrial and Engineering Chemistry)
Numerous student prizes

MEMBERSHIP: 6800 (fellows, associates, graduates, subscribers, students)

321   Royal Australian College of Dental Surgeons Inc.
William Bland Centre, 229 Macquarie Street, Sydney, N.S.W. 2000
Telephone: (02) 232 3059

SECRETARY: R. Harris (Honorary Secretary)

SUBDIVISIONS
State and regional committees in Vic., Qld., S.A., W.A. and New Zealand and United Kingdom.

HISTORY: Founded on 14th March, 1965.

PURPOSE: To advance the science and art of dentistry; to encourage study and research in the field of dental science and cognate subjects.

INTERESTS: Dental science and practice; post-graduate education.

ACTIVITIES: Convocations at intervals of 2-3 years. Regional scientific meetings annually.

PUBLICATIONS
Annals of the Royal Australian College of Dental Surgeons (following Convocation)
Regulations covering examinations
Reading lists and study guides for candidates taking examinations
Annual Report

AWARDS
F.G. Christensen Memorial Prize

MEMBERSHIP: 720 (fellows and honorary fellows)

322   Royal Australian College of General Practitioners
43 Lower Fort Street, Sydney, N.S.W. 2000
Telephone: (02) 27 3244, 27 8845

SECRETARY: Dr. F.M. Farrar (Secretary General)

SUBDIVISIONS
New South Wales Faculty - 43 Lower Fort Street, Sydney, 2000
Queensland Faculty - G.P.O. Box 1498, Brisbane, 4001
South Australia Faculty - 183 Tynte Street, North Adelaide, 5006
Tasmanian Faculty - 64 Hampden Road, Battery Point, Tas. 7000.
Victorian Faculty - 'Trawalla', 22 Lascelles Avenue, Toorak, Vic. 3142.
Western Australia - 28 Broadway, Nedlands, 6009

AFFILIATIONS
Family Medicine Programme (4th Floor, 70 Jolimont Street, Jolimont, Vic. 3002)

HISTORY: Founded in 1958

PURPOSE: The advancement of high standards of general practice in Australia

INTERESTS: Educational interests include teaching of undergraduates, vocational training of graduates for general practice, and preparation for the examination for membership of the college and continuing education of practising members. Other interests are the conduct of research in and into general practice, promotion of preventive medicine at the personal doctor-patient level, practice management instruction.

ACTIVITIES: Annual general meeting, council meetings, Australian General Practitioners Convention (3 times per year).

PUBLICATIONS
Australian Family Physician (12 times yearly)

AWARDS
Francis Hardey Faulding Memorial Research Fellowship
Rose-Hunt Award
Prize in community medicine.

MEMBERSHIP: Approximately 3000 (associates, members, fellows)

323   Royal Australian College of Ophthalmologists
27 Commonwealth Street, Sydney, N.S.W. 2010
Telephone: (02) 61 7006

SECRETARY: J.W. Fair (Executive Secretary)

SUBDIVISIONS
Qld. - Dr. W.V. Hefferan, Secretary, 131 Wickham Terrace, Brisbane, Qld. 4000 (Telephone: (07) 221 0360)
W.A. - Dr. I.McL. North, Secretary, 8 Emerald Terrace, West Perth, W.A. 6005 (Telephone: (092) 21 6866)
S.A. - Dr. J.H. Pellew, Secretary, 104 Brougham Place, North Adelaide, S.A. 5006
Tas. - Dr. R. Westmore, Secretary, 66 York Street, Launceston, Tas. 7250 (Telepnone: (003) 31 7951)
Vic. - Dr. L. Jones, Secretary, 17 Roslyn Street, Brighton Beach, Vic. 3186 (Telephone: (03) 96 5556)
N.S.W. - Dr. E.M. Gregory, Secretary, 22 Florence Street, Strathfield, N.S.W. 2135 (Telephone: (02) 602 8066)

HISTORY: The Ophthalmological Society of Victoria was formed in 1899 and the Ophthalmological Society of N.S.W. in 1910. The Ophthalmological Society of Australia (BMA) was founded in 1938. The Australian College of Ophthalmologists was formed from the latter two societies in 1969. The 'Royal' prefix was granted in 1977.

PURPOSE: To encourage the advancement of knowledge and exchange of ideas in ophthalmology, and to maintain high standards of training in ophthalmology as an independent specialty. The College supervises training and examination for membership of the College, a postgraduate specialist qualification recognised by medical boards in Australia and in other countries.

INTERESTS: The College advises statutory authorities in all aspects of vision, blindness and eye health, and educates and warns the public on matters of visual safety. It administers the National Trachoma and Eye Health Program, which screens and treats people for trachoma in remote parts of Australia. Members participate in training and continuing education of ophthalmologists and other medical personnel, and serve in overseas aid programmes, as well as working voluntarily for the National Trachoma and Eye Health Program.

ACTIVITIES: Australian Scientific Meeting; Annual Branch meetings.

PUBLICATIONS
Australian Journal of Ophthalmology (3 times a year)
Ophthalmologists' Exchange (4 times a year)

LIBRARY: At the Royal Victorian Eye and Ear Hospital. N.S.W. Branch library at Sydney Eye Hospital.

AWARDS
The Ophthalmic Research Institute of Australia provides funds for ophthalmic research. The College offers 5 prizes a year to undergraduates in ophthalmology.

MEMBERSHIP: 550 (ordinary, honorary, trainee associate)

324   Royal Australian Institute of Architects
2A Mugga Way, Red Hill, A.C.T. 2603.
Telephone: (062) 73 1548

SECRETARY: D. Kindon (Secretary); D. Bailey (Executive Director)

SUBDIVISIONS
New South Wales Chapter including Newcastle and Country Divisions (A.C. Reynolds, Secretary, 196 Miller Street, North Sydney, N.S.W. 2060).
Victorian Chapter including Geelong Division (P.A. Sorel, Secretary, 30 Howe Crescent, South Melbourne, Vic. 3205).
Queensland Chapter including North Queensland Division (Mrs. P. Parker, Secretary, 243 Coronation Drive, Milton, Qld. 4064).
South Australian Chapter (R.D. Hastwell, Secretary, 191 Melbourne Street, North Adelaide, S.A. 5006).
Western Australian Chapter (Mrs. K. Langoolant, Secretary, 22 Altona Street, West Perth, W.A. 6005).
Tasmanian Chapter (Secretary, 97 Murray Street, Hobart, Tas. 7000).
Australian Capital Territory Chapter (Secretary, P.O. Box 468, Canberra City, A.C.T. 2601).
Northern Territory Committee (Secretary, P.O. Box 1017, Darwin, N.T. 5794).

HISTORY: Founded in 1930

PURPOSE: To advance architecture; to represent the architectural profession; to serve the public by improving the environment and raising living standards; to preserve professional integrity; to serve and promote the interests of the membership; to foster public appreciation of architecture; to advance the standards of arctitectural education, training, practice and research; to recognise and reward architectural merit.

ACTIVITIES: Annual General Meeting, RAIA Convention, Prescribed General Meetings, Chapter and Area Committees (twice yearly), Institute Council Meetings (twice yearly), Chapter Council and Area Committee Meetings (monthly).

PUBLICATIONS
Architecture in Australia (bi-monthly)
RAIA News (quarterly)

AWARDS
RAIA Gold Medal Award
RAIA Silver Medal Award
A.S. Hook Memorial Address
St. Regis - A.C.I. Scholarship
Alcoa of Australia Award
Royal Doulton Research Grant
W.H. Robertson Travel Grant

MEMBERSHIP: 5000 members and 900 student members

325   Royal Australian Nursing Federation
2nd Floor, 132-136 Albert Road, South Melbourne, Vic. 3205
Telephone: (03) 699 8087

SECRETARY: Ms. M.E. Patten (Federal Secretary)

SUBDIVISIONS
Victorian Branch - Miss S. Maddocks (Secretary), 431 St. Kilda Road, Melbourne, 3004.
South Australian Branch - Miss B. Bond (Executive Secretary), Nurses' Memorial Centre, 18 Dequetteville Terrace, Kent Town, S.A. 5067
New South Wales Branch - Mrs. K. Zepps (Secretary), 55 Hereford Street, Glebe, N.S.W. 2037
Tasmanian Branch - Mrs. E.M. Gibson (Secretary), 182 Macquarie Street, Hobart, 7000
Queensland Branch - Miss B. A. Power (Executive Secretary), G.P.O. Box 1289, Brisbane, 4001
Northern Territory Branch - Mrs. J. Wilkinson (Administrative Officer), P.O. Box 3429, Darwin, N.T. 5794; Miss L. Thompson (Secretary, Alice Springs Sub-branch), P.O. Box 882, Alice Springs, N.T. 5750
Western Australian Branch - Miss N. Yelverton (Executive Secretary), P.O. Box 117, West Perth, 6005
Australian Capital Territory Branch - Mrs G. Svoboda (Secretary), Box 418 P.O., Canberra City, 2601

AFFILIATIONS
Council of Australian Government Employee Organizations
Australian Council of Salaried and Professional Associations
International Council of Nurses

HISTORY: Founded in 1922. 'Royal' prefix granted in 1955.

PURPOSE: To protect and promote the industrial and professional interests of nurses; to safeguard and promote the quality of nursing service.

INTERESTS: Industrial relations with specific reference to nurses; health and welfare services and manpower planning with specific references to nursing and nurses.

ACTIVITIES: State and national conferences; annual Federal Council meeting; regular meetings at branch level of councils, special interest groups.

PUBLICATIONS
Australian Nurses' Journal (monthly)
RANF Review (Queensland)

LIBRARY: Technical library at national office.

MEMBERSHIP: 35 771 members

326   Royal Australian Planning Institute
P.O. Box 263, Canberra City, A.C.T. 2601
Telephone: (062) 48 8777

SECRETARY: D.M. Davis (Executive Secretary)

SUBDIVISIONS
Divisions in New South Wales, Victoria, Queensland, South Australia, Western Australia, Tasmania, Australian Capital Territory

AFFILIATIONS
Royal Town Planning Institute
New Zealand Planning Institute

HISTORY: Founded in 1951 by the amalgamation of separate institutes which had developed earlier in some state capitals. In Melbourne, the Planning Institute of Australia was founded in 1944, in Adelaide the Town Planning Institute of South Australia formed in 1947, while in Sydney the Town and Country Institute of Australia commenced in 1934.

PURPOSE: To advance the study of regional and town planning and encourage the development of urban and rural areas in the best interests of the community.

ACTIVITIES: Biennial congress; monthly meetings on a state basis; summer schools.

PUBLICATIONS
Royal Australian Planning Institute Journal (quarterly)
Calendar, divisional journals and newsletters.

MEMBERSHIP: 1,380 (fellows, affiliates, members, students)

327 Royal College of Obstetricians and Gynaecologists, Australian Council
8 LaTrobe Street, Melbourne, Vic. 3000
Telephone: (03) 347 5877

SECRETARY: A.G. Bond (Honorary Secretary)

SUBDIVISIONS
State committees in all states and Australian Capital Territory.

AFFILIATIONS
International Federation of Gynaecology and Obstetrics

HISTORY: Royal College of Obstetricians and Gynaecologists founded in London in 1929, as a Commonwealth body. In 1932 reference committees in each dominion were set up to advise the Council of the College of local conditions. The Australian Regional Council was elected in 1947 and a constitution adopted in 1949. The word 'Regional' was deleted from the title in 1966.

PURPOSE: The encouragement of the study of the advancement of the science and practice of obstetrics and gynaecology.

ACTIVITIES: Australian congress (biennial); advanced courses in obstetrics and gynaecology in alternate states (biennial); scientific meetings in each state, combined New South Wales-Queensland and combined Victoria-Tasmania scientific meetings held annually.

PUBLICATIONS
Australian and New Zealand Journal of Obstetrics and Gynaecology

LIBRARY: Maguire Library housed at Royal Women's Hospital Carlton, Vic.

AWARDS
Fotheringham Research Fellowships
Australian Council, R.C.O.G. Part-time Research Grants
Robert Marshall Allan Prize
Australian Council R.C.O.G. Prize in Obstetrics and Gynaecology (for student at Papuan Medical College)
William Morton Lemmon Travel Grant
Brown-Craig Travelling Fellowship

MEMBERSHIP: 750 (members, fellows)

328 Royal College of Pathologists of Australia
82 Windmill Street, Sydney, N.S.W. 2000
Telephone: (02) 241 2493

SECRETARY: Dr. R.A. Osborn (Hon. Secretary)

HISTORY: Founded in 1956

PURPOSE: To promote the study of the sciences and practice of pathology in relation to medicine; to encourage research in pathology and ancillary sciences; to bring together pathologists for their common benefit and for scientific discussions and demonstrations; and to disseminate knowledge of the principles and practice of pathology in relation to medicine by such means as may be thought fit; to consider and advise as to any course of study and technical training and to diffuse any information calculated to promote and ensure the fitness of persons desirous of qualifying for membership of the College; to institute and provide lectures, seminars, symposia and demonstrations upon sciences pertinent to the practice of pathology for the benefit of members of the College and to invite to admit to such lectures, seminars, symposia and demonstrations persons who are not members of the College on such occasions and on such conditions as shall be deemed expedient by the College.

PUBLICATIONS
Pathology

MEMBERSHIP: 806 (fellows, honorary fellows, associate fellows)

329 Royal Geographical Society of Australasia, Queensland Inc.
177 Ann Street, Brisbane, Qld 4000
Telephone: (07) 221 2074

SECRETARY: J.H. Griffiths

HISTORY: Founded in 1885. Charter 'Royal' granted in 1886.

PURPOSE: The special collection of material for compilation of a reliable geography of Australasia.

ACTIVITIES: Monthly lectures; camps-field work studies for secondary school students in Grades 8 to 12.

PUBLICATIONS
Queensland Geographical Journal
Royal Geographical Society of Australasia, Queensland Incorporated 'Magazine'

AWARDS
Geography prizes to university students
Prizes for Geographical Contests organised by Geography Teachers Association of Queensland.

MEMBERSHIP: Approximately 500 (honorary life, life, ordinary student, overseas, corporate members)

330 Royal Geographical Society of Australasia (S.A. Branch) Incorporated
State Library Building, North Terrace, Adelaide, S.A. 5000

SECRETARY: M.C. Grant

HISTORY: Founded 10th July, 1885

PURPOSE: Advancement of all aspects of geographical science, the collection of historical records of geographical interest and the dissemination of knowledge relating to these by means of public lectures and publications.

ACTIVITIES: Monthly general meetings, guest lectures, occasional special purpose meetings of seminars.

PUBLICATIONS
Proceedings of the Royal Geographical Society of Australasia (S.A. Branch) Incorporated (annually)
Occasional publications (e.g. *To the Desert with Stuart* ed. K. Peake-Jones)

LIBRARY: Extensive collection of 16th to 20th century geographical works, with emphasis upon 19th century and Australiana. Includes a wide range of bibliography and military history. Rare books and manuscripts in process of cataloguing. Journals include many foreign language publications.

AWARDS
John Lewis Prizes and Medals (Bronze medals annually to students and gold medal occasionally to a notable geographer)

MEMBERSHIP: Approximately 300 (ordinary, student, country, corresponding, honorary life, institutional members)

331   Royal Historical Society of Victoria
14th Floor, City Mutual Life Building, 459 Collins Street, Melbourne, Vic. 3000
Telephone: (03) 62 1929

SECRETARY: Mrs. E.V. Pullin

SUBDIVISIONS
Bendigo Branch

AFFILIATIONS
135 local historical societies.

HISTORY: Founded 1909 with which is incorporated the Victorian Branch of the Royal Geographical Society of Australasia (incorporated 1920). In 1952, Royal Charter was granted.

PURPOSE: To encourage the study of history, especially of Australian history. To promote the complication and presentation of authentic records relating in Australia.

ACTIVITIES: Biennial conference, historical convention biennially on alternate years; annual seminar for local historical societies; monthly lectures.

PUBLICATIONS
Victorian Historical Journal (quarterly)
Indexes to magazines; newsletter (10 months in year).

LIBRARY: Library maintained for use of members and for research by public.

MEMBERSHIP: 1,200 (metropolitan, student, country, family, corporate members, schools, libraries)

332   Royal Horticultural Society of New South Wales
G.P.O. Box 4728, Sydney, N.S.W. 2001

SUBDIVISIONS
Floral Art Section
Indoor Plant Section
Geranium and Garden Perennial Section

AFFILIATIONS
98 affiliated Societies.

HISTORY: Founded in 1862 as the Horticultural Society of New South Wales. 'Royal' prefix granted in 1931.

PURPOSE: The encouragement, improvement and development of horticulture in New South Wales.

ACTIVITIES: Monthly meetings; section meetings held to cater for the more specialised interests of members.

PUBLICATIONS
Better Gardening (quarterly)
Horticultural Guide and Standard Reference Book

LIBRARY: Library of approximately 200 volumes.

AWARDS
Walter G. Gates Memorial Medal
John Thomas Baptist Medal
Certificate of preliminary commendation
Award of Merit

MEMBERSHIP: 510 (individual, country, joint, family, honorary, life members,

333 Royal Meteorological Society, Australian Branch
Clunies Ross Memorial Foundation, 191 Royal Parade, Parkville, Vic.
3058
Telephone: (03) 347 6077

SECRETARY: P.G. Price (Bureau of Meteorology, Box 1289K, Melbourne, Vic. 3001)

HISTORY: Founded by action of Fellows of the Royal Meteorological Society residing in Australia, 1973.

PURPOSE: To advance meteorology and related sciences.

INTERESTS: Atmospheric and oceanographic physics, fluid mechanics, geography, geomorphology, biometeorology.

ACTIVITIES: Monthly meetings, conferences arranged as need arises.

PUBLICATIONS
Journal of the Royal Meteorological Society (quarterly)
Weather (monthly)

MEMBERSHIP: 300 (fellows, foreign members, students, corporate members)

334 Royal Society of New South Wales
Science Centre, 35 Clarence Street, Sydney, N.S.W. 2000
Telephone: (02) 29 1496

SECRETARY: M.J. Puttock (General); Mrs. M. Krysko v. Tryst (Editorial)

SUBDIVISIONS
New England (University of New England)
South Coast (Wollongong University)

HISTORY: Originated in 1821 as the Philosophical Society of Australasia. After an interval of inactivity it was resuscitated in 1850 under the name Australian Philosophical Society. In 1856 the name was changed to Philosophical Society of New South Wales. In 1866 the Society assumed its present title and was incorporated by Act of Parliament of New South Wales in 1881.

PURPOSE: Promotion of science, art, literature, and philosophy.

INTERESTS: Astronomy, botany, chemistry, geology, geophysics, geochemistry, mathematics and physics.

ACTIVITIES: General monthly meetings open to the public, symposia, summer schools for senior secondary school students. Liversidge Lecture (chemistry), Pollock Memorial Lecture (mathematics), Clarke Memorial Lecture (geology).

PUBLICATIONS
Journal and Proceedings of the Royal Society of New South Wales

LIBRARY: Serials library of 50,000 volumes, collection of rare books.

AWARDS
James Cook Medal
Walter Burfitt Prize
W.B. Clarke Medal
Royal Society of New South Wales Medal
Edgeworth David Medal
Archibald D. Olle Prize

MEMBERSHIP: 452 (honorary, ordinary, life, associate members)

335   Royal Society of Queensland
University of Queensland, St. Lucia, Qld. 4067.
Telephone: (072) 70 0111

SECRETARY: Dr. D. Doley

SUBDIVISIONS
Townsville

HISTORY: Founded in 1859 as Queensland Philosophical Society

PURPOSE: The furtherance of the natural and applied sciences especially by means of original research.

ACTIVITIES: A minimum of four general meetings held March to November. Symposium held annually in conjunction with ANZAAS Qld Division.

PUBLICATIONS
Proceedings of the Royal Society of Queensland
Occassional Proceedings of Symposia

LIBRARY: Extensive library maintained

AWARDS
Queensland Science Teachers Association Science Contest

MEMBERSHIP: 320 (honorary life, ordinary, life, associate members)

336   Royal Society of South Australia Incorporated
State Library Building, North Terrace, Adelaide, S.A. 5000
Telephone: (08) 223 5360

SECRETARY: Dr. B.J. Cooper

HISTORY: Founded as Adelaide Philosophical Society in 1853; granted Royal Charter in 1880 and name changed to Royal Society of South Australia.

PURPOSE: To provide a forum, source of publication and a scientific library for contributors to many disciplines of the natural sciences.

INTERESTS: Botany, zoology, geology, palaeontology, anthropology, soil science

ACTIVITIES: Regular ordinary meetings held monthly April to November.

PUBLICATIONS
Transactions of the Royal Society of South Australia

LIBRARY: Extensive library of scientific serials maintained

AWARDS
Scientific Research and Endowment Fund
Verco Medal

MEMBERSHIP: 351 (fellows, honorary fellows, life fellows)

337   Royal Society of Tasmania
Tasmanian Museum, Argyle Street, Hobart, Tas.
(G.P.O. Box 1166M, Hobart, 7001)
Telephone: (002) 23 2696

SECRETARY: D. Gregg

SUBDIVISIONS
Northern Branch, Queen Victoria Museum, Launceston, Tas. 7250

HISTORY: Founded in 1843

PURPOSE: The advancement of science

INTERESTS: Science generally and Tasmanian history

ACTIVITIES: Monthly meetings; irregular conferences.

PUBLICATIONS
Papers and Proceedings of the Royal Society of Tasmania (annual)

LIBRARY: Library housed at University of Tasmania

AWARDS
Royal Society of Tasmania Medal
Clive Lord Memorial Medal
R.M. Johnston Memorial Medal

MEMBERSHIP: 536 (ordinary, life, associate, honorary members)

338 Royal Society of Victoria
9 Victoria Street, Melbourne, Vic. 3000
Telephone: (03) 347 4728

SECRETARY: Prof. A.B. Wardrop

HISTORY: The Philosophical Institute of Victoria was formed in 1855 by the amalgamation of the Victorian Institute for the Advancement of Science and the Philosophical Society of Victoria, both of which were founded in 1854. In 1859 the Society's hall was built and the title 'Royal' was bestowed.

PURPOSE: The advancement of science.

INTERESTS: Science in general with some leaning towards the natural sciences (geological and biological) and education in science.

ACTIVITIES: Monthly meetings from March to December; symposia

PUBLICATIONS
Proceedings of the Royal Society of Victoria

LIBRARY: Extensive library maintained

AWARDS
Royal Society of Victoria Medal

MEMBERSHIP: 640 (honorary, life, ordinary members)

339 Royal Society of Western Australia Inc.
Western Australian Museum, Francis Street, Perth, W.A. 6000
Telephone: (092) 28 4411

SECRETARY: M.W. and G. Perry (Joint Honorary Secretaries)

HISTORY: Founded in 1897 as the Mueller Botanical Society. In 1903 name changed to the Western Australian Natural History Society and in 1909 to Western Australian Natural History and Science Society. Present title was adopted in 1914.

PURPOSE: To promote and assist in the advancement of science in all its branches

INTERESTS: Natural history of Western Australia, in particular geology, botany, zoology and archaeology.

ACTIVITIES: Monthly meetings, March to December.

PUBLICATIONS
Journal of the Royal Society of Western Australia (published 4 times per year)
Proceedings of the Royal Society of Western Australia (monthly newsletter)

LIBRARY: Library of 6,000 volumes maintained

AWARDS
Royal Society Medal (awarded every 4 years)

MEMBERSHIP: 265 (ordinary, honorary, associate members)

340 Royal Zoological Society of New South Wales
Taronga Zoo, Mosman, N.S.W. 2088
Telephone: (02) 969 7336

PURPOSE: To promote and advance the science of zoology; to protect, preserve and study the indigenous and introduced animals of Australia.

ACTIVITIES: Monthly council meetings; monthly meetings of each section.

PUBLICATIONS
Australian Zoologist
Koolewong
Proceedings of the Royal Zoological Society of New South Wales

LIBRARY: Library maintained at Society's rooms, Toronga Zoo.

MEMBERSHIP: 2,224 (ordinary, associate, junior members)

341 Royal Zoological Society of South Australia, Inc.
Frome Road, Adelaide, S.A. 5000
Telephone: (08) 267 3255

SECRETARY: W.E. Lancaster (Director)

HISTORY: Established in 1878 as the South Australian Acclimatization Society. The Zoological Gardens were officially opened in 1883.

PURPOSE: The establishment and maintenance of Zoological Gardens and other areas and the procuring of specimens thereof; the establishment and maintenance of colonies of native animals and birds whose numbers are becoming seriously depleted in South Australia; the holding of periodical meetings and the publication of reports and proceedings of the Society and such other activities as may be desirable for the furthering and spreading knowledge of zoology; co-operation with other learned societies and organizations.

ACTIVITIES: Council meetings; annual general meeting; periodic meetings of members.

LIBRARY: Library maintined and available to members.

MEMBERSHIP: 410 (honorary life, life ordinary and junior members)

342 Rural Media Association of South Australia
Stock Journal Publishers Ltd., 11 Cannon Street, Adelaide, S.A.
(Box 2249 G.P.O., Adelaide, 5001)
Telephone: (08) 51 4481

SECRETARY: D.L. East

AFFILIATIONS
Australian Council of Agricultural Journalists
Rural Press Club (Queensland)
Farm Writers and Broadcasters Society (New South Wales and Victoria)

HISTORY: Founded 25th July, 1972

PURPOSE: To provide a forum for agricultural journalists.

ACTIVITIES: Monthly meetings

MEMBERSHIP: 48 (full members)

343   Science Teachers Association of N.S.W.
8 Calbina Road, Earlwood, N.S.W. 2206
Telephone: (02) 78 4330

SECRETARY: Dr. J.N. Pendlebury

SUBDIVISIONS
Albury, Armidale, Bathurst and Mitchell Region, Illawarra, Mid-North Coast, North West, Western.

AFFILIATIONS
Australian Science Teachers Association
Joint Council of N.S.W. Professional Teachers Associations

HISTORY: Reformed in 1949

PURPOSE: To promote and stimulate the study and teaching of science; to create a fellowship amongst those engaged in science education; to provide a meeting ground and forum for members of the science teaching profession in its various fields; to encourage and provide for the publication of learned papers.

ACTIVITIES: Conferences, general meetings, seminars, workshops, social gatherings.

PUBLICATIONS
Science Education News

MEMBERSHIP: 1000 (full, associate, students)

344   Science Teachers Association of Queensland
care of- Brisbane Education Centre, P.O.Box 84, North Brisbane, Qld. 4000
Telephone: (07) 349 7033 ext 420

SECRETARY: Dr. I.S. Costin

SUBDIVISIONS
Branches at Toowoomba, Rockhampton and Townsville.

HISTORY: Founded in 1945

PURPOSE: To co-operate with all those concerned in the education process; to consider the place and scope of science in education and to give specific attention and education in science.

ACTIVITIES: Conference of Science Teachers Association of Queensland (CONSTAQ) held annually in August. Monthly meetings.

PUBLICATIONS
STAQ Newsletter (monthly Feb.-Nov.)
Queensland Science Teacher (4 per year)

LIBRARY: Library housed at Brisbane Education Centre

AWARDS
Science contest for school students.

MEMBERSHIP: 430 (full members, students, associates)

345 Science Teachers Association of Tasmania
P.O. Box 477, G.P.O., Launceston, Tas. 7250.
Telephone: (003) 31 3333

SECRETARY: P.S. Manchester

SUBDIVISIONS
Northern, North-west, Southern

AFFILIATIONS
Laboratory Technicians Association of Tasmania
Australian Science Teachers Association

HISTORY: Founded in 1948

PURPOSE: To foster an interest in Science Education and to consider the problems of the teaching of scientific subjects; to provide a forum for discussion and exchange of information on Science Education and modern developments in the field of science; to act as an advisory body on relevant matters to the Schools Board of Tasmania; to publish the Science Teachers' Association of Tasmania Newsletter 'Static', and in this, and other ways to keep members abreast of development in Science Education and in the field of science; to promote research into the teaching of Science and to encourage members to undertake research in the fields of science and science education; to conduct an annual 'Science Talent Search' among school children in Tasmania; to investigate matters of interest to science teachers such as conditions of teaching, loading, laboratory design, and the development and introduction of new science courses; to pursue such activities as the State Council of the Association shall from time to time deem fit.

ACTIVITIES: State Council Meetings (7 per year); branch meetings, CONSTAT Conferences (yearly)

PUBLICATIONS
S.T.A.T.I.C.

AWARDS
Science Talent Search Contest

MEMBERSHIP: 110 (metropolitan, country, student, honorary life membership)

346 Science Teachers Association of Victoria
191 Royal Parade, Parkville, Vic. 3052
Telephone: (03) 347 2537

SECRETARY: G.P. White

SUBDIVISIONS
Branches in the following districts - Ballarat, Gippsland, Glenelg (Hamilton), Goulburn Valley (Shepparton), Mid-Murray (Swan Hill), North-Eastern (Benalla), Western District (Warrnambool), Wimmera (Horsham), Mallee (Mildura).

HISTORY: Founded in 1943

PURPOSE: To assist science teachers and further all aspects of science education.

ACTIVITIES: Monthly council meetings; annual general meeting; organised conferences relevant to science.

PUBLICATIONS
Lab Talk (6 issues per year)
Contact (5 issues per year)

AWARDS
Annual science talent search, open to all school children (awards made).

MEMBERSHIP: 1230 (individuals, associates 'A', schools, libraries)

347 Society of Automotive Engineers - Australasia
National Science Centre, 191 Royal Parade, Parkville, Vic. 3052
Telephone: (03) 347 2220

SECRETARY: J. E. R. d'Helin (General Secretary)

SUBDIVISIONS
Tasmanian Division - Mr. J.S. McKenna, Secretary, G.P.O. Box 1252N, Hobart, Tas. 7001
(Telephone: (002) 345 8111).
Queensland Division - Mr. D.J. Wagner, Secretary, P.O. Box 1891, Brisbane, Qld. 4001 (Telephone:
(07) 221 1511).
New South Wales Division - Mr. R.H. Sims, Secretary, 50 Cross Street, Baulkham Hills, N.S.W. 2153
(Telephone: (02) 290 0123).
New Zealand Division - Mr. J. Murphy, Secretary, IBM House, 155 The Terrace, Wellington, N.Z.
(Telephone: 55 5188).
South Australian Division - Mr. M. Mathews, Secretary, 3 Fern Avenue, Tea Tree Gully, S.A. 5091
(Telephone: (08) 51 0301).
Victorian Division - Mr. G. Crawford, Secretary, 191 Royal Parade, Parkville, Vic. 3052 (Telephone:
(03) 347 2220).
Western Australian Division - Mr. D. Thomson, Secretary, P.O. Box 47, Mosman Park, W.A. 6012
(Telephone: (092) 35 1141).

HISTORY: Founded in 1927 as the Australian Institute of Automotive Engineers. Title changed in 1946
to the Institute of Automotive and Aeronautical Engineers and the present title adopted in 1966.

PURPOSE: To promote, encourage and co-ordinate the science and practice of automotive aeronautical
and transportation engineering in all its ramifications.

ACTIVITIES: Monthly lecture meetings of all Divisions and Groups; frequent seminars and series of
lectures in most capital cities. Annual national conventions. Irregular international conferences with
overseas societies or institutions; technical and other committee meetings.

PUBLICATIONS
SAE - Australasia (bi-monthly)
SAE - Australasia News (monthly)
SAE - Australasia Recommended Practices (technical manuals)
SAE - Australasia Technical Paper Abstracts
SAE - Australasia Publications and Technical Papers Index

LIBRARY: Reference library maintained for members.

AWARDS
Rodda Award
Batchelor Award
O'Shannessy Award
Hartnett Award
Gas Turbine Award

MEMBERSHIP: Approximately 2,750 (members, associate members, associates, students, affiliated
companies)

348 Society of Chemical Industry of Victoria
Clunies Ross House, 191 Royal Parade, Parkville, Vic. 3052
Telephone: (03) 347 7911

HISTORY: The oldest chemical society in Australia. Founded in 1900

PURPOSE: To further the work and image of the chemical and allied industries in Australia, to afford
its members opportunities of meeting and discussing matters connected with applied and industrial
chemistry, generally to advance the cause of the chemical industry in Victoria.

ACTIVITIES: Technical meetings throughout the year

AWARDS
Society of Chemical Industry Awards (to students)
Plant-of-the-Year Award

MEMBERSHIP: 273 (private, company, life, honorary, retired members)

349 Society of Dyers and Colourists of Australia and New Zealand

Ciba - Geigy Australia Limited, Box 9, Northland Centre, Preston, Vic. 3072
Telephone: (03) 480 2533

SECRETARY: A.N. Lawson (Hon. General Secretary)

SUBDIVISIONS
Vic. (including Geelong Sub-Section), N.S.W., S.A., W.A., New Zealand (Auckland, Christchurch).

HISTORY: Founded in 1932

PURPOSE: To promote the advancement of science and technology, especially in the theory and practice of the tinctorial arts.

ACTIVITIES: Monthly meeting in most sections; biennial conferences.

PUBLICATIONS
Textile Journal of Australia

MEMBERSHIP: 720 (honorary; ordinary, country, junior members)

350 Society for Growing Australian Plants

21 Robb Street, Revesby, N.S.W. 2212
Telephone: (02) 771 4082

SECRETARY: R.T. Page

SUBDIVISIONS
New South Wales Region - R.T. Page (Secretary), 21 Robb Street, Revesby, 2212
Queensland Region - Mrs D. Brown (Sectretary), 79 Birley Street, off Wickham Terrace, Brisbane, 4000
Victorian Region - Miss E.R. Bowman (Secretary), 4 Homebush Crescent, Hawthorn, 3123
Tasmanian Region - Mrs. D.H. Gill (Secretary), Box 1353 P, G.P.O., Hobart, Tas. 7001
Canberra Region - Mrs. J. Benyon (Secretary), P.O. Box 207, Civic Square, A.C.T. 2608
South Australian Region - Mr. A. Peart (Secretary), Box 1592, G.P.O., Adelaide, S.A. 5001
Western Australian Wildflower Society (Inc.) - Mrs. K. Edmonds (Secretary), P.O. Box 64, Nedlands, W.A. 6009

AFFILIATIONS
Western Australian Wildlife Society (Inc.)

HISTORY: Founded in 1957

PURPOSE: To preserve Australian native flora by propagation and cultivation, either in its native state or in private gardens, or public places.

INTERESTS: Growing Australian plants; excursions of botanical interest; provision of advice on propagation and cultivation of native flora; planting of trees and shrubs in parks and reserves.

ACTIVITIES: Biennial conference; monthly meetings of regional societies.

PUBLICATIONS
Australian Plants

MEMBERSHIP: 7 regional societies

351   Society of Hospital Pharmacists of Australia
34 Hopetown Grove, Ivanhoe, Vic.
(P.O.Box 125, Heidelberg, 3084)
Telephone: (03) 45 0411 (extn 575)

SECRETARY: B. R. Miller

SUBDIVISIONS
State branches in each capital city throughout Australia.

HISTORY: Founded in 1942

PURPOSE: To build a strong, united, nation-wide organization of professional hospital pharmacists whoare dedicated to the principle of achieving and maintaining the highest professional pharmaceuticalstandards in Australia.

INTERESTS: Practical interest in all facets of hospital pharmacy involvement, i.e. dispensing, drug information,nursing education; post graduate education for hospital pharmacists; viz. diploma course, fellowship course based on administrative roles and clinical pharmacology.

ACTIVITIES: State branch conferences held biennially , federal conferences in the alternate year. State branch meetings held monthly, federal council meetings twice per annum.

PUBLICATIONS
Australian Journal of Hospital Pharmacy (published 4 times per year)

AWARDS
Squibb Fellowship Bursary
Abbott Laboratories Fellowship Bursary
Roche Scholarship
Boots Travel Fellowship
Travenol Award
David Bull Laboratories Award
Sigma Prize
Burroughs Wellcome Prize
Merck Sharp and Dohme Travel Award
Lilly International Fellowship

MEMBERSHIP: 852 (members, fellows, students, trainees)

352   Society of Leather Technologists and Chemists
Austral Finishes Pty. Ltd., 19 Wilson Street, Botany, N.S.W. 2019

SECRETARY: J.Gotch

AFFILIATIONS
Leather Guild
American Leather Chemists Association

HISTORY: Founded in 1897 as the International Society of Leather Trades Chemists, name changed to Society of Leather Trades Chemists in 1951, and in 1972 changed to the Society of Leather Technologists and Chemists.

PURPOSE: To promote and publish research and discussion into the chemistry of leather manufacture and all things pertaining to this.

ACTIVITIES: About 6 meetings per year

MEMBERSHIP: 71 (full, associate, local associate members)

353   **Society of Licensed Aircraft Engineers and Technologists (Aust.)**
P.O. Box 339, Mascot, N.S.W. 2020
Telephone: (02) 522 7138

SECRETARY: A.N. Campbell

AFFILIATIONS
International Federation of Airworthiness (foundation member)

HISTORY: Founded in 1950 as a branch of Society of Licensed Aircraft Engineers in U.K. Reformed as an autonomous Australian society in 1958.

PURPOSE: The advancement of the aircraft engineer; to improve the safety of aviation.

ACTIVITIES: Monthly council meetings; technical meetings; conducting aircraft engineering training courses.

PUBLICATIONS
Aircraft

AWARDS
Annual apprentice prize to Sydney Technical College.

MEMBERSHIP: 160 (fellows, associate fellows, members, associates, companions, students, affiliated companies)

354   **Society for Social Responsibility in Science (A.C.T.)**
P.O. Box 48, O'Connor, A.C.T. 2601
Telephone: (062) 46 5682

SECRETARY: Dr. R.J. Bartell

HISTORY: Founded in 1970

PURPOSE: To alert natural and social scientists, the public and decision-makers to the social consequences and implications of scientific developments.

PUBLICATIONS
Papers and submissions published at frequent intervals.

MEMBERSHIP: 130 (ordinary, student, family, library members)

355   **Soil and Water Conservation Society of Victoria**
593-615 Springvale Road, Springvale South, Vic.
(Box 104, Springvale 3171)
Telephone: (03) 89 0711

SECRETARY: P.F. FitzSimons

AFFILIATIONS
Natural Resources Conservation League of Victoria

HISTORY: Founded on 13 April, 1972.

PURPOSE: To promote the investigation of soil and water conservation problems and to present the views of the Society to the League for appropriate action; to bring together farmers, officers of the Soil Conservation Authority and other Government bodies, academics and teachers, persons operating in financial and commercial fields, and any other persons who are interested in soil and water conservation; the Committee shall arrange activities to further the objects of the Society as may be expedient.

ACTIVITIES: Annual and Special General Meetings, Committee Meetings two to four times per year, field days, seminars and film or lecture nights.

PUBLICATIONS
Soil and Water Conservation Society Newsletter

MEMBERSHIP: 500 (ordinary, associate, family)

356 South Australian Ornithological Association
South Australian Museum, North Terrace, Adelaide, S.A. 5000

AFFILIATIONS
Royal Australasian Ornithologists Union

HISTORY: Founded in 1899; journal first published in 1914.

PURPOSE: To promote the study and conservation of Australian birds; recording the results of research in regard to all aspects of bird life.

INTERESTS: Ornithology, conservation, legislation.

ACTIVITIES: Monthly meetings; day trips to localities of interest; weekend camp-outs

PUBLICATIONS
South Australian Ornithologist (twice yearly)
Quarterly newsletter

LIBRARY: Extensive library of Australian and overseas ornithological journals and books.

MEMBERSHIP: 490 (honorary, life, ordinary, junior members)

357 South Australian Science Teachers Association
163A Greenhill Road, Parkside, S.A. 5063.

SECRETARY: B.J. Burford

SUBDIVISIONS
Local Branches - Riverland, Northern and Eyre Penninsula, Lower North, Mid North, Yorke Penninsula, South-east

HISTORY: Founded in 1941

PURPOSE: To promote science teaching

ACTIVITIES: Conference (annual), branch conferences and meetings.

PUBLICATIONS
SASTA Journal
SASTA Newsletter

AWARDS
Annual science fair for students

MEMBERSHIP: 850 (individual, associate, corporate, student)

358 Standards Association of Australia
Standards House, 80 Arthur Street, North Sydney, N.S.W.
(P.O. Box 458, North Sydney, 2060)
Telephone: (02) 929 6022

SUBDIVISIONS
Victorian Branch, Clunies Ross House, 191 Royal Parade, Parkville, 3052
Queensland Branch, 447 Upper Edward Street, Brisbane, 4000
South Australian Branch, 11 Bagot Street, North Adelaide, 5006
Tasmanian Branch, 181 Collins Street, Hobart, 7000
Western Australian Branch, Science House, 10 Hooper Street, West Perth, 6005
Newcastle Branch, Howard Smith Chambers, Watt Street, Newcastle, N.S.W. 2300

HISTORY: The two associations, Australian Commonwealth Engineering Standards Association, founded in 1922, and the Australian Commonwealth Association of Simplified Practice founded in 1927, were amalgamated in 1929 as the Standards Association of Australia.

PURPOSE: To prepare and promote the general adoption of standards relating to structures, commodities, materials, practices, operations, matters and things and to undertake activities ancillary to this particular purpose.

ACTIVITIES: Conferences and meetings; annual council meeting. Approximately 1,500 meetings each year of technical committees in the fields indicated above.

PUBLICATIONS
Australian Standards (new and revised as published from time to time)
Annual List of Australian Standards
Annual report, monthly information sheet.

LIBRARY: Libraries maintained

MEMBERSHIP: 5200 subscribing members, 10 000 committee members

359   Statistical Society of Australia
A.N.U. Survey Research Centre, P.O. Box 4, Canberra, A.C.T. 2601
Telephone: (062) 49 4400

SECRETARY: K.R.W. Brewer

SUBDIVISIONS
Branches in N.S.W., Canberra, Vic., S.A., W.A.

HISTORY: Founded in 1962.

PURPOSE: To further the study and application of statistical theory and methods in all branches of learning and enterprise.

ACTIVITIES: Local branch meetings. Statistical Conference held every two years. N.S.W. Branch arranges a two-day Symposium annually.

PUBLICATIONS
Australian Journal of Statistics
Statistical Society of Australia Newsletter

AWARDS
Branches issue their own prizes

MEMBERSHIP: 700 (honorary life, ordinary, student)

360   Sydney University Chemical Engineering Association
Department of Chemical Engineering, University of Sydney, Sydney, N.S.W. 2006
Telephone: (02) 660 8455

HISTORY: Founded in 1952

PURPOSE: To encourage professional development and social contacts amongst chemical engineering graduates and other professional people of similar interests.

INTERESTS: Chemical engineering, economics

ACTIVITIES: Two symposia per year

MEMBERSHIP: 535 (life)

361   Sydney University Chemical Society
School of Chemistry, University of Sydney, N.S.W. 2006
Telephone: (02) 660 0522 (extn 2732)

HISTORY: Founded in 1929

PURPOSE: To foster and maintain an interest in pure chemistry among its members by reading papers on original research topics and holding general discussions on outstanding chemical problems.

PUBLICATIONS
Monthly newsletter

MEMBERSHIP: 220 (original, ordinary, honorary, life members)

362   Sydney University Medical Society
Blackburn Building, D06, University of Sydney, Sydney, N.S.W. 2006
Telephone: (02) 660 0522 (extn 2482)

HISTORY: Founded in 1886

PURPOSE: To provide a common meeting ground for teachers, graduates and undergraduates in the Faculty of Medicine; to further the interests of members and to represent their views; to maintain the traditions of the University and the Faculty; to develop scientific and general knowledge; to promote and maintain co-operation between medical students and medical societies throughout Australia and internationally.

ACTIVITIES: Council meetings; annual general meeting; A.M.S.A. Convention (held conjointly with other medical societies throughout Australasia); Lambie-Dew Oration.

PUBLICATIONS
S.U.M.S. Journal (annually)
Senior Year Book (annually)
Innominate (about 6 per annum)

AWARDS
Clinical Years Bursary Fund
War Memorial Library Fund
'Robin May' Memorial Prize

MEMBERSHIP: 1,493 undergraduate members

363   Sydney University Psychological Society
Psychology Department, Box 80, The Union, University of Sydney, Sydney, N.S.W. 2006.
Telephone: (02) 660 0522 ext. 2864

SECRETARY: J. Patrick

PURPOSE: To promote interaction between those interested in psychology, to provide a forum for discussions, to provide machinery for staff-student interaction, and social functions.

ACTIVITIES: Monthly meeting held during university terms

MEMBERSHIP: 250

364 Sydney University Veterinary Society

Faculty of Veterinary Science, University of Sydney, Sydney, N.S.W.
2006

SECRETARY: Ms A. Wise

AFFILIATIONS
Australian Veterinary Students Association

PURPOSE: To provide a common meeting ground for veterinary graduates and undergraduates.

ACTIVITIES: Annual Australian Veterinary Students Association Conference

PUBLICATIONS
Centaur (annually)

AWARDS
Two prizes for entries in 'Centaur'.

MEMBERSHIP: 400 (full, honorary members)

365 Tasmanian Conservation Trust Incorporated

102 Bathurst Street, Hobart, Tas.
(G.P.O. Box 684G, Hobart, 7001)
Telephone: (002) 34 5543

SECRETARY: Dr. J. Kirkpatrick

SUBDIVISIONS
Southern Branch - Mr. J. Swain, care of - G.P.O. Box 684G, Hobart, Tas. 7001.
Northern Branch - Mrs. M. Cameron, care of - P.O. Box 1072, Launceston, Tas. 7230.
Circular-Head Branch - Mr. A.G. Rockliff, care of - P.O. Box 259, Smithton, Tas. 7330.
North West Branch - Miss C. Kerslake, 18 Surrey Street, Devonport, Tas. 7310.

HISTORY: Founded in 1968; full time director appointed in 1974.

PURPOSE: To make every effort to ensure that the land, water and other resources are used with wisdom and forsight; to foster and actively to assist in the conservation of distinctive fauna and important natural and archaeological features; to take action in the interests of promoting conservation

INTERESTS: Nature conservation, environmental control, urban development, state planning.

ACTIVITIES: Monthly meetings of state council, branches, committees and executives. Annual General Meeting, annual symposium, field trips.

PUBLICATIONS
Circulars (10 per year), symposium papers, incidental reports, government submissions

MEMBERSHIP: 700 (ordinary, family, student, subscriber, life, honorary members)

366 Tasmanian University Agricultural Science Society

Agricultural Faculty, University of Tasmania, Box 252, G.P.O., Hobart, Tas. 7001.
Telephone: (002) 23 0561

SECRETARY: Miss C.E. Young

HISTORY: Founded in 1962

PURPOSE: To act as a unifying force among the students and to promote cooperation and exchange of ideas with students of this and other universities; to effect formal liaison with staff members of the Faculty; to cater for the social interests of the students generally.

ACTIVITIES: Two ordinary meetings per year and annual general meeting.

MEMBERSHIP: 45

367   Technical Association of the Australian and New Zealand Pulp and Paper Industry
see Appita

368   Telecommunication Society of Australia
Box 4050, G.P.O., Melbourne, Vic. 3001
Telephone: (03) 630 7650

SECRETARY: N.G. Ross

SUBDIVISIONS
Branches in all capital cities.

HISTORY: Founded in 1874 as the Telegraph Electrical Society, Melbourne. Name changed to Postal Electrical Society of Victoria in 1908 and Telecommunication Society of Australia in 1959.

PURPOSE: The diffusion of knowledge of the telecommunication, broadcasting and television services of Australia by means of lectures, discussions, publications and other means.

ACTIVITIES: Meetings and lectures in state capital cities and country centres, arranged by state branches

PUBLICATIONS
Telecommunication Journal of Australia (3 per annum)
Australian Telecommunication Research (2 per annum)
Australian Telecommunication Monographs (occasional)

AWARDS
Prizes issued to outstanding students of telecommunication oriented courses (Certificate courses at Colleges of Advanced Education)

MEMBERSHIP: Approximately 7000 (ordinary members, subscribers, associate, life members)

369   Television Society of Australia
Box 1712 P, G.P.O., Melbourne, Vic. 3001.
Telephone: (03) 231 1528

SECRETARY: A. J. Hardess (Hon. Secretary)

SUBDIVISIONS
Branches in Melbourne, Sydney and Perth.

AFFILIATIONS
Educational Television Association of Australia
Royal Television Society of Great Britain

HISTORY: Founded in Melbourne in 1950

PURPOSE: To assist in the development of television as an art.

ACTIVITIES: Monthly meetings of the Council of the Society; bi-monthly meeting at the Sciences Club.

PUBLICATIONS
Television
Penguin Awards (incorporating the Shell Award for Television Documentary and A.F.D.C. Awards)

LIBRARY: Library maintained

MEMBERSHIP: 700 (patron, honorary, ordinary members, associates)

370 Textile Society of Australia
594 St. Kilda Road, Melbourne, Vic. 3004
Telephone: (03) 51 0221

SECRETARY: I. Steuart

SUBDIVISIONS
Victorian Country Liaison Officers - J.S. Gregory (Wangaratta), Mario Bettanin (Shepparton).

HISTORY: Founded in 1945

PURPOSE: To promote the profession and practice of textile technology in the general interest of its members and the textile industry.

ACTIVITIES: Monthly meetings of members; monthly meetings of Committee of Management.

PUBLICATIONS
Textile Journal of Australia

LIBRARY: Personal library maintained at office.

AWARDS
Cash awards to most successful student annually at Melbourne College of Textiles and at Gordon Institute of Technology (Textile College)

MEMBERSHIP: 279 (full members, honorary life members, country members, junior or student members)

371 Timber Development Association (N.S.W.) Limited
525 Elizabeth Street, Sydney, N.S.W.
(P.O. Box M34, Sydney Mail Exchange, 2012)
Telephone: (02) 699 1388

SECRETARY: L.H. Martin (Executive Director)

HISTORY: Founded in 1937

PURPOSE: Promotion of timber both local and imported.

PUBLICATIONS
Promotional and technical publications.

MEMBERSHIP: Approximately 500 (associate and full members)

372 Town and Country Planning Association of Victoria (Inc.)
Victorian Environment Centre, 324 William Street, Melbourne, Vic. 3000
Telephone: (03) 329 5516

SECRETARY: Mrs. D.E. Waters (Administrative Secretary)

HISTORY: Founded in 1914

PURPOSE: Promotion of town and country planning

INTERESTS: Planning, conservation and environment protection.

ACTIVITIES: Monthly workshops, seminars

PUBLICATIONS
Space (irregular magazine)

AWARDS
Sir James Barrett Award (annually)
Certificate of Planning Achievement (annually)
R.A. Gardner Oration (annually)

MEMBERSHIP: 700 (ordinary members, municipalities, business organizations, government departments)

373 Tropical Grassland Society of Australia
CSIRO Cunningham Laboratory, Mill Road, St. Lucia, Qld. 4067
Telephone: (07) 370 7121

SECRETARY: V.G. Corry

SUBDIVISIONS
Central Coast Section, Mackay, Qld.

HISTORY: Founded in 1963

PURPOSE: To further knowledge in all aspects of the production, management and the use of tropical and sub-tropical pastures and forages and to provide members with opportunities for the interchange of ideas and experiences relating thereto.

ACTIVITIES: Generally an annual general meeting and three annual field day meetings.

PUBLICATIONS
Tropical Grasslands (3 issues per year)
Newsletter of the Tropical Grassland Society of Australia (4 issues per year)

LIBRARY: Limited facilities. Literature pertaining to research in grasslands.

MEMBERSHIP: 720 (private, company members)

374 University Geographical Society
Department of Geography, University of Western Australia, Nedlands, W.A. 6009
Telephone: (092) 80 2698

SECRETARY: C.J. Cluck

HISTORY: Founded in March, 1964.

PURPOSE: To enable geography students to interrelate socially and educationally.

INTERESTS: Ecology, environmental protection, urban planning.

ACTIVITIES: Field excursions, visiting lecturers, social activities

PUBLICATIONS
Real World (bi-annually)

MEMBERSHIP: Approx. 140

375 University of New South Wales Chemical Engineering Association
University of New South Wales, P.O. Box 1, Kensington, N.S.W. 2033
Telephone: (02) 663 0351 extn 3109

SECRETARY: R. Bowrey

HISTORY: Founded in 1962

PURPOSE: To promote scientific meetings, symposia and graduate retraining in chemical engineering.

MEMBERSHIP: Approximately 400 (life, honorary, ordinary, student members)

376 University of Queensland Veterinary Students Association

Veterinary Students' Common Room, Veterinary School, University of
Queensland, St. Lucia, Qld. 4067
Telephone: (07) 71 2287

SECRETARY: S. Tonge

HISTORY: Founded in about 1951

PURPOSE: To further the interests of, and promote good fellowship among veterinary students and
generally advance veterinary science in the state.

ACTIVITIES: Annual students' conference, annual general meetings, ordinary general meetings, special
general meetings.

PUBLICATIONS
Apsyrtus (annually)
Speculum (bimonthly)

MEMBERSHIP: Approximately 395 (annual, life members)

377 Victorian Medical Postgraduate Foundation

'Trawalla', 22 Lascelles Avenue, Toorak, Vic. 3142
Telephone: (03) 24 0671

SECRETARY: I.S. Russell (Acting Director)

HISTORY: Founded in 1920 by the Victorian Branch of the British Medical Association. Present name
adopted in 1976, previously Melbourne Medical Postgraduate Committee.

PURPOSE: To promote and develop facilities for postgraduate study in medicine and its allied sciences.

ACTIVITIES: Committee meets quarterly. Conferences.

PUBLICATIONS
Victorian Medical Postgraduate Foundation Handbook (annual)
Directory of Internships, Residencies and Registrarships Available in Hospitals in Victoria (annual)
Anatomical Abstracts (irregular)
Conference on First Year Medical Graduate Training Programme
Foundation Newsletter (quarterly)

AWARDS
Gordon-Taylor Scholarship

MEMBERSHIP: 59 members consisting of representatives of the main University affiliated teaching
hospitals, Colleges, Associations, Deans of the Faculty of Medicine at the University of Melbourne and
Monash University, and a number of co-opted members.

378 Victorian Society of Pathology and Experimental Medicine

191 Royal Parade, Parkville, Vic. 3052
Telephone: (03) 347 6077

SECRETARY: Miss X. Dennett

HISTORY: Founded in 1936

PURPOSE: To advance pathology, experimental medicine and allied sciences and to facilitate discussion
between workers in these fields.

ACTIVITIES: Symposia and guest lectures.

MEMBERSHIP: 150 members

379 Victorian Society for Social Responsibility in Science

This society was descended on November 30th, 1976 and its assets divided equally between ANZAAS and the Australian Conservation Foundation Inc.

380 Victorian State Foresters' Association

Forests Commission of Victoria, 1 Treasury Place, Melbourne, Vic. 3002
Telephone: (03) 63 0321 (extn 1002)

SECRETARY: I.W. Wild

AFFILIATIONS
Victorian Public Service Association

HISTORY: Founded in 1920's

PURPOSE: To maintain a high standard of forestry practice and professional ethics and to provide a means of discussion of forestry matters.

INTERESTS: General forestry matters, industrial welfare of members

ACTIVITIES: Annual conference and periodic regional meetings.

PUBLICATIONS
Newsletter (periodic)

AWARDS
Annual travel award; prize for best field excursion reports by second and third year students at Victorian School of Forestry.

MEMBERSHIP: 450 members

381 Waite Agricultural Sciences Club

Waite Agricultural Research Institute, Glen Osmond, S.A. 5064
Telephone: (08) 79 7901

SECRETARY: R.R. Lamacraft

HISTORY: Founded in 1928 as the Agricultural Sciences Club of the Waite Institute. Present name adopted in 1961

PURPOSE: To endeavour to keep members in touch with research work being carried out on the Waite campus and to review selected fields of interest.

ACTIVITIES: Annual all-day symposium.

MEMBERSHIP: All scientific and technical workers located on the Waite campus.

382 Water Research Foundation of Australia

School of Civil Engineering, University of New South Wales, Kensington, N.S.W.
(P.O. Box 47, Kingsford 2032.)
Telephone: (02) 663 4257

SECRETARY: K.W. Eather

SUBDIVISIONS
Offices in each state

HISTORY: Founded in 1951 as a non-profit limited liability company

PURPOSE: To initiate and support research.

INTERESTS: All problems associated with water conservation and use.

ACTIVITIES: Symposia at infrequent intervals

PUBLICATIONS
Water Research Foundation of Australia. Bulletin
Water Research Foundation of Australia. Report

LIBRARY: Specialist Water Reference Library

AWARDS
Grants to support research at Australian universities

MEMBERSHIP: 959

383   Waterworks Trusts Association of Victoria
Rigby House, 15 Queens Road, Melbourne, Vic. 3004
Telephone: (03) 26 4421

SECRETARY: J.D. Fagan

HISTORY: Founded in 1899

PURPOSE: To watch over and protect the interests, rights and privileges of waterworks trusts; to advise and instruct waterworks trusts in matters of doubt and difficulty; to take action in relation to any legislation affecting waterworks trusts.

ACTIVITIES: Annual session and two executive committee meetings each year

PUBLICATIONS
Annual Report

MEMBERSHIP: 190 waterworks trusts.

384   Weed Science Society of New South Wales
P.O. Box K287, Haymarket, N.S.W. 2000.
Telephone: (02) 631 0655, 80 4971 (A.H.)

SECRETARY: W.J. Burke

AFFILIATIONS
Council of Australian Weed Science Societies
Affiliated with similar weed societies in Qld., Vic., S.A. and W.A.

HISTORY: Founded in 1966

PURPOSE: To promote wider interest in weeds and weed control; to provide the opportunity for exchange of technical information among weed workers.

ACTIVITIES: Symposia held irregularly; approx.one every two years.

PUBLICATIONS
Proceedings of the Weed Society of N.S.W. (approx. every 18 months)
Newsletter (approx. every 3 months)

AWARDS
Annual prize for best student in weed science in fourth year of the Agricultural Science course at Sydney University.

MEMBERSHIP: 125 (ordinary, honorary, corporate members)

385   Weed Science Society of South Australia

Ian Clunies Ross Centre, Australian Mineral Foundation, Conyngham Street, Glenside, S.A. 5065
Telephone: (08) 79 7821

SECRETARY: M. McKay, care of- ICI Australia, P.O. Box 75, Cowandilla, S.A. 5033

HISTORY: Founded in 1970.

PURPOSE: To promote wider interest in weeds and their control; to provide the opportunity for exchange of ideas and information.

INTERESTS: All weeds, weed control and weed research.

ACTIVITIES: General meeting (two-monthly); executive meeting (monthly); sub-committee meetings as needed.

PUBLICATIONS
Newsletter and minutes to all members

AWARDS
Issued by Executive Committee when deemed necessary

MEMBERSHIP: 70 (ordinary, honorary, corporate members)

386   Weed Society of Western Australia

P.O. Box 190, Victoria Park, W.A. 6100
Telephone: (092) 67 0111

SECRETARY: P.A. Rutherford

HISTORY: Founded in 1976.

PURPOSE: To provide a means of improving interchange of information and experience between all workers in the weed industry.

INTERESTS: Weed identification, biology, control.

ACTIVITIES: Bimonthly meetings. Conference proposed for 1979.

PUBLICATIONS
Newsletter

MEMBERSHIP: 97 (ordinary, honorary, corporate)

387   West Australian Nutgrowing Society

225 Onslow Road, Shenton Park, W.A.
(P.O. Box 27, Subiaco 6008)
Telephone: (092) 81 8656

SECRETARY: Ms. C. Blackwell

SUBDIVISIONS
Members own a co-operative, West Australian Nut Supplies Co-operative Ltd, which handles any commercial interests and also supports the Society's Research Fund

HISTORY: Founded in 1975.

PURPOSE: To promote and assist in the growing of nut-bearing plants in every appropriate way.

INTERESTS: Nut horticulture, production, marketing.

ACTIVITIES: Irregular. A number of field trips each year.

PUBLICATIONS
Quandong (quarterly)
WANS Yearbook (annual)

AWARDS
Research fund currently being set up

MEMBERSHIP: 350

388 Western Australian Association for the Promotion of Education and Research in the Dairy Industry Inc.
Farmers Union of W.A., Inc., 239 Adelaide Terrace, Perth, W.A. 6000.
Telephone: (092) 25 2933

SECRETARY: E. Munch-Peterson

HISTORY: Founded on 29th Sept., 1966

PURPOSE: To provide scholarships, exhibitions, cadetships and bursaries; to provide technical advice and assistance; to disseminate information, publish technical information; to assist financially students at conferences.

INTERESTS: Dairying industry in W.A.

MEMBERSHIP: 52 (ordinary)

389 Western Australian Mental Health Association (Inc.)
311-313 Hay Street, Subiaco, W.A. 6008
Telephone: (092) 81 1986

SECRETARY: Mrs. J. Meharry, Executive Secretary, Community Development Centre, Selby Street, Shenton Park,W.A. 6008.

HISTORY: Founded in 1960

PURPOSE: To promote positive mental health and aid mentally ill.

INTERESTS: Volunteer groups in hospitals; public forums, seminars; 311 Club for ex-psychiatric patients.

ACTIVITIES: Monthly executive meetings; quarterly council meetings; annual general meeting.

PUBLICATIONS
Concern (monthly newsletter)
Help Is At Hand - Information Booklet No.1 (Towards a Better Understanding of Psychiatric Illness)

390 Western Australian Naturalists' Club (Inc.)
63-65 Merriwa Street, Nedlands, W.A. 6009

SECRETARY: O. Mueller

SUBDIVISIONS
Branch at Mundaring

AFFILIATIONS
National Trust of Australia
Tree Society
Australian Conservation Foundation Incorporated
Western Australian Conservation Council
International Council for Bird Preservation

HISTORY: Founded in 1924

PURPOSE: To encourage the study of natural history in all its branches and to endeavour to prevent the wanton destruction of native flora and fauna

ACTIVITIES: Monthly meetings; monthly field excursions; occasional weekend camps; annual wildlife show (one week) in the Perth Town Hall

PUBLICATIONS
Western Australian Naturalist Handbooks (quarterly)

LIBRARY: Club library

MEMBERSHIP: 800 (senior, junior, honorary members, honorary life members)

391   Western Australian Psychology Students Association
Department of Psychology, University of Western Australia, Nedlands, W.A. 6009

SECRETARY: J.M. Hewson

AFFILIATIONS
National Association of Psychology Students of Australia (NAPSA)

PURPOSE: To encourage and facilitate the study of psychology by senior students; to have a representative body with Psychology Department to assist student solidarity; to establish and maintain communications with staff; to have formal organization to facilitate the holding of special events

ACTIVITIES: Annual NAPSA conferences

PUBLICATIONS
Newsletter

392   Western Australian Shell Club
P.O.Box T1623, G.P.O., Perth, W.A. 6001

HISTORY: Founded in 1965

PURPOSE: To study of molluscs and conservation

ACTIVITIES: Monthly meetings at W.A. Museum.

PUBLICATIONS
W.A. Shell Collector (quarterly)
Monthly newsletter

MEMBERSHIP: 100 (members, juniors, overseas members)

393   Wildlife Conservation Society (Riverina and North-eastern Victorian)
Ettamogah Sanctuary, Hume Highway, Lavington, N.S.W.
(P.O.Box 600, Albury, N.S.W. 2640)
Telephone: (058) 25 1473

SECRETARY: Mrs. H. Peck

SUBDIVISIONS
Nature education centre at Ettamogah

HISTORY: Founded in 1967

PURPOSE: To encourage proper management of resources.

INTERESTS: Nature education and conservation

ACTIVITIES: Monthly meetings.

MEMBERSHIP: Approximately 100

394   Wildlife Preservation Society of Australia
Box 3428, G.P.O., Sydney, N.S.W. 2001

SECRETARY: Miss I. Gallagher

AFFILIATIONS
National Trust of Australia
National Parks Association of New South Wales
International Union for Conservation of Nature
International Council for Bird Preservation

HISTORY: Founded in 1909. The Naturalists' Society of New South Wales amalgamated in 1964

PURPOSE: To achieve the dedication of an adequate national park and nature reserve system in each state; the preservation of representative natural environments; public education in appreciating wildlife; a co-ordinated national plan for future conservation development.

ACTIVITIES: 10 general meetings per year; monthly excursions.

PUBLICATIONS
Australian Wildlife
Annual report; quarterly newsletter

LIBRARY: Library currently at Dew Field Studies Centre, 'Wirrimbirra' Sanctuary, Bargo

MEMBERSHIP: 650 (ordinary, associate, corporate, life members)

395   Wildlife Preservation Society of Queensland (Inc.)
Room 70-72, 4th Floor, 240 Queen Street, Brisbane, Qld.
(G.P.O. Box 2030, Brisbane, 4001)
Telephone: (07) 221 6376

SECRETARY: Mrs. G. MacCartie

SUBDIVISIONS
Branches at Bundaberg, Cairns, Caloundra, Dalby, Gladstone, Gold Coast, Hinchinbrook (Ingham), Maryborough- Moonaboola, Pittsworth, Proserpine, Toowoomba, Townsville

HISTORY: Founded in 1962

PURPOSE: The preservation of the fauna and flora of Australia by educating the community, particularly the young, in an understanding of the principles of conservation and preservation, by discouraging wanton destruction of any part of the fauna or flora; co-operation with other bodies.

INTERESTS: Creation of national parks and reserves; preservation of the Great Barrier Reef from exploitation; preservation of species of native flora and fauna threatened with extinction.

ACTIVITIES: Bi-monthly general meeting; monthly council meeting; monthly Sunday bush walks

PUBLICATIONS
Wildlife in Australia

LIBRARY: Sir Joseph Banks Memorial Library

AWARDS
Bursary to Science Teachers annual competition; prizes to schools

MEMBERSHIP: Approximately 2000 (single, joint, junior members, societies and associations)

396 Wildlife Research Group (Queensland)
108 Outlook Crescent, Bardon, Qld.
(P.O. Box 867, Fortitude Valley, 4006)
Telephone: (07) 36 0061

SECRETARY: G.J. Roberts

HISTORY: Founded in 1963

PURPOSE: To increase current awareness and knowledge with respect to Australian wildlife and associated habitat and strive for their conservation

INTERESTS: The study and conservation of Australian fauna, vertebrate and invertebrate; the protection of habitat, particularly via national park submission.

ACTIVITIES: Regular meetings; conferences arranged for particular issues.

PUBLICATIONS
Occasional publications on specific issues

MEMBERSHIP: 28 members from university and government institutions

397 Wireless Institute of Australia
2
517 Toorak Toad, Toorak, Vic.
(P.O. Box 150, Toorak 3142.)
Telephone: (03) 24 8652

SECRETARY: P.B. Dodd

SUBDIVISIONS
Divisions in all states of Australia
W.I.A. Youth Radio Clubs Scheme (training of youth in electronics)
W.I.A. Project Australis (construction and control of amateur communications satellites)
Affiliated Radio Amateur Clubs

HISTORY: Founded in 1910

PURPOSE: To encourage experimentation in electronics as applied to amateur radio communications on HF, VHF and higher frequencies; to represent the Amateur Radio Service and the Amateur Satellite Service domestically and internationally to the respective regulatory authorities; to promote amateur radio and to impart training and instruction in radio and allied subjects; to publish monthly membership journal 'Amateur Radio'.

ACTIVITIES: Monthly meetings in each state; annual convention (federal). Technical classes in most states.

PUBLICATIONS
Amateur Radio (monthly)

MEMBERSHIP: 5000 (full, associate members, students, life honorary members)

398 World Energy Conference. Australian National Committee
State Electricity Commission of Victoria, Monash House, 15 William Street, Melbourne, Vic.
(Box 2765Y, G.P.O., Melbourne 3001)
Telephone: (03) 615 3931

SECRETARY: A.M. Sharp

HISTORY: Founded in 1924 at the same time as the founding of the International organization.

PURPOSE: To make arrangements for meetings organised by the World Energy Conference, and for the presentation of papers; to promote the attendance of Australian representatives at meetings of the World Energy Conference; to maintain, through the Central Office of the World Energy Conference and by direct intercourse and correspondence, liaison with the other National Committees of the Conference; to supply to members information concerning the activities of the conference; generally to promote the declared Objects of the World Energy Conference.

ACTIVITIES: Annual General Meeting held in March; Executive Committee Meetings as required.

PUBLICATIONS
Annual Report is published by the World Body

MEMBERSHIP: 35 (full, honorary)

399   World's Poultry Science Association, Australian Branch
Poultry Research Station, Seven Hills, N.S.W.
(P.O. Box 11, Seven Hills 2147.)
Telephone: (02) 622 6322

SECRETARY: R.N. Macindoe

SUBDIVISIONS
New South Wales - P.O. Box 11, Seven Hills 2147.
New England - P.O. Box 547, Tamworth, N.S.W. 2340.
Newcastle - P.O. Box 1179, Gosford South, N.S.W. 2250.
Queensland - care of- Department of Primary Industry, William Street, Brisbane, 4000
Victoria - Department of Agriculture, Division of Animal Industry, Box 4041, G.P.O., Melbourne, Vic. 3001.
South Australia - care of- Parafield Poultry Research Centre, P.O.Box 3, Salisbury, S.A. 5018
Western Australia - care of- Poultry Branch, Department of Agriculture, Jarrah Road, South Perth, W.A. 6151

HISTORY: The Australian Branch W.P.S.A. became established in 1956 and the first regional conference was organized in 1959 in co-operation with the University of Sydney.

PURPOSE: To further the interest of the poultry industry through all phases including research, teaching, dissemination of knowledge and investigation into breeding, production and marketing. To facilitate in all possible ways the exchange of knowledge and experience among people who are contributing to the advancement of the various branches of the poultry industry.

ACTIVITIES: Australasian Convention every four years; monthly and bi-monthly meetings held by all sub-branches throughout Australia. World body meets every four years at the World's Poultry Science Convention.

PUBLICATIONS
World's Poultry Science Journal (quarterly)

AWARDS
Australian Poultry Award (annually)

MEMBERSHIP: 500 (life, individual, affiliated, student members)

400   Other Societies
The following societies were approached, but entries had not been received at time of publication.

AFFILIATIONS
Association of Architects, Engineers, Surveyors and Draftsmen of Australia
Asthma Foundation of New South Wales
Astronomical Amateurs Club of Moreton Bay
Astronomical Society of Tasmania
Australasian Airline Flight Engineers Association
Australian Academy of Forensic Sciences
Australian Coal Association
Australian Council on Smoking and Health
Australian Federation of Family Planning Associations
Australian Forest Development Institute
Australian Institute of Pest Control Ltd.
Australian Liquified Petroleum Gas Association
Australian Minerals Industry Research Association
Australian and New Zealand Architectural Science Association
Australian Welding Institute
Bird Banders Association of Australia
Conservation Society of New South Wales
Council of Australian Weed Science Societies
Commonwealth Professional Surveyors Association
Electronics Association of Australia
Goulburn Astronomers Club
Illawarra Astronomical Society
Institute of Materials Handling, N.S.W. Division
Institution of Electrical Engineers, Qld. Organisation
Institution of Electrical Engineers, S.A. Organisation
Institution of Electrical Engineers, W.A. Organisation
New England Solar Energy Society
Queensland Littoral Society
Remote Sensing Association of Australia
Society of Manufacturing Engineers (Melbourne Chapter)
South Australian Tuberculosis Association
Thoracic Society of Australia
Town and Country Planning Association, S.A. Inc.
Weed Science Society of Victoria

List of Initials

A.A.C.B.	Australian Association of Clinical Biochemists
A.A.D.	Australian Association of Dieticians
A.A.E.S.	Australian Agricultural Economics Society
A.A.G.	Australian Association of Gerontology
A.A.H.P.S.	Australasian Association for the History and Philosophy of Science
A.A.M.T.	Australian Association of Mathematics Teachers
A.A.N.	Australian Association of Neurologists
A.A.O.T.	Australian Association of Occupational Therapists Inc.
A.A.P.	Association of Australasian Palaeontologists
A.A.P.	Australasian Association of Philosophy
A.A.Q.	Astronomers Association of Queensland
A.A.S.	Australian Academy of Science
A.A.S.	Australian Acoustical Society
A.A.S.	Australian Association of Surgeons
A.A.S.H.	Australian Association of Speech and Hearing
A.A.S.W.	Australian Association of Social Workers
A.A.T.A.	Australian Animal Technicians' Association
A.A.T.S.	Australian Academy of Technological Sciences
A.B.S.	Australian Biochemical Society
A.C.A.	Australasian Corrosion Association
A.C.A.	Australian Chiropody Association (Vic.)
A.C.A.	Australian Chiropractors Association, A.C.T. Council
A.C.A.	Australian College of Allergists
A.C.A.	Australian Consumers' Association
A.C.A.D.	Association for Computer Aided Design Limited
A.C.D.	Australasian College of Dermatologists
A.C.E.R.	Australian Council for Educational Research
A.C.F.	Australian Conservation Foundation Incorporated
A.C.H.P.E.R.	Australian Council for Health, Physical Education and Recreation
A.C.H.S.	Australian Council on Hospital Standards
A.C.M.A.	Australian College of Medical Administrators
A.C.M.S.	Australian Clay Minerals Society
A.C.S.	Australian Cancer Society
A.C.S.	Australian Ceramic Society
A.C.S.	Australian Computer Society Incorporated
A.C.T.A.O.T.	Australian Capital Territory Association of Occupational Therapists
A.C.V.S.	Australian College of Veterinary Scientists
A.D.A.	Australian Dental Association
A.D.F.A.	Australian Dried Fruits Association
A.E.S.	Australian Entomological Society
A.E.S.A.	Agricultural Engineering Society [Australia]
A.E.V.A.	Australian Electrical Vehicle Association
A.F.A.P.T.S.	Australian French Association of Professional and Technical Specialists
A.F.C.C.	Australian Federation of Construction Contractors
A.F.I.	Australian Foundry Institute (New South Wales Division)
A.F.M.B.E.	Australian Federation for Medical and Biological Engineering
A.F.M.S.	Australian Farm Management Society
A.F.M.W.	Australian Federation of Medical Women
A.F.P.A.	Australian Fire Protection Association

A.F.S.A.	Asthma Foundation of South Australia Inc.
A.G.A.	Australian Gas Association
A.G.I.A.	Australian Geosciences Information Association
A.G.S.	Australian Geomechanics Society
A.G.T.A.	Australian Geography Teachers' Association
A.I.A.S.	Australian Institute of Agricultural Science
A.I.B.	Australian Institute of Building
A.I.B.S.	Australian Institute of Building Surveyors
A.I.C.	Australian Institute of Cartographers
A.I.E.A.	Australian Institute of Engineering Associates Limited
A.I.F.S.T.	Australian Institute of Food Science and Technology
A.I.H.	Australian Institute of Horticulture Incorporated
A.I.H.A.	Australian Institute of Hospital Administrators
A.I.H.S.	Australian Institute of Health Surveyors
A.I.I.P.	Australian Institute of Industrial Psychology
A.I.L.A.	Australian Institute of Landscape Architects
A.I.M.	Australasian Institute of Metals
A.I.M.	Australian Institute of Management
A.I.M.F.	Australasian Institute of Metal Finishing
A.I.M.M.	Australasian Institute of Mining and Metallurgy
A.I.M.P.E.	Australian Institute of Marine and Power Engineers
A.I.M.T.	Australian Institute of Medical Technologists
A.I.N.	Australian Institute of Navigation
A.I.N.D.T.	Australian Institute of Non-Destructive Testing
A.I.N.S.E.	Australian Institute of Nuclear Science and Engineering
A.I.P.	Australian Institute of Packaging
A.I.P.	Australian Institute of Petroleum Ltd.
A.I.P.	Australian Institute of Physics
A.I.P.R.	Australian Institute of Parks and Recreation
A.I.Q.S.	Australian Institute of Quantity Surveyors
A.I.R.	Australasian Institute of Radiography
A.I.R.A.C.H.	Australian Institute of Refrigeration, Air Conditioning and Heating (Inc.)
A.I.S.A.	Australian Institute of Systems Analysts
A.I.S.C.	Australian Institute of Steel Construction
A.I.S.T.	Australian Institute of Science Technology Inc.
A.I.U.S.	Australian Institute of Urban Studies
A.K.F.	Australian Kidney Foundation
A.L.A.E.A.	Australian Licensed Aircraft Engineers' Association
A.L.D.A.	Australian Lead Development Association
A.L.I.	Australian Leather Institute
A.L.S.	Australian Littoral Society
A.M.A.	Australian Medical Association
A.M.A.	Australian Meteorological Association Inc.
A.M.D.A.P.I.	Association of Medical Directors to the Australian Pharmaceutical Industry
A.M.S.	Australian Mammal Society Incorporated
A.M.S.	Australian Mathematical Society
A.M.S.A.	Australian Marine Sciences' Association
A.M.S.A.N.Z.	Aviation Medicine Society of Australia and New Zealand
A.N.A.	Australian Nurserymen's Association Limited

A.N.C.L.D.	Australian National Committee on Large Dams
A.N.Z.A.A.S.	Australian and New Zealand Association for the Advancement of Science Incorporated (ANZAAS)
A.N.Z.C.P.	Australian and New Zealand College of Psychiatrists
A.N.Z.S.E.R.C.H.	Australian and New Zealand Society for Epidemiology and Research in Community Health
A.N.Z.S.N.M.	Australian and New Zealand Society of Nuclear Medicine
A.N.Z.S.O.M.	Australian and New Zealand Society of Occupational Medicine
A.N.Z.S.O.S.	Australian and New Zealand Society of Oral Surgeons
A.O.A.	Australian Optometrical Association
A.O.A.	Australian Orthopaedic Association
A.O.Q.C.	Australian Organisation for Quality Control
A.P.A.	Australian Paediatric Association
A.P.A.	Australian Physiotherapy Association
A.P.E.A.	Association of Professional Engineers, Australia
A.P.E.A.	Australian Petroleum Exploration Association Ltd.
A.P.F.M.	Australian Postgraduate Federation in Medicine
A.P.H.A.	Australian Pneumatic and Hydraulic Association
A.P.P.I.T.A.	Appita
A.P.P.S.	Australian Physiological and Pharmacological Society
A.P.P.S.	Australian Plant Pathology Society
A.P.S.	Australian Psychological Society
A.P.S.A.	Association of Professional Scientists of Australia
A.P.S.A.	Australian Pharmaceutical Sciences Association
A.R.E.A.	Australian Remedial Education Association
A.R.S.	Australian Rangeland Society
A.S.A.	Astronomical Society of Australia
A.S.A.	Australian Society of Anaesthetists
A.S.A.P.	Australian Society of Animal Production
A.S.A.-W.	Astronomical Society of Albury-Wodonga
A.S.B.S.	Australian Systematic Botany Society
A.S.C.C.	Australian Society of Cosmetic Chemists
A.S.C.E.P.	Australasian Society of Clinical and Experimental Pharmacologists
A.S.D.T.	Australian Society of Dairy Technology (Inc.)
A.S.E.	Australasian Society of Engineers
A.S.E.	Australian Society of Endontology
A.S.E.G.	Australian Society of Exploration Geophysicists
A.S.F.	Astronomical Society of Frankston
A.S.F.	Australian Speleological Federation
A.S.F.B.	Australian Society for Fish Biology
A.S.G.	Astronomical Society of Geelong
A.S.H.	Astronomical Society of the Hunter
A.S.H.	Australian Society of Herpetologists
A.S.L.	Australian Society for Limnology
A.S.M.	Australian Society for Microbiology Inc.
A.S.M.R.	Australian Society for Medical Research
A.S.N.S.W.	Anthropological Society of New South Wales
A.S.N.S.W.	Astronomical Society of New South Wales
A.S.O.	Australian Society of Orthodontists
A.S.O.R.	Australian Society for Operations Research Incorporated
A.S.P.	Australian Society for Parasitology

A.S.P.	Australian Society of Periodontology
A.S.P.	Australian Society of Prosthodontists
A.S.P.P.	Australian Society of Plant Physiologists
A.S.Q.	Anthropological Society of Queensland
A.S.Q.	Astronomical Society of Queensland
A.S.R.B.	Australian Society for Reproductive Biology
A.S.S.A.	Academy of the Social Sciences in Australia
A.S.S.A.	Anthropological Society of South Australia Incorporated
A.S.S.A.	Astronomical Society of South Australia Inc.
A.S.S.S.	Australian Society of Soil Science Incorporated.
A.S.T.A.	Australian Science Teachers Association
A.S.V.	Anthropological Society of Victoria
A.S.V.	Astronomical Society of Victoria
A.S.W.A.	Anthropological Society of Western Australia
A.S.W.A.	Astronautical Society of Western Australia Inc.
A.S.W.A.	Astronomical Society of Western Australia, Inc.
A.T.A.	Agricultural Technologists of Australasia
A.T.A.	Australian Tunnelling Association
A.T.D.A.	Australian Telecommunications Development Association
A.T.M.A.	Australian Technical Millers Association
A.U.R.I.S.A.	Australian Urban and Regional Information Systems Association
A.V.A.	Australian Veterinary Association
A.W.R.A.	Australian Welding Research Association
A.W.W.A.	Australian Water and Wastewater Association
A.Z.D.A.	Australian Zinc Development Association
B.A.S.	Ballarat Astronomical Society
B.A.S.	British Astronomical Society, N.S.W. Branch
B.A.S.	Bundaberg Astronomical Society
B.O.C.	Bird Observers Club
B.S.F.A.	Building Science Forum of Australia
B.S.R.A.B.	British Society of Rheology; Australian Branch
C.A.A.N.S.W.	Commercial Apiarists' Association of New South Wales
C.A.F.T.A.	Council of Australian Food Technology Associations Inc.
C.A.S.	Canberra Astronomical Society
C.A.S.A.N.Z.	Clean Air Society of Australia and New Zealand
C.C.A.A.	Cement and Concrete Association of Australia
C.C.S.A.	Conservation Council of S.A. Inc.
C.C.W.A.	Conservation Council of Western Australia Inc.
C.G.S.	Canberra Gem Society Inc.
C.I.	Combustion Institute (Australian Section)
C.I.A.	Concrete Institute of Australia
C.I.T.	Chartered Institute of Transport
C.L.S.A.	Contact Lens Society of Australia
C.S.A.N.Z.	Cardiac Society of Australia and New Zealand
C.S.I.R.O.O.A.	CSIRO Officers' Association
D.G.S.M.W.R.F.A.	David G. Stead Memorial Wildlife Research Foundation of Australia
D.I.A.	Diecasting Institute of Australia
E.S.A.	Ecological Society of Australia, Incorporated
E.S.A.	Endocrine Society of Australia

E.S.A.A.	Electricity Supply Association of Australia
E.S.A.N.Z.	Ergonomics Society of Australia and New Zealand Inc.
E.S.A.V.	Environment Studies Association of Victoria
E.S.E.A.N.S.W.	Electricity Supply Engineers' Association of N.S.W.
E.S.Q.	Entomological Society of Queensland
F.A.R.	Foundation for Australian Resources
F.C.A.A.A.	Federal Council of Australian Apiarists' Associations
F.N.C.V.	Field Naturalists' Club of Victoria
F.N.S.S.A.	Field Naturalists' Society of South Australia Inc.
F.P.A.(W.A.)	Forest Products Association (W.A.)
F.T.A.N.S.W.	Food Technology Association of New South Wales
F.T.A.T.	Food Technology Association of Tasmania
G.A.A.	Gemmological Association of Australia
G.B.R.C.	Great Barrier Reef Committee
G.D.O.	Guild of Dispensing Opticians (Australia) Limited
G.S.A.	Genetics Society of Australia
G.S.A.	Geological Society of Australia Inc.
G.T.A.N.S.W.	Geography Teachers' Association of New South Wales
H.G.A.	Horological Guild of Australasia
H.I.A.	Housing Industry Association
H.P.A.	Hospital Physicists' Association (Australian Regional Group)
I.A.A.	Inventors' Association of Australia Limited
I.A.A.N.Z.	Institute of Actuaries of Australia and New Zealand
I.A.G.	Institute of Australian Geographers
I.A.M.E.	Institute of Automotive Mechanical Engineers
I.A.W.P.R.	International Association on Water Pollution Research. Australian National Committee
I.C.E.	Institution of Chemical Engineers, Australian National Committee
I.C.E.	Institution of Civil Engineers, Victorian Local Association
I.C.R.M.F.	Ian Clunies Ross Memorial Foundation
I.D.C.A.	Industrial Design Council of Australia
I.D.E.A.	Institute of Diesel Engineers of Australia (Inc.)
I.D.I.A.	Industrial Design Institute of Australia
I.E.A.	Institution of Engineers, Australia
I.E.E.	Institution of Electrical Engineers, N.S.W. Overseas Committee
I.E.E.	Institution of Electrical Engineers, Tasmania
I.E.E.	Institution of Electrical Engineers, Victorian Organization
I.E.I.	Institute of Electrical Inspectors
I.E.S.A.	Illuminating Engineering Societies of Australia
I.F.	Institute of Fuel (Australian Membership)
I.F.A.	Institute of Foresters of Australia Inc.
I.G.E.A.	Institution of Gas Engineers (Australia)
I.I.C.A.	Institute of Instrumentation and Control Australia
I.I.E.	Institute of Industrial Engineers
I.I.R	International Institute of Refrigeration. Australian National Committee
I.M.	Institution of Metallurgists (Australian Region)
I.M.E.	Institute of Marine Engineers, Australia-New Zealand Division
I.M.E.	Institution of Mechanical Engineers (Australian Branch)
I.M.H.	Institute of Materials Handling, South Australian Division
I.M.H.	Institute of Materials Handling, Victorian Division

I.M.H.	Institute of Materials Handling, Western Australian Division
I.P.E.	Institution of Production Engineers, Australian Council
I.P.T.	Institute of Photographic Technology
I.Q.A.	Institute of Quality Assurance (Australian Federal Committee)
I.R.A.S.E.	Institute of Refrigeration and Air-Conditioning Service Engineers (Australian Council)
I.R.E.E.A.	Institution of Radio and Electronics Engineers Australia
I.R.S.A.	Industrial Relations Society of Australia
I.S.A.	Institution of Surveyors, Australia
I.S.E.S.	International Solar Energy Society, Australian and New Zealand Section
I.W.S.	Institute of Wood Science (Australian Branch)
J.C.A.S.	James Cook Astronomical Society
L.E.S.A.	Licensing Executives Society of Australia
L.G.	Leather Guild
L.S.N.S.W.	Linnean Society of New South Wales
L.V.A.S.	Latrobe Valley Astronomical Society
M.A.A.	Microfilm Association of Australia Limited
M.A.R.I.A.	Marine Aquarium Research Institute of Australia
M.A.S.	Monash Astronautical Society
M.L.S.N.S.W.	Medico Legal Society of New South Wales
M.S.A.	Malacological Society of Australia
M.S.G.V.	Management Services Group of Victoria
M.S.N.S.W.	Meteorological Society of N.S.W.
M.S.V.	Medical Society of Victoria
M.U.E.S.C.	Melbourne University Engineering Students' Club
M.U.S.S.S.	Melbourne University Science Students' Society
N.A.T.A.	National Association of Testing Authorities, Australia
N.C.A.S.	National Capital Agricultural Society
N.C.C.N.S.W.	Nature Conservation Council of New South Wales
N.C.S.S.A.	Nature Conservation Society of South Australia (Inc.)
N.H.F.A.	National Heart Foundation of Australia
N.Q.N.C.	North Queensland Naturalists Club
N.R.C.L.V.	Natural Resources Conservation League of Victoria
N.S.A.	Nutrition Society of Australia
N.S.C.A.	National Safety Council of Australia
N.S.W.F.O.C.	New South Wales Field Ornithologists Club
N.S.W.H.P.C.S.	New South Wales Horticultural Propagation Co-operative Society Ltd.
N.S.W.I.E.R.	New South Wales Institute for Educational Research
O.A.A.	Orthoptic Association of Australia
O.C.C.A.A.	Oil and Colour Chemists' Association, Australia
O.G.F.S.T.	Organic Gardening and Farming Society of Tasmania
O.O.A.N.S.W.	Opticians and Optometrists Association of N.S.W.
O.R.I.A.	Ophthalmic Research Institute of Australia
O.S.N.S.W.	Orchid Society of N.S.W. Ltd.
P.E.S.A.	Petroleum Exploration Society of Australia
P.G.A.	Pharmacy Guild of Australia
P.I.A.	Plastics Institute of Australia Inc.
P.I.E.C.	Packaging Industry Environment Council
P.M.A.A.	Port Macquarie Astronomical Society
P.M.F.	Postgraduate Medical Foundation, University of Sydney

P.S.A.	Pharmaceutical Society of Australia
P.S.A.A.V.	Provincial Sewerage Authorities Association of Victoria
P.S.A.N.Z.	Pharmaceutical Association of Australia and New Zealand
P.S.N.S.W.	Pharmaceutical Society of New South Wales
P.S.S.A.	Pharmaceutical Society of South Australia, Incorporated
P.S.T.	Pharmaceutical Society of Tasmania
P.S.V.	Paediatric Society of Victoria
P.S.V.	Pharmaceutical Society of Victoria
P.S.W.A.	Pharmaceutical Society of Western Australia
Q.C.C.	Queensland Conservational Council
Q.I.E.R.	Queensland Institute for Educational Research
Q.N.C.	Queensland Naturalists' Club
Q.S.S.C.T.	Queensland Society of Sugar Cane Technologists
R.A.C.C.A.A.	Refrigeration and Air Conditioning Contractors Association of Australia
R.A.C.D.S.	Royal Australian College of Dental Surgeons Inc.
R.A.C.G.P.	Royal Australian College of General Practitioners
R.A.C.I.	Royal Australian Chemical Institute
R.A.C.O.	Royal Australian College of Ophthalmologists
R.A.C.P.	Royal Australasian College of Physicians
R.A.C.R.	Royal Australasian College of Radiologists
R.A.C.S.	Royal Australasian College of Surgeons
R.A.H.S.S.A.	Royal Agricultural and Horticultural Society of South Australia Inc.
R.A.I.A.	Royal Australian Institute of Architects
R.A.N.F.	Royal Australian Nursing Federation
R.A.O.U.	Royal Australasian Ornithologists Union
R.A.P.I.	Royal Australian Planning Institute
R.A.S.	Royal Aeronautical Society (Australian Division)
R.A.S.N.S.W.	Royal Agricultural Society of New South Wales
R.A.S.T.	Royal Agricultural Society of Tasmania
R.A.S.W.A.	Royal Agricultural Society of Western Australia (Inc.)
R.C.O.G.	Royal College of Obstetricians and Gynaecologists, Australian Council
R.C.P.A.	Royal College of Pathologists of Australia
R.G.S.A. (S.A.)	Royal Geographical Society of Australasia (S.A. Branch) Incorporated
R.G.S.A.Q.	Royal Geographical Society of Australasia, Queensland Inc.
R.H.S.N.S.W.	Royal Horticultural Society of New South Wales
R.H.S.V.	Royal Historical Society of Victoria
R.M.A.S.A.	Rural Media Association of South Australia
R.M.S.	Royal Meteorological Society, Australian Branch
R.S.A.A.	Rail Sleeper Association (Australia)
R.S.N.S.W.	Royal Society of New South Wales
R.S.Q.	Royal Society of Queensland
R.S.S.A.	Royal Society of South Australia Incorporated
R.S.T.	Royal Society of Tasmania
R.S.V.	Royal Society of Victoria
R.S.W.A.	Royal Society of Western Australia Inc.
R.Z.S.N.S.W.	Royal Zoological Society of New South Wales
R.Z.S.S.A.	Royal Zoological Society of South Australia, Inc.
S.A.A.	Standards Association of Australia
S.A.E.A.	Society of Automotive Engineers - Australasia

S.A.O.A.	South Australian Ornithological Association
S.A.S.T.A.	South Australian Science Teachers Association
S.C.I.V.	Society of Chemical Industry of Victoria
S.D.C.A.N.Z.	Society of Dyers and Colourists of Australia and New Zealand
S.G.A.P.	Society for Growing Australian Plants
S.H.P.A.	Society of Hospital Pharmacists of Australia
S.L.A.E.T.	Society of Licensed Aircraft Engineers and Technologists (Aust.)
S.L.T.C.	Society of Leather Technologists and Chemists
S.S.A.	Statistical Society of Australia
S.S.R.S.	Society for Social Responsibility in Science (A.C.T.)
S.T.A.N.S.W.	Science Teachers Association of N.S.W.
S.T.A.Q.	Science Teachers Association of Queensland
S.T.A.T.	Science Teachers Association of Tasmania
S.T.A.V.	Science Teachers Association of Victoria
S.U.C.E.	Sydney University Chemical Engineering Association
S.U.C.S.	Sydney University Chemical Society
S.U.M.S.	Sydney University Medical Society
S.U.P.S.	Sydney University Psychological Society
S.U.V.S.	Sydney University Veterinary Society
S.W.C.S.V.	Soil and Water Conservation Society of Victoria
T.A.A.N.Z.P.P.I.	Technical Association of the Australian and New Zealand Pulp and Paper Industry
T.C.P.A.V.	Town and Country Planning Association of Victoria (Inc.)
T.C.T.	Tasmanian Conservation Trust Incorporated
T.D.A.	Timber Development Association (N.S.W.) Limited
T.G.S.A.	Tropical Grassland Society of Australia
T.S.A.	Telecommunication Society of Australia
T.S.A.	Television Society of Australia
T.S.A.	Textile Society of Australia
T.U.A.S.S.	Tasmanian University Agricultural Science Society
U.G.S.	University Geographical Society
U.N.S.W.C.E.A.	University of New South Wales Chemical Engineering Association
U.Q.V.S.A.	University of Queensland Veterinary Students Association
V.M.P.F.	Victorian Medical Postgraduate Foundation
V.S.F.A.	Victorian State Foresters' Association
V.S.P.E.M.	Victorian Society of Pathology and Experimental Medicine
W.A.A.P.E.R.D.I.	Western Australian Association for the Promotion of Education and Research in the Dairy Industry Inc.
W.A.M.H.A.	Western Australian Mental Health Association (Inc.)
W.A.N.C.	Western Australian Naturalists' Club (Inc.)
W.A.N.S.	West Australian Nutgrowing Society
W.A.P.S.A.	Western Australian Psychology Students Association
W.A.S.C.	Waite Agricultural Sciences Club
W.A.S.C.	Western Australian Shell Club
W.C.S.	Wildlife Conservation Society (Riverina and North-eastern Victorian)
W.E.C.	World Energy Conference. Australian National Committee
W.I.A.	Wireless Institute of Australia
W.P.S.A.	Wildlife Preservation Society of Australia
W.P.S.A.	World's Poultry Science Association, Australian Branch
W.P.S.Q.	Wildlife Preservation Society of Queensland (Inc.)

W.R.F.A.	Water Research Foundation of Australia
W.R.G.	Wildlife Research Group (Queensland)
W.S.N.S.W.	Weed Science Society of New South Wales
W.S.S.S.A.	Weed Science Society of South Australia
W.S.W.A.	Weed Society of Western Australia
W.T.A.V.	Waterworks Trusts Association of Victoria

Names Index

Numbers refer to entries

Publications Index

Numbers refer to entries

Awards Index

Numbers refer to entries

Subject Index

Numbers refer to entries